IN TRANSITION

IN
TRANSITION

From the Harvard Business School Club of New York
Personal Seminar in Career Management

MARY LINDLEY BURTON
RICHARD A. WEDEMEYER

CENTURY
BUSINESS

First published in the USA in 1991 by Harper Business

First published in the UK in 1992 by Century Business
An imprint of Random Century Group Ltd
20 Vauxhall Bridge Road, London SW1V 2SA

Random Century Group Australia (Pty) Ltd
20 Alfred Street, Milsons Point
Sydney, NSW 2061, Australia

Random Century Group New Zealand Ltd
18 Poland Road, Glenfield
Auckland 10, New Zealand

Random Century Group South Africa (Pty) Ltd
PO Box 337, Bergvlei, South Africa

Printed and bound in Great Britain by
Butler & Tanner Ltd, Frome and London

The right of Mary Lindley Burton and Richard A. Wedemeyer to be
identified as the authors of this work has been asserted by them
in accordance with the Copyright, Designs and Patents Act, 1988.

A catalogue record for this book is available
from the British Library.

ISBN 0–7126–9801–9

To the members of the
Harvard Business School Club of Greater New York
who have given encouragement to the Career Seminar, and in particular

JOHN C. FAULKNER

whose willingness to support a new approach to career
transitions made the Career Seminar possible.

CONTENTS

PART III
MARKETING YOURSELF IN THE JOB SEARCH

ACKNOWLEDGMENTS

Mary and Dick are grateful to the many people who have contributed to this book. Participants in the Career Seminar gave inputs that helped shape it, and those who agreed to have their comments and quotes used in the text greatly enhanced the content. The officers and staff of the Harvard Business School Club of Greater New York, particularly Ron Weintraub, Ken Powell, Ennius Bergsma, Stephen Wald, Burt Alimansky, Nancy Lane, and Jack Faulkner, provided ongoing support for the Seminar, which in turn made the book possible. A special recognition is due Carl R. Boll, who initiated career guidance to New York HBS alumni and provided that service for over two decades, and to Rich Payne, who maintained the tradition and passed it on to us.

Virginia Smith, our editor, catalyzed and gently guided the book as it took shape. Nancy Trichter guided us through the unfamiliar territory of publishing. Susan Saunders, Linda Shirley, Elizabeth Striker, and Jean Davis Taft gave invaluable assistance in preparing the manuscript. Linda Kirby and Nancy Barger were generous with their useful comments and input to the Myers-Briggs Type Indicator chapter.

Mary owes a special debt to the many individuals she has worked with over the last twelve years in her role as career strategy consultant. Her opportunity to work with many Career Seminar participants one-on-one and in smaller groups enabled us to bring individual stories into *In Transition*. But more than the specific quotes, each person shared a part of the reality of being in between—and those direct accounts have shaped the process distilled into this book.

Mary would also like to thank each friend and family member who provided a levening word or humorous pickup through a full year of managing a practice and writing a book. And to Joan and Jacky, who continually parted the clouds, made the pathway straight, and held high the light, she expresses special gratitude.

Dick is indebted to two wonderful women, without whom this book would not have been possible. Shirlee Hamm Wedemeyer, his first wife, supported and encouraged him during his mid-career crisis in spite of her considerable fears and the heart condition that eventually ended her life in 1980. Jane Wedemeyer, his wife, helpmate, and best friend, furthered the book with her belief in the project and incredible patience during his countless hours at the word processor and in the office. Dick also thanks his two children, Laura and Trevor, from whom he has learned much about the more important things in life.

Dick expresses his gratitude to Jim Henson, Jane Henson, and all his colleagues and associates for their support. Being a part of the wonderous world of the Muppets has facilitated his personal growth and greatly enhanced his sensitivity to the complex subject of people in organizations. Bonnie Brown, Jessie Turberg, and Alex Platt are continuing sources of help in keeping life in perspective.

And lastly, Mary and Dick acknowledge one another as colleague and friend. Neither could have guessed when they met in 1980 that a decade later they would have spent more than 500 hours together teaching the Career Seminar, let alone countless more hours in the writing of this book. The journey has had its challenges but overall continues to facilitate their mutual growth, a gift they both cherish.

INTRODUCTION

Career doubts and difficulties are not unusual for managers, although this fact may be obscured by the prerequisite managerial facade: confident, buttoned-down, in control. Managers in career difficulty often conclude, "I'm the only one who's having problems coping. There must be something wrong with *me.*" *In Transition* is for just such a manager. As the economy presents increasingly severe challenges, more managers than ever are wrestling with career-related problems: industries are contracting, and the probability of working for one company for most of one's professional life is dwindling. Many managers are examining their careers not because "something is wrong" with them but because external realities demand it. For others, issues once associated with a midlife reevaluation arise earlier. Highly educated, well-trained managers expect a lot from their jobs—far more than just a paycheck.

But whether you are "in transition" as a result of the white-collar recession or because an inner voice is calling for change, we invite you to take a ring-side seat at the Harvard Business School Club of New York's Career Seminar. Over the past ten years we have worked with over 1,000 managers in the HBSCNY Career Seminar. They represent a range of industries and functions—CEOs, consultants, small business managers, chief financial officers, money managers, human resources managers, strategic planners, product managers, investment bankers, MIS professionals. In developing a process for this audience, we brought our own perspectives as Harvard MBAs, our knowledge of the business world, and a keen understanding of the difficult early stages of career transitions. We offer no magic techniques in this book, but the process of career assessment and action works. It has been validated and found to be effective in the seminar time and again by bright, experienced, skeptical, even cynical managers of all ages and situations. It will work for you—provided you do your part.

"Confidence building" is how I'd describe the seminar. I came to it thinking that I was alone in the world and found people in similar situations—capable, good-quality people—who were not only dealing with the situation but enthused about it.

DIRECTOR, CUSTOMER SERVICES, HBS '69

Career transitions are never painless. In most situations a career embodies many facets of a manager's life: it's a source of revenue (for necessities and for luxuries that provide pleasure and status), a means of self-expression, a source of personal identity, and for many a primary means of making acquaintances. In short, your *livelihood* incorporates many of the elements of your life. A manager feels on top of the world when the job is going smoothly. When a deal falls through, however, or a manager is passed over for promotion or loses a job, the news can hit at the very core of his or her identity:

I felt devalued, frightened, abandoned, angry, devastated. The well-meaning consolation "It's only a job!" produced a bitter response: "No, it's my life. It's me!"

VP SALES, INDUSTRIAL PRODUCTS, HBS '61

We believe not only that every manager is far more than his or her present or most recent job but that each has the ability to orchestrate a career transition. One of the basic concepts underlying the HBSCNY Career Seminar is that many managerial skills are readily transferable to the career assessment and self-marketing process. *In Transition* will draw heavily on your experience and mind-set: on your management expertise to develop an effective, self-directed campaign; on your analytical talents to gain useful insights and reach important conclusions; on your marketing experience to adapt to new market conditions; and on your skill at conceptualizing and articulating ideas to present yourself as a valuable resource. *In Transition* reveals that the terrain you traverse during a career change is not as foreign or hostile an environment as it may first appear.

The *In Transition* process identifies parallels between marketing and the job search:

- *Know your product.* The first rule of selling is particularly applicable here: *you* are the product. So the first phase of your work is a series of self-exploration and self-awareness exercises.
- *Know your market.* During the important but often ignored market research phase you investigate fields and functions to determine the fit between you-the-product and a particular market segment's needs. The second phase of your work is a careful market assessment.

- *Market yourself.* An effective self-marketing campaign is your key to a new situation. The third phase of the process begins when you develop a detailed and rigorously scheduled marketing campaign. In the implementation of your campaign you make known your availability (for a limited time only) to sectors of the market (employers) that need what you are offering.

We stress three additional points:

- Your existing marketing training, skills, and experience can be used to your advantage in the job market, with only a few significant modifications.
- Finding a good match between you-the-product—your needs and your product benefits—and a particular organization's needs is a manageable, step-by-step process that takes advantage of your business acumen.
- The benefits of the process continue long after securing a new position. Being aware of your priorities and attributes gives you a reference point for making decisions on the job and in your personal life.

The book is divided into three parts:

Part 1

The first part of *In Transition* presents the five basic concepts underlying the process and offers guidance in how to use the book depending on your individual situation. It describes commonly encountered impediments to a successful transition, and concludes with a technique to get your campaign off to a good start.

Part 2

The second part of *In Transition* takes you through the self-exploration and self-awareness process. First we ask you to consider common impediments to self-exploration in order to clear the way for a productive self-assessment. Then we take you through the exercises used in the HBSCNY Career Seminar:

- The Forks in the Road
- Life Mission
- Priorities and Trade-offs
- To See Ourselves as Others See Us
- Your Style, Your Values, and Your Motivational Hierarchy

- Your Organizational Fit Profile
- Your Skills Audit[1]
- Personal Constraints

The results of each exercise become part of your product specification file, which is refined into a concise description of you-the-product—your goals, priorities, capabilities, environmental tolerances, performance characteristics, and price tag.

Part 3

In the third part of *In Transition* you develop a self-marketing campaign, a far more effective and constructive method of securing a new job than the mendicant approach. As in any effective marketing effort, you first examine the market for you-the-product (developed in Part 2) and identify prospective users. We describe a market assessment process in which you identify functions, fields, and positions of visceral interest, develop a line of questioning based on the results of the exercises you completed in Part 2, and conduct investigative interviews to determine the fit between you-the-product and your areas of interest.

Your objective in this phase is to determine the realities: how well you would *fit* within a given field or function and, based on supply and demand, your *odds* of securing employment within your time frame. At the end of the market assessment phase, you will have a distilled list of fields or positions that represents your target market.

The next step is writing out your marketing campaign—a blueprint for your selling effort that includes defined phases, your goals for each, the specific tactics you will employ to achieve those goals, and your timetable. You'll also design and test your sales tools (including product literature such as your resumé, supplements, and the various types of letters appropriate to your campaign) and cultivate the channels of approach to key decision makers. Part 3 also contains practical suggestions for implementing your self-marketing campaign: chapters on the realities of the job search; networking (the way most managers find their jobs); resumés, letters, and ads (debunking traditional wisdom and offering some proven techniques); interviewing (something that most managers do poorly); recruiters (how to use them without ever being used); career help for hire;

[1]To complete the core exercise in Part 2 you must have *The New Quick Job-Hunting Map* workbook by Richard N. Bolles. Your bookstore can order it from these distributors: Ingram Book Company or Baker & Taylor Books. Or you may order it from Ten Speed Press, Box 7123, Berkeley, CA 94707 (415-845-8414). Do it now!

and closing the sale. The final chapter of Part 3 offers a comprehensive checklist to keep you organized and moving forward during this transition process.

Along the way, we'll include comments from HBS graduates[2] who have experienced the transition process. Our hope is that something said by a seminar participant will be particularly meaningful for each of you reading this book. When that happens, you will experience one of the primary benefits of the HBSCNY Career Seminar: the opportunity to share the realization that other managers have had similar thoughts, doubts, and breakthroughs. We are grateful to each person who allowed a portion of his or her journey to be shared.

[2]To ensure confidentiality, job titles, industries, and years of graduation have been slightly altered.

I

PUTTING THINGS INTO PERSPECTIVE

1

THE PREMISES AND
THE PAYOFF

THE FIVE PREMISES

The career transition process advocated in this book and used effectively by the many managers who have attended the Harvard Business School Club of New York Career Seminar is based on five premises.

The Process Is Much of the Prize

In the self-awareness portions of the transition process, you will review your patterns, articulate your goals, and reacquaint yourself with your abilities. New insights will change the way you see yourself in relation to your environment. The process of defining your product specifications also will help you form a picture of yourself—not the ideal you or the person that others wish you to be, but the real you. Having a clear sense of those product attributes allows you to present yourself to other people in a highly effective and credible manner.

Each Person Is a Unique Being in a Unique Situation

This premise precludes the idea of applying one set of rules to every individual or situation. In the HBSCNY Career Seminar we tell attendees that although they may have come for answers, our role is to help them identify the questions and issues most critical to their respective situations. This approach works, time and time again, because once it is allowed to function, a manager's internal guidance system is wise and capable.

> *I came to the Career Seminar to find a job and came away with a whole new concept of success—in terms of things that really mattered to me*

rather than others. In my last job I had a lot of success in terms of company recognition but virtually no satisfaction. Now I have a much better handle on what's important to me.

—Managing Director, consulting, HBS '84

Career Difficulties Are Often an Invitation to Change

Most people have a hand in creating their career difficulties. Such self-sabotaging behavior is often obvious to everyone except the person involved, who may vehemently deny playing any role in his or her misfortunes. Consider this comment by a manager recalling an early stage in his professional life:

> *I had problems with my boss's boss. I had been put in charge of the administration of the annual meeting, a big show. It's not the kind of work that turns me on, and I didn't take it seriously. No one ever told me this was very important. I felt it was just an administrative thing to be done—to be delegated—so I could do the important stuff, and I guess I didn't give it the attention I should have. This guy put out the word that he wanted me out of there. I felt very screwed: I'm smart, I'm bright, and I was cut off. I think this guy made a big mistake.*

Division President, manufacturing, HBS '74

The annual meeting was clearly important to several very influential senior managers, and yet this intelligent manager misread, or ignored, their signals.

Such behavior represents cues from your internal guidance system that you need to either change how you cope with the workplace or change where you work. When heeded at an early stage, these cues can prompt you to make changes in a relatively painless and constructive manner. When ignored, such cues become increasingly insistent, until inappropriate behavior creates a crisis situation that is impossible to ignore.

> *My boss screamed mercilessly at anyone who provoked his anger. I found him to be a very threatening individual, and anticipating his tirades made me very jumpy. In retrospect, I lived out a self-fulfilling prophecy: his expectation that I would make a mistake became my expectation, and eventually I did make a mistake. One too many sets of figures didn't add up, and the boss told me that he had had it with me. I don't recall that I made even one mathematical mistake while I was at my former job.*

VP, commercial banking, HBS '65

Career difficulties can lead you to resolve unhealthy situations. Many people look back at career crises and admit, "Even though it involved a lot of pain, it was the best thing that could have happened to me."

Your Intuition Has a Role to Play in the Career Process and in Your Next Job

Some managers find this precept difficult to accept. Managers who are highly skilled in logical and analytical thinking are most comfortable with a career process that draws exclusively on those analytical skills. But developing your *intuitive* skills is the challenge at hand. Acknowledging your intuition's existence and its legitimate role in decision making is the first step. Your career process will yield far more if your logical and intuitive powers work hand in hand. And once in the new job, that combination will continue to be a very effective management tool.

> *My rational thought process ran my life for twenty-five years while I successfully ignored what my gut instinct was trying to tell me. Finally I tripped myself up and was left with no choice but to listen. At first I had difficulty believing and trusting that internal guidance system you talk about in the Seminar, but then I could see that when I used it, things fell into place. Now I am careful to keep my intellect and intuition in balance.*
>
> VICE PRESIDENT, WALL STREET, HBS '71

You Already Have the Skills to Find the Right Road

The search for the right career move is not as mysterious as it might seem.

- You can define the product: you. This is not the superficial you but the *entire* you, including your talents, attributes, values, motivations, preferences, and disinclinations.
- You can define the market: the industries, fields, or functions that are a good fit for the entire you and offer sufficiently good odds of entry and success.
- You can design and carry out a classic marketing campaign for the product: you. It may take some time and involve some repositioning or trading off of nonessentials. But a successful campaign is something well within your abilities and experience to accomplish.

Finding the best fit does not mean tailoring your resume and your pitch according to what jobs are available. The goal is a fit that is good for *you:* that's why you first define you-the-product. The world of work offers a wide range of customers for your product; your task is to decide who you *choose* to sell to, at what price, and for what trade-offs. In the market assessment phase you'll evaluate what your markets of interest are buying and how to reach them, but not, we hope, from the perspective of a chameleon who changes colors to fit the occasion.

THE PAYOFF: SELF-ACCEPTANCE, SUCCESS, AND HAPPINESS IN YOUR JOB AND YOUR LIFE

We recommend a life reassessment. You may think that this sounds like a good idea after you have a new job, but *now* may be a better time. One of our favorite bumper stickers reads, "I'm lost, but I'm making good time!" Before you're immersed in a new job—on call all day to management, racing the clock and your appointment calendar—make sure you are headed where you want to be going. Treat yourself to the benefits of a tested process. Harness your intuition. Recover yourself.

The goal is to achieve fulfillment in more areas of your life. By identifying and satisfying your highest priorities and accepting the necessary trade-offs, you've created conditions that allow you to be more satisfied with your life. By defining what *you* feel success is, you can direct your energies toward attaining objectives that are consistent with your deepest values. And by approaching this transition methodically, you're on the road to succeeding in what is most important to you.

HOW TO USE THIS BOOK

We'll assume you fall into one of two categories—currently in transition or employed. Whatever your situation, we suggest that you read Part 1 to put yourself in the right frame of mind for this transition and then skim the entire book. Slow down and savor any section that seems particularly interesting. Then, depending on your situation, we recommend that you proceed according to the following plan.

Currently in Transition

My Change of Status Happened Recently

Read Chapter 20, "A Recap of the *In Transition* Process: A Checklist." Then, start at the beginning of the book and work systematically through the entire *In Transition* process. As a morale builder, fast-forward to two activities—Your Intrinsic Skills, step 2 (Chapter 7), and Networking, step 1 (Chapter 14). Follow the directions for making a comprehensive list of accomplishments and contacts. These exercises put your career in better perspective, get you back in touch with your areas of competence, and remind you of the many people you know who represent a source of help.

I Have Been Between Jobs for Some Months

Read Chapter 3—"The CEO and the Board of Directors of Your Job Search"—for directions on building the most important board in your life, the team that will sustain you as you move through *In Transition.* Commit to appointing that board and calling a board meeting to review your plan of attack. You may find that you're right on course, or you may need to start with Part 2. Take action now! And read Chapter 13 on "Realities of the Job Search" for a reminder of what comes with the territory.

It's Been Too Long, and I'm Pretty Desperate

Read Chapter 10 on "Constraints to Achieving Your Ideal Job" to identify possible roadblocks to your moving forward. Take action steps within your control: strengthen your selling skills, tackle any psychological impediments to effective marketing, and revisit your priorities. Read Chapter 18 on "Career Help for Hire" and consider hiring a good coach.

Employed

I Anticipate a Job Transition

You are in an excellent position to take full advantage of the *In Transition* process. Start with Chapter 5, "Life Mission, Priorities, and Trade-offs," and complete each exercise in Part 2. Start your self-assessment now. You have an opportunity to do it right: don't wait until you're in a crisis mode.

I Don't Anticipate a Transition, But I'm Uneasy about My Career Direction

Read Part 2 straight through before doing any exercises, to identify the source of your uneasiness. Are you not moving toward your life goals? Do you have no time for your priorities? Is your operating style wrong for the job? Is there a skills mismatch or a poor fit with the organization? Decide whether you are *sufficiently* uneasy to undertake a process of self-examination; if so, begin with the exercises in Chapter 5, "Life Mission, Priorities, and Trade-offs."

I'm Content But Want to Improve My Career Savvy

Read Chapter 6, "Styles, Values, and Motivations," Chapter 8, "Organizational Fit and Politics," and Chapter 9, "To See Ourselves as Others See Us." These three chapters discuss the important determinants of career savvy: knowing your own style (a manifestation of your values and motivations), understanding the styles of others, and recognizing the rules of the road in an organization.

As you browse through this book, pay attention to subsection titles and "nuggets," which highlight important topics. Also try to use the cross-references, which direct you to other useful sections. For those who have time for only a skim, we hope that a nugget or case quote may be sufficiently intriguing to prompt you to slow down and give your career the attention it deserves.

"CONGRATULATIONS ON YOUR GOOD NEWS"

Unlike most of our case histories this one does not use pseudonyms. Dick Wedemeyer recounts this experience regularly in the HBSCNY Career Seminar because it illustrates so much of what we believe about the transition process:

> It had finally happened! As I drove home, I dreaded talking with Shirlee, my wife, about the future. Earlier in the day I had telephoned her to share the bad news: an organizational change was eliminating the small subsidiary company I worked for. Soon I would be jobless. Three years ago it had seemed like a good decision to leave the security of a large company and move our family to take a job that had glowing prospects for challenge and income. Then the market sagged. The past year had been awful, and now the parent company had pulled the plug—a regretful but not surprising decision.
>
> As I pulled into the driveway, I saw the car of one of our dearest friends, Maria Teresa. My first thought was, "Damn, I don't want to spread the news all over town. I hope Shirlee hasn't told her."
>
> "Congratulations on your good news!" said Maria Teresa as I walked through the door. I was stunned. What was she talking about? "I'm so happy you're getting out of that stupid job that's been causing you so much grief." First I felt a rush of anger: how dare she make fun of my

misfortune! But in a flash I shared her insight: the job had not been right for me, and a part of me shared Maria Teresa's relief. There still would be scary times ahead, but—thanks to the perception of a friend—part of me could now perceive the good news.

We hope that this book does for you what Maria Teresa did for Dick: help put things in perspective and reveal the "good news" contained in whatever career difficulty you find yourself. Welcome to the start of the most exciting and life-enhancing period of your life!

2

PITFALLS AND IMPEDIMENTS

All managers have career problems at one time or another. And intelligent, competent managers sometimes lose their ability to manage or respond effectively to those career difficulties. Listen to this seminar participant:

> *I know something is wrong—because I've been trying to get a job since last fall, and I don't seem to be making progress. I think I'm waiting to be offered a job rather than going in with a clear idea of the job I want. I'm not selling. I'm losing enthusiasm, getting tired of it—I've been down a lot of blind alleys. I know I'm not aggressive in my follow-up. The bottom line is I haven't identified what I am really seeking.*
>
> VP, COMMERCIAL BANKING, HBS '70

Perhaps you can recall similar experiences in your career or the careers of your acquaintances. The point is clear: even the most experienced manager does not automatically bring to bear management skills when faced with career difficulties.

The following seven factors may contribute to this phenomenon of reduced coping ability:

1. Being at loose ends professionally is *unfamiliar territory*. It seems foreign and unresponsive to your accustomed practices.
2. Your initial reaction may be a feeling of *helplessness*. This perceived helplessness—a severe contrast to the sense of control you experienced previously—may become a reality.
3. Without a job you're on the *outside looking in*, an abrupt change from the collegiality and key-role stature you recently enjoyed. Such distance from others can lead to alienation from self.
4. This *wasn't part of your plan:* the plausible scenarios you had foreseen did not include this eventuality. An attitude of "I don't belong in this situation" encourages denial and interferes with effective coping.

5. You may be encumbered by difficulties in dealing with a sense of *failure*. Bear in mind that *to fail* is a verb, *failure* is a noun, and "I'm a failure" is a state of mind. Failure is a normal part of life; you're not a failure until you give up trying.
6. You may believe in the *stigma of joblessness*—that a person's importance is related to his or her job and that therefore someone without a job is without value. If you believe this on the upswing, when you have that high-status job, you're bound to feel the repercussions on the downswing.
7. You may believe in the *lily-pad-to-lily-pad* fallacy: a competent manager steps from one job to the next (ever upward, of course) without missing a beat or—heaven forbid—being unemployed. This perception has little to do with reality, but it can cause you to question your own competence when your transition goes less than smoothly.

Examined coolly and rationally, any or all of the above factors may seem laughable. But for anyone who goes through a period of joblessness, these factors can be powerful, painful, and disruptive. Their power stems in part from their subtle influence. When they are held up for scrutiny, they begin to lose their potency.

COMMON PITFALLS

The seven factors listed above cause many capable managers to mishandle career difficulties. Some all-too-common errors in judgment and the resulting behavior choices are discussed below.

Pitfall 1: Adopting the "Keep It Quiet" Syndrome

The first inclination of many managers with career problems is to keep mum: no discussions with co-workers, friends, or—not uncommonly—spouse or significant other. This manifestation of the stigma of joblessness was captured by these two managers in transition:

> *I'm not giving out that I'm at home. . . . I'm hesitating to let my friends know that I'm in this situation.*
>
> VP, REAL ESTATE, HBS '84

> *Our minister told me today that three parishioners who are out of work have sworn their wives to secrecy about their situation, and he feels there may be others that even he doesn't know about.*
>
> ADMINISTRATIVE DIRECTOR, SERVICE INDUSTRY, HBS '66

The *In Transition* process ultimately depends on marketing—letting prospective employers know that you are available. The "keep it quiet" syndrome keeps this information from circulating. Whatever your personal circumstances, the current widespread and highly visible no-fault dismissals brought about by massive corporate contractions have resulted in the layoffs of many capable, responsible, respectable managers just like you. Your situation is not unique, so don't be tempted to keep it a secret.

Pitfall 2: Going for the Quick Fix

Let's face it: most people prefer to take the short, easy route. Look at the self-help section in your bookstore. The titles offer seductive promises: "Quick! Simple! Fast! Painless! Inexpensive!" "Everything you need to know about . . ." Headhunters sometimes approach managers in transition with an offer that promises to fix everything:

> *There I was in Philadelphia, and a search guy came after me for a job in Chicago . . . the appeal was the job as Chief Financial Officer of a company, which I thought had good opportunities for the future. Also, he intimated that the company would go public, and I would be a part of it. Well, it was a disaster! I hadn't done my homework independently as to their marketplace position, the real chances. I jumped too quickly at something that sounded ideal.*
>
> VP FINANCE, ELECTRONICS, HBS '60

In Transition makes no claims to offer quick fixes or simple answers. A quick read through this book might yield insights and suggestions you can use immediately, but as we say in the seminar, the process requires you to commit a significant amount of your time and energy. What you gain from the process depends on what you put in.

Quick fixes are seductive—and treacherous. The tendency to postpone addressing career difficulties until they reach crisis proportions, the insidious stigma of joblessness, and the specter of loss of revenue all exert strong pressures on you to polish up the resumé, reach for the address book, find another job fast—to take what's available.

> *I was offered a place on a short-term finance team started by a person brought over from a competitor. I took it because it was there, because I only had one other lead, and I felt the world was coming to an end.*
>
> VP, FINANCIAL SERVICES, HBS '77

*I took the first offer in—within two months, even with seven months'
severance from my previous employer. This company was a real money
machine—and they paid me well. But once our senior management felt
there wasn't that much new business down the road, those of us brought
in to build the business were let go.*

VP, FINANCIAL SERVICES, HBS '82

In many instances quick fixes quickly fail. Their greater cost, however,
is the lost opportunity to reexamine your past for tendencies to avoid in
the future. If you give yourself the opportunity to analyze your career
path, you will find some common threads, perhaps a tendency to take the
first offer, difficulty in dealing with a particular type of person or situation,
or self-sabotaging tendencies. Once you are aware of such patterns, you're
on the way to being fortified against making the same mistake in future
transitions and on the next job.

NUGGET: Resist the temptation of the quick fix. Consider your decision-making history (see Chapter 4). Are you succumbing to a familiar
life pattern that often backfires? Are you encountering a psychological
constraint (see Chapter 10) masquerading as good financial sense? Review any decision with your board before acting (see Chapter 3).

Pitfall 3: Taking Irrelevant or Invested Advice

Another common mistake is accepting questionable advice from others.
Everyone you talk with—family, friends, co-workers, even strangers—has
career experience and expertise to offer and has an opinion on what you
should do. The danger comes from failing to determine to what extent
another person's experience is relevant to your particular situation. All too
often, it is not.

*I'm getting a lot of conflicting feedback from my friends—like "You're
giving up too soon on the corporate world" and "To take part-time work
is crazy." In an earlier period when I did freelance only, I couldn't relax
and just get into it; I felt lonely and disconnected, with too little structure
in my life. However, that was ten years ago . . . at this stage, I'd really
like to give my own business a shot.*

STRATEGIC PLANNER, PUBLISHING, HBS '81

*As soon as I was let go my parents and friends started putting a lot of
pressure on me. "You should be doing several interviews a day." "Don't*

consider any changes, it's easier to get the same kind of job you had."
The HBSCNY Career Seminar was a big help in turning a deaf ear to
this well-meaning advice of people who just wanted to get me back to
work. The result was a career change, which was the best thing that could
have happened.

VP, CORPORATE PLANNING, HBS '81

Those well-meaning friends may not even be aware of their biases.

Authoritative—but questionable—advice also comes from people
who are ostensibly "more experienced"—people who you feel know what
is better for you than you yourself. You may feel constrained to at least
listen to and possibly heed such advice. Some influential individuals may
have jobs to offer:

A headhunter called and said, "It's not your usual insurance com-
pany—it's very go-go." I visited the offices, and they were very run
down. I decided, "Here's a start-up—I'm getting a form of equity, a
good salary, a bonus opportunity." I wished away a lot—boss, environ-
ment, experience not on my resume—this headhunter was a very good
salesman.

VP, SYSTEMS, HBS '75

I decided to accept the job. And then the calls came from senior execu-
tives at my company. All these important people telling me how impor-
tant I was—"You're a person with a vision. You want to move mountains;
you have such a wonderful career here; you'll lead this company one day."
I began to think, "Maybe I could be president, if I stayed right where I
was!" I was listening to others rather than myself. I took the new job, but
not without a few second thoughts.

PARTNER, ADVERTISING, HBS '79

Seek advice assertively, sort through it carefully, and use it wisely. Ask,
"How relevant is this input to *my* situation?" Guard against advice from
people with vested interests or agendas different from yours. The best
validation is receiving the same advice from several well-qualified sources.
Standing by *your* self-understanding and well-considered course of action
will pay off, as it did for this manager:

After years working for a large corporation, I started out on my own—
feeling good about the decision. Then I met with this prospective cli-
ent who took an hour trying to hire me into his company and giving
some very persuasive arguments against my decision to work alone. It
really shook me—but then I went back over the results of my self-

awareness work and was reassured I had made the right decision. Things have worked out wonderfully for me—I am so thankful I stuck to my resolve.

INDEPENDENT CONSULTANT, INFORMATION SERVICES, HBS '81

Pitfall 4: Heeding Conventional Wisdom

Conventional wisdom may be even more difficult to resist than irrelevant or invested advice. Rather than one person's opinion, conventional wisdom is ostensibly a body of knowledge that has stood the test of time. Any one piece of conventional wisdom may be valid for some people in some circumstances. The fallacy, once again, is in thinking that one piece of wisdom applies to a variety of situations. The following common career maxims illustrate the importance of not taking any piece of conventional wisdom to be true in all times and circumstances.

It's Easier to Get a Job When You Have a Job
Contraindications:

- The negative connotations of being in transition have lessened considerably in the past decade.
- A serious job campaign is a full-time job; it is hard to carry out an effective job search if you are employed.
- An employee at the end of his or her rope on the job may come across as the last-angry-manager on interviews, thereby prolonging if not altogether precluding a successful job campaign.
- For job changers in certain positions, conflicting desires to maintain confidentiality and find new work will protract the search.
- At some point it may be more constructive to leave the old job and conduct the job campaign full time and unconstrained. This seminar participant was close to that point:

I must take the time. I'd rather be on the job while I'm looking, but I'm behind. I had a ten-day business trip, and I've made no calls. I must turn what we have done in the self-assessment process into action.

DIRECTOR OF MARKETING, FINANCIAL SERVICES, HBS '83

And in fact, on leaving her high-pressure, travel-intense position, she moved her search into high gear and moved into a new industry within a few months.

Never Admit to Being Out of Work When You're Networking or Interviewing
Contraindications:

- The downside of being dishonest about your current status far outweighs any question of convenience or comfort.
- The key is to position your circumstances in a way that neutralizes the situation.
- Exploiting every opportunity to discuss your campaign requires being out in the world, confident of your abilities and gifts. Hiding your status erodes your confidence:

  "It's getting harder to remember who knows and who doesn't."

  "The interviewer was very understanding after I tripped myself up about still working, but it killed my chances."

If You're Older, Don't Put Your Age or Date of College Graduation on Your Resumé
Contraindications:

- When a manager encounters a resumé without dates, age becomes an issue.
- A candidate telegraphing the message, "My age is a problem," undercuts important selling points.
- A job seeker uncomfortable or apologetic about his or her age does not make a positive impression.
- If you have the maturity and wisdom that come with years of experience, feature your age as an advantage. The employer looking specifically for youth won't appreciate the assets of someone with a longer career. Don't waste your time or exhaust your self-esteem on such targets.

If Your Job History Lacks Continuity, Use a Functional Resumé Format That Omits a Chronological List of Employers and Titles
Contraindications:

- Put yourself in the prospective employer's place. A functional resumé without any chronological data prompts the question, "What is this candidate hiding?"
- A functional resumé format is appropriate in some cases (see Chapter 15), but always include a brief chronology of your work history to avoid raising suspicions.

Control the Interview to Demonstrate Your Managerial Abilities
Contraindications:

- Effective interviewing involves exerting sufficient influence to ensure that you highlight your sales points, but think back to candidates you have interviewed. Remember those whose misguided efforts to control the conversation resulted in their leaving a negative impression?

  "Assertive is one thing. That guy was pushy bordering on obnoxious."

  "I was tempted to say, 'Let's trade seats. You seem to want to run this interview.' "

- Effective interviewing involves integrating relevant information *while* demonstrating your ability to relate to the interviewer.
- Challenging an interviewer's right to control the situation by engaging in a power struggle is inappropriate.

Beware of conventional wisdom. Make your own determination about whether any maxim is wise—or simply conventional.

Pitfall 5: Deferring Your Career Work

Since few managers relish addressing career issues, the tendency is great to put off this work:

  "I'll pick up the search when I'm ready—in a few weeks or months."

  "I'll be away on vacation next week. I can make calls from there."

  "I'm very involved in fund-raising for my college and don't have any time to spare."

  "It's hard to get motivated. I'm in a fur-lined rut."

Career difficulties often escalate to the crisis stage because managers tend not to address them—even ignore them—at an early stage. Ignore career issues at your own peril: they seldom go away and usually reappear with amazing regularity until you tackle them head on.

Pitfall 6: Delegating Your Career Work

When career difficulties become too obvious to ignore, many managers look to someone else for solutions. It's a natural response, especially for the manager accustomed to delegating "detail work." We strongly advise against delegating your career work. In the employment pages of the *Wall Street Journal* and other publications you'll find ads placed by "career management" firms with seductive pitches:

If you don't have the time to conduct your own job campaign . . .

Get maximum market exposure in the shortest time.

We offer access to top-level positions that are never advertised.

Let us manage your career campaign.

A personalized marketing strategy.

And managers succumb:

I went to them, paid the fee, and got a wonderful package for a search that promised to save me time—letters to associations, labels, search firms. We sent out eighty letters to headhunters, and then I sat back and hoped for the best. Nothing happened, of course. It was foolish, but I couldn't bring myself to call companies directly.

VP Systems, financial services, HBS '75

We strongly advise against delegating career work for two reasons. First, many firms offering to do the work for you are more expert at promoting their product than delivering results. Typically, the fee is a lump sum, possibly characterized as a retainer with the remaining percentage of salary on the new job to be paid over the first year of employment. Firms may promise custom treatment, listings of openings, and introductions, but the contract rarely guarantees anything more specific than the fee to be paid—by you, in advance. Our guideline is simple: if you ever pay for career counseling, the safest way is on an hour-by-hour basis.

We have a second reason for recommending that you not delegate your career work: as mentioned in the introduction, a premise of *In Transition* is that the process is part of the prize. The self-exploration and development portion of the process is a personal and rewarding exercise; it must be done by you, using proven techniques and outside benchmarks. Who is best equipped to determine your priorities, to select your next field or function, or to develop your marketing strategy? We believe firmly that *you* are the best person to be at the helm. The resumé you evolve and test is a much more effective selling document than one that is ghost written. The self-awareness and confidence you develop during the process make you a much more credible and effective interviewer. This is not to say you should go it *alone* (see Chapter 3); a well-chosen coach and an appropriate advisory board can be invaluable. And you may enlist assistance from specialty service firms (typing services, for example), such as those discussed in Chapter 18. But it's *your* process, and you should manage it yourself.

YOUR FIRST STEP: ON YOUR OWN BUT NOT ALONE

Many of the techniques covered in this book are best done by yourself, for yourself. But it need not be a lonely experience. Quite the contrary! *In Transition* shows you how to manage your career transition with the same confidence you've enjoyed in your best job experience. It shows you how to establish a support system that will bolster and advise you. So whatever your state and condition as you start this book, give yourself a pat on the back. You are addressing your career in a serious, professional manner.

3

THE CEO AND BOARD OF DIRECTORS OF YOUR JOB SEARCH

For the manager accustomed to extensive staff support and the power and authority to make things happen, the diminution of stature that results from a job loss is particularly difficult. Managers in transition must perform many functions they previously left to others and may not have attempted in years. This strikes many as inefficient, and in frustration they let minor obstacles become major impediments to their effectiveness. Word processors, fax machines, and automatic dialers reduce the amount of mundane work, but the job search remains a hands-on experience in which you wear *all the hats.* Handle this reality as a challenge—as an unpleasant but necessary reality to be dealt with constructively—and you'll come out ahead.

But for most managers in transition, more threatening than additional clerical duties are isolation and loss of power. An isolated job changer often experiences a downward spiral in self-confidence. The absence of colleagues to provide perspective and the loss in authority to dictate the course of events diminish a manager's sense of self-worth and competence. Implementing a marketing campaign—particularly selling oneself—becomes increasingly difficult, which in turn leads to experiences of rejection by the market, further diminished confidence and self-worth, and so forth, downward and inward.

THE CEO CONCEPT

For the HBSCNY Career Seminar, we have developed what we call the CEO concept to deal with these realities. Consider the CEO of a corporation. Although to the public this captain of industry may seem to have a great deal of power and control, those familiar with business recognize that the CEO has limited control over the environment in which the corporation operates. The CEO's role is to analyze the marketplace, assess the strengths and weaknesses of the corporation, and determine the course of action that will result in the greatest return on assets with the least downside risk from liabilities. The CEO's job, then, is to steer the energies and resources of the corporation in the right direction.

The role of a manager in a job transition resembles that of the CEO. The job changer cannot control the environment but *can* channel his or her energies and resources in the direction that has the greatest prospect of yielding good returns. By taking an active managerial stance, the job-changer-turned-CEO regains that vital sense of control, an effective antidote to the feeling of powerlessness that can undermine the search.

NUGGET: The attitude of the manager who adopts the CEO concept will positively affect both the quality and duration of this career transition.

Promote yourself to CEO in charge of your job search. Your "corporation" has assets and liabilities, strengths and weaknesses. It contains a valuable combination of capabilities for a particular segment of the marketplace. Recognize and affirm that your functions and responsibilities are those of a CEO:

- To assess the strengths and weaknesses of your "corporation,"
- To direct all of its energies and activities in a carefully designed strategy in line with your assessment, and
- To reach those sectors of the market where your strengths are most valuable and your liabilities least limiting.

Like any CEO, you cannot control the environment. You *can* make the decision to focus on the elements under your control, primarily time and energy, to ensure they are used effectively rather than diffused and depleted. Once you embrace the CEO concept, you begin to address your situation with increasing assurance because the job search starts to feel like manageable territory. One more thing is needed, and it is the essential complement to every successful CEO—a board of directors. So your first task as CEO of your own corporation is to establish your board.

YOUR BOARD OF DIRECTORS

A good board of directors supports the CEO in three ways:

- Helping the CEO to maintain objectivity,
- Providing access to a broad range of outside information and re-sources, and
- Giving the CEO support and encouragement.

NUGGET: These benefits are critical to anyone in the job search: *objectivity* keeps the proper perspective throughout your campaign; *outside information and resources* augment your own network; and *support and encouragement* ensure an energized and steady pace. You need a board!

How do you form a board? Probably the most difficult step is convincing yourself you need a board. Consider your alternatives. You could go it alone—a real temptation for many managers who pride themselves on their objectivity, connections, and inner-directed, optimistic outlook. You could rely on your spouse. You might even hire a career counselor to provide objective inputs, special information sources, and all-important support.

Imagine a president or prime minister without a cabinet. Imagine a college president who consults only her spouse. None of those scenarios makes sense if the objective is the most effective decision making with the best possible information available. On the job, you recognized the value of multiple data sources and bouncing ideas off a number of people. It's not fair to load too much on any one set of shoulders, especially those of a spouse or significant other who may be experiencing considerable stress given your new situation. He or she may even have mixed emotions about being thrust unwillingly into the role of board-of-one.

Still not convinced? Listen to a veteran job seeker:

What the Seminar taught me was to think like a CEO: be realistic about your short suits so they don't trip you up, and be very clear about your strengths and play to them. When you go for a certain goal, you may or may not attain it—it's a question of fit and luck—but if you keep at the process you will be successful. And it worked for me. I love what I'm doing, and it's going very well.

DIRECTOR, PUBLISHING INDUSTRY, HBS/PMD '87

Now to the practicalities of forming a board.

1. Make a list of about ten candidates for your board. Include as broad a range of types as possible: some close friends, preferably representing a variety of lines of work and talent; individuals who are not close friends but whose judgment and business acumen you respect; and people in fields of particular interest to you.
2. Run your list by a few friends and advisers to make sure you haven't overlooked some good candidates or included potentially inappropriate ones. Do not omit someone because you feel that he or she would probably decline.
3. Set up a grid that enables you to rate each of your board members. Be sure each candidate has the three essential criteria listed below and at least one of the specialty criteria. When forming your board, aim to have one member with each of the specialty criteria.

Essential Criteria

☐ This candidate is someone I would listen to and whose input I would take seriously. I would not easily dismiss views from this board member.

☐ This candidate is a straight shooter and can be counted on to give honest and thoughtful feedback. This candidate would be a good sounding board.

☐ This candidate has no investment in my following a particular path. My self-actualization, as I define it, is a goal this candidate can wholeheartedly support.

Specialty Criteria

☐ This candidate believes in me unconditionally. I can honestly say that in a range of situations, over a number of years, this candidate has always been supportive and affirming.

☐ This candidate is available and accessible. Work and life pressures are not so great that I will rarely be able to make contact to avail myself of this candidate's views.

☐ This candidate is well placed and has a grasp of arenas or issues I am considering at this time of transition (a sector of the business world, the not-for-profit world, starting a business, balancing family and professional life).

☐ This candidate knows me very well. This candidate knows the questions I would rather not ask and asks them. I can't fool this candidate. He or she will keep me mindful of reality.

☐ This candidate complements my own strengths: where I have a blind spot, this candidate has perception; where I might rush the process, this candidate would challenge my hurry.

4. Draft a script to use in approaching your board candidates. Explain the CEO concept and your need for a well-qualified board. Make it clear what each person's role will be, reviewing the selection criteria used and stressing the contribution he or she could make. Specify the time commitment involved: this will vary according to the board member's situation. You might ask one for ten minutes on the phone each week, another for a bimonthly breakfast at a convenient

---

SAMPLE SCRIPT

Hi, _____. [Begin with brief personal inquiries, if appropriate.] I know you're busy, so I'll be brief. As you may know, I'm in the middle of a career transition; it's a fascinating process, which I'd enjoy telling you about some time. Right now I'm setting up a board of advisers—to bounce around ideas, test concepts, and keep me objective during this process. One of my ground rules is respect for the amount of time each person might be able to devote to this. It could be ten minutes per week on the phone or a periodic breakfast meeting— something comfortable for both sides. [_____ have already agreed to be board members.]

As I was considering people who might serve on this board, you came to mind because you would bring _____ [cite specifics from your essential or specific criteria]. Having that kind of advice and support to call on occasionally would be of great benefit. Would you consider joining my board?

[Listen carefully to the response, and gauge your next move accordingly. Respond with:] I'm pleased you are amenable to the concept. Let's work out a timing arrangement so that this won't become a burden to you.

[or:] I can appreciate the pressures you're under. And I'm glad I had an opportunity to update you on my status. Let's keep in touch.

location, a third for a one-hour face-to-face consultation monthly to touch base. Be sure you have board members in all three categories of availability.

5. Contact each candidate, starting with the ones most likely to say yes. Be concise (that's why you have the script), and structure a role appropriate to each candidate's situation, to ensure you will not feel awkward about contacting board members.

How are board candidates likely to react? How would *you* react if in the middle of your regular routine someone came to you with a unique idea about reassessing his or her career in a well thought out and organized fashion? In some cases, you would be intrigued, especially if you had been thinking about *your* career and had concluded that it might be time for a personal reexamination. You might respond similarly if someone you know, your teenager or a friend, were facing an upcoming career choice. In other cases, you would be wary, concerned that you were being asked to do more than your already busy schedule would allow.

In fact, that is exactly what happens when you recruit board members. In some cases you'll hear, "Count me in," and in others you'll be turned down. Those who have tried this approach have been pleasantly surprised at the results. They have formed boards of highly qualified people who, if used sparingly and regularly, helped the job seeker's campaign. As a side benefit, board members have learned something about the *In Transition* process.

Not surprisingly, you often make friends in the process of finding a job. Two Harvard Business School graduates described it this way:

If I had gotten nothing else out of our group, the friendship my wife and I have with Larry is worth everything. His new job is about twenty-five minutes from our home, and occasionally he stops by on the way home for dinner with us. He just helped us upgrade our computer—for a fee, of course. He is a real addition to our lives.
DIRECTOR OF CORPORATE RELATIONS, ACADEMIA, HBS '79

My board was great! At the beginning I was a little apprehensive about opening up, but even more apprehensive about not getting a job. The people really supported me—and cared enough to pounce on me if I started acting inappropriately. That was over six years ago, and we still stay in touch. When you get to know someone on that level, the relationship is better than most superficial business relationships.
PERSONNEL DIRECTOR, CONSUMER PRODUCTS, HBS '68

Long after the job search has ended, board members remain part of your network of colleagues. The friendships made and strengthened in the career transition process—because it is a time of vulnerability, exploration, and discovery—are deep friendships.

A TIME OF GROWTH AND OPPORTUNITY

> *In the middle of the journey of our life*
> *I came to my senses in a dark forest,*
> *for I had lost the straight path.*
> —Dante, Divine Comedy

Few people welcome change, especially if they are in reasonably comfortable circumstances and change does not suggest obvious advantages. Some changes are akin to movement over familiar ground toward a clear goal: during those changes anxiety is balanced by exhilaration. This book is about life changes related to one's career—an important part of any manager's identity. These are seldom pleasant journeys, particularly at the outset:

> *I just couldn't get motivated, and nothing was pushing me. I wasn't fortunate enough to get fired, so I went on and on until the dull ache of dissatisfaction became unbearable.*
> Associate, management consulting, HBS '77

To find yourself at a dead end in a career that isn't fulfilling is never a pleasant experience. However, as you become more intrigued at the prospect of a *better* work situation, we hope the transition process itself becomes more attractive—even enjoyable. Because this is *your* journey, designed to enhance your well-being and fulfillment, it can be a refreshing experience:

> *My job search was the first thing that I had done totally for myself in as long as I can remember. It had some very anxious and scary times to it, but there were also days when I felt so exhilarated that I would stop and say to myself, "Damn, I'm really enjoying this!"*
> Director of Administration, service industry, HBS '68

Even if your career transition was precipitated by the unpleasant shock of losing a job, bear in mind that many people look back and say,

Getting laid off was the best thing that could have happened to me. It gave me the impetus and license to do with my life what I had wanted to do but hadn't the courage.
STRATEGIC PLANNER, COMMUNICATIONS, HBS '80

Much depends on your point of view. As one seminar participant put it,

For me, everything fell into place when I realized I wasn't "looking for a job"—I was sorting through opportunities.
TECHNICAL SALES, INDUSTRIAL PRODUCTS, HBS '78

Many people have difficulty with any kind of *ending*. The end of something pleasurable and valued involves a loss, as does the end of anything known, familiar, or routine. Letting go can be difficult even when the end was your choice; if it was not your choice, letting go can prove to be a major challenge. Scrutinize your deep-seated reactions to this ending. They may be connected less to the realities of the present situation than to your conditioned response to all endings.

NUGGET: Endings are a normal part of each person's life and often serve a positive function: giving up one thing opens up the way for another. However much you have enjoyed a chapter in a favorite book, to move on to the next chapter you have to turn the page. To hold on is to be trapped.

Few veterans describe their job searches as among the most pleasurable experiences in their lives. But every search has some positive aspects that should not be overlooked:

1. A transition is one of the few times in your life when all of your professional focus is on you. All too often your priorities and interests may have been overshadowed by the needs of your employer and other affiliations.

   I dragged myself to the first session of the Career Seminar—out of work and really depressed. As I listened to what was being discussed, a little voice inside of me said, "Focusing on me *could be very stimulating. It might even be fun!" I walked out of there with a completely different attitude. And that little voice was correct: the process was one of the most meaningful things I have done in my life.*
   GENERAL PARTNER, INVESTMENT BANKING, HBS/AMP '78

2. Similarly, during a transition you can develop a panoramic, 360-degree perspective. The possibilities open to you need not be limited

to your present position, circumscribed by your past or otherwise narrowed. Like a traveler returning from a journey, you will look at life with a fresh perspective.

3. A job search gives you the opportunity to meet many good people in the course of your networking and interviewing. Some will become friends, and many will be useful contacts in your new role:

   I did a lot of networking during my search, and was careful to keep each contact informed of my progress. When I decided to become an independent consultant, I had an instant list of prospects—and a number of them are now clients.

   INDEPENDENT CONSULTANT, HBS '85

4. You have a rare opportunity to scrutinize and improve your techniques for relating with others. To sense how others perceive you and to empathize with their positions in a transaction is an invaluable asset for professional life. This manager flagged an old pattern:

   After I had been at the job for maybe three or four months, my boss told me I was coming on too strong and was ruffling some feathers. This was an old problem and I think related to my strong desire to want to be successful in my career. It was the "Don't get in my way; I'm on my way to becoming president or partner or whatever" syndrome.

   VP, COMMERCIAL BANKING, HBS '65

   Aware of the problem, he was on his way to resolving it.

5. Your job search is a chance to assess how realistically you deal with situations that "hooked" you in the past.

   I do believe there is a better job out there. I think it's time for a change, but there are only four people in my office: I'm indispensable. I think I need to quit or take a sabbatical to get this job search done. The problem is I'm liked here, I'm needed, and I've been here from the beginning. And I don't want to walk away. That's a pretty strong set of hooks, isn't it?

   VP, INVESTMENT BANKING, HBS '81

   My boss is no genius, I make no bones about it, but he has been successful at everything he's done. I've worked for him for the last eight years, and I would not turn on him now. In fact, I would probably run down Fifth Avenue for his next venture if he asked. I'm not being very realistic, I guess, but that's the truth.

   MANAGEMENT CONSULTANT, CONSUMER PRODUCTS, HBS '59

   Maybe you're hooked on being indispensable or on a particular type of boss. This is the time to evaluate the consequences and explore any limits to your professional growth.

6. During the job search, counterintuitive as this sounds, you may learn to become more comfortable with being open in your dealings with

your friends, colleagues, and even casual acquaintances. That heightened capacity to interrelate can lead to stronger and more meaningful relationships.

7. A transition is a time to grow in self-acceptance—to take more satisfaction from your skills and attributes and become less preoccupied with your short suits. This seminar participant had lost sight of his special qualities:

What am I unsatisfied with about myself? Not being more academic, more quantitatively oriented. Not getting into the models, the theory, the unpragmatic stuff. Not being a nastier person, able to be more aggressive, burn bridges. Not being able to be more intense. Not being able to project something I don't feel or believe. Being a bit lazy.

ASSOCIATE, M&A, INVESTMENT BANKING, HBS '80

If your most recent work situation was a poor fit with your skills and attributes, now is the time to reclaim your unique strengths and abilities.

8. A transition is a time to build the next chapter of your professional life on a firm foundation—on your core values, your immediate priorities, and your cherished skills. Avoid the self-doubts captured by this manager:

I have this fear of becoming "smaller" if I go with a small company, that I'll have less opportunity to be messianic or worldly. Yet am I riding on working for a big firm, having gone to a top graduate school? With the new company, will I still have major responsibilities outside? Will I still have the freedom to do what I want and be who I want? I know I define myself in terms of how people perceive me.

GROUP VP, PACKAGED GOODS, HBS '80

9. A transition is a time to regain balance in your life:

My first priority is personal growth, by which I mean opening up many more facets of life to myself—books, people, learning more about life, experiencing more emotions.

VP, FINANCIAL SERVICES, HBS '73

We extend our sincere wish that your career transition may be a journey filled with memorable adventures on a road that leads you to increased fulfillment and well-being.

II

GETTING TO KNOW
YOU—THE PRODUCT

4

THE SELF-EXPLORATION AND SELF-ASSESSMENT PROCESS

In the previous chapters we stressed that in developing a self-marketing campaign, the first and most critical step is to fully understand *you*, the product. The goals of your self-exploration and self-assessment should include enhancing your self-understanding and self-appreciation, clarifying your long-term life goals and near-term priorities, and gaining fresh insights into your assets and liabilities, particularly your *underutilized* potential. A well-done self-assessment enables you to better use your strengths and to chart a course leading to a job where your long suits are critical to success and your short suits irrelevant. The seven chapters in this section are designed to facilitate that process by acquainting you with self-assessment tools and techniques.

A word of caution. If you are at all typical, you may be strongly tempted to skip over this self-assessment section to get to the "heart of the process"—self-marketing, in Part 3. From many years of experience in the HBSCNY Career Seminar we know most managers tend to opt for the action-oriented over the reflective—or even more daunting, the *introspective*. The vast majority of "happy ending" feedback from seminar participants, however, has emphasized the benefits of the self-assessment portion of the process.

> *What I learned in the self-assessment was a big factor in finding this new position and affirming it is the right field and company for me.*
> MANAGER, BUSINESS DEVELOPMENT, HBS '82

> *The most useful part of the Seminar by far was the self-assessment phase—who I am, where I should be headed. It helped me realize that I had lost touch with my true objectives: I had been pursuing achievements for their own sake rather than because I enjoyed them.*
> MANAGEMENT CONSULTANT, HBS '87

It was not easy to throw away the image of me the chief executive, but doing so was key to success and happiness.

INVESTMENT BANKER, HBS '68

Put on your CEO hat. You would never start a marketing campaign without thoroughly assessing the product and its markets. In business, periodic audits and other organizational self-assessments are normal and appropriate. Likewise, as CEO of your career transition, your self-assessment is the appropriate first step of the process.

You may be wondering, "Who can be both auditor *and* object of an audit? And how do I do this?" This is not just checking up on a plant in some remote location; this is delving into portions of yourself that are infrequently, if ever, exposed. Once there, you must then assess what you find and draw valid conclusions from the results of your exploration.

Don't be intimidated. The self-assessment process can be an exciting and fulfilling journey. It need not be done all at one time, but once started, self-exploration and assessment can become an ongoing process that informs your decisions and enhances your satisfaction in everything you do. So as you move through the self-awareness exercises in Part 2, if at any time you feel inclined to fast-forward to Part 3, remind yourself, "This is essential product research."

As you begin to see the first results of your exercises, you will form some tentative conclusions, an approximation of you-the-product. As further results come in, you can compare and integrate these into your first approximation—or form a new image to test against your first. You will repeat this process until the characterization of you rings true to you and to the people close to you whose help you have enlisted in the process (see the discussion on building a board of directors in Chapter 3).

Most formal management training is heavily skewed toward the logical and sequential, even though some of the most able managers draw on good instincts and are known for their intuitive decision making. As you go through the self-assessment process, *trust the input of your instincts and intuition.* Your internal guidance system was influential in getting you into this process, so use it *with* your logical reasoning skills to obtain the best possible results. Keep in mind this HBSCNY Career Seminar participant's insights:

I know from experience that my intuition gives me valuable guidance, leading to conclusions I am more committed to and function better within. Even with that certainty, it is easier *for me to remain in the*

*comfort and familiar territory of logic and analysis, so getting out of my
head and into my gut requires discipline.*
                              CFO, SMALL ENTERPRISE, HBS '83

IMPEDIMENTS TO SELF-ASSESSMENT

The fact that introspection does not come readily to some managers has
been amply demonstrated over a decade of teaching the HBSCNY Career
Seminar. Each session of the seminar is divided into two parts: in the first
half we explore some facet of self-awareness, and in the second half we
deal with the pragmatic, nuts-and-bolts aspects of the job search. The
design is intentional: many people come for the practical pointers and—at
least at the outset—are only reluctantly willing to sit through the self-
awareness module. Most become increasingly intrigued and then con-
verted. A few, on realizing the initial topic, quietly close their attaché
cases and head for the door.

Before you start, read the following list of commonly encountered
factors that can impede *your* self-assessment—or defeat it entirely. We'll
examine these factors in more detail in Chapter 10, "Constraints to
Achieving Your Ideal Job."

Resistance to Change

Just as any organizational group resists criticism of its current practices
and suggestions for change, many managers resist the self-assessment
process—even when it is done by someone as trustworthy as themselves.
Look back at instances in your career when you examined a department
with an eye to recommending improvements. Remember the resistance
and reluctance you encountered? That same attitude can hinder your
self-assessment. As one Career Seminar participant said,

> *It's comfortable here. And I have no vision of where I'd go, no idea of
> the ideal job. It's very elusive. If I had a burning desire, probably I'd have
> more interest in this process. I'm not risk-oriented; inertia plays a role. I
> want to work things out in my own organization.*
>   MARKETING MANAGER, MANUFACTURING, HBS '69

If you encounter that same reaction in yourself as you go through the
process, be understanding. Give yourself credit for undertaking this pro-

cess in a professional fashion; recognize that your resistance is normal; and periodically take a break!

Why Probe?

Most managers are not prone to introspection. The archetypal manager is incisive and action-oriented, not a Hamlet paralyzed by conflicting inner thoughts. Such a manager writes bulleted memos, makes timely decisions, exercises authority, and sees that things are neatly wrapped up. This seminar participant is typical:

> *I'm sixteen years out of HBS: I thought going there was a good idea. Then I went to Wall Street: I thought that was a good idea. I have been on Wall Street for sixteen years, and I have no idea of who I am or should be. I haven't stopped to think about this stuff.*
>
> VP, FINANCIAL SERVICES, HBS '71

In highly competitive environments, self-assurance is always an asset, self-reflection sometimes a liability. You may not feel managerial during this process, particularly if you've been action-oriented most of your career.

Numbness Is My Armor

A high tolerance for long hours, no positive feedback, and a great deal of stress is essential for survival in some work situations:

> *The professionalism of this field requires total commitment: my life is not my own. The work is all-consuming, and I'm trying to balance a new family, which I am categorically* unwilling to trade off. *I'm totally stressed out.*
>
> CFO, INVESTMENTS, HBS '67

> *What does my boss want me to do? Leveraged buy-outs and mezzanine subordinated debt deals—not my thing! Can I do it? Yes. After all, I've done Paris Island.*
>
> VP, COMMERCIAL BANKING, HBS '71

To be an effective worker or to make a difficult job more tolerable, you may have stopped listening to your inner thoughts a long time ago. If you start listening to those thoughts in order to become more self-aware, you may have to reassess why you're in your current situation.

Lost Investment

If getting to where you are has taken most of your life and a lot of sacrifices, you may not want to find out that you should be somewhere else:

> I'm not that old, and frankly I can't see staying where I am. But I have fifteen years of my life invested here.
> MANAGER OF SHIP DESIGN AND CONSTRUCTION, HBS '66

What if your self-assessment suggests a whole *new career?* What if your intrinsic skills are ideally suited for running a small service business, and you've been in Fortune 50 companies for decades? What if a field of genuine interest doesn't even "require" a graduate school degree?

Don't Mess with My Façade!

Some managers, sensing they are in precarious shape, don't want to touch anything. Like a fake castle in a movie set, they look solid and impressive from the outside, but inside they feel held together with bailing wire:

> My current schedule, not to mention the stress, makes this process feel very overwhelming. I'm not sure why I'm procrastinating. Maybe I don't dare add anything to my platter.
> DIRECTOR, HUMAN RESOURCES, RETAILING, HBS '80

The fear that tampering with anything will cause your whole façade to collapse can derail a good self-assessment.

Shoulds and Oughts

A very subtle impediment to self-assessment is a deeply held belief that "I'm doing what I *should* be doing":

> I have family as my number one priority and future income as number two. I'm the pacesetter for the family; I'm the only one making a lot of money. I feel like I should be paying for my nieces' and nephews' college education.
> CONSULTANT, STRATEGIC PLANNING, HBS '80

Whether it is working for you or not, such a course—perhaps defined by family expectations or societal pressures—seems impossible to change.

Unfinished Business

In the context of self-assessment, *unfinished business* refers to unresolved issues in a manager's life that limit his or her options:

> *Money is very important to my parents—and that is hard for me to shake.*
> *I would have looked at different careers except for that issue.*
> ASSOCIATE, MANAGEMENT CONSULTING, HBS '84

> *I haven't come to grips with issues from my last job, so they're getting in the way.*
> CONSULTANT, STRATEGIC PLANNING, HBS '80

Dealing with unfinished business may include shaking a superimposed value that society, your peers, or your parents stress. It may mean acknowledging a pattern or an addiction. Unfinished business can threaten a good self-assessment by closing off avenues of exploration and discussion.

Do any of the above impediments ring a bell? Stay aware of these potential roadblocks as you go through this section. If you find yourself turning away from the process, reread the above list and see if you can pinpoint what is happening. Are you giving in to any false assumptions? Determine to stay on course. Consult your trusted advisers for strategies to get past your impediments. Persevere!

YOUR PRODUCT SPECIFICATION FILE

We suggest that you set up a convenient system for collecting the results of each of your self-awareness exercises. We'll call it your *product specification file*. This may be a set of manila files, a notebook, or any other convenient setup. It will eventually contain:

1. Forks in the Road Exercise
   A. Raw Data
   B. Themes

2. Eulogy Exercise
   A. Essay
   B. Distillation Lists
   C. Action Items: If . . . Then . . . To Do's
   D. Questions for Market Assessment

3. Priorities Exercise
   A. Initial Ranking
   B. Priority Cards
   C. Priority Grid
   D. Top Six Priorities
   E. Action Items: Must Haves/Must Avoids
   F. Questions for Market Assessment

4. Styles, Values, and Motivations Profiles
   A. Raw Data
   B. Questions for Market Assessment

5. Skills Audit
   A. Accomplishments List, Total
   B. Seven Accomplishments, Described
   C. Audit Results
   D. Questions for Market Assessment

6. Organizational Fit Requirements
   A. Raw Data
   B. Questions for Market Assessment

7. Constraints
   A. Profile
   B. Conclusions

Keep it flexible! Although the term *product specification file* is a useful reminder that you are working to fully characterize you-the-product, it can be misleading in one regard. You can list the fixed set of properties that characterize an inanimate object, but developing your specifications is an *evolutionary* process. With each exercise you will learn more about what matters to you and why, your predictable choices in work situations, and your natural skills. Be sure to leave sufficient space in your file for modifications and enhancements.

Bear in mind as you fill up your product specification file that you are operating in the shadow of *old* product specifications. Although never formally articulated, that old set of specs has defined you for many years. Perhaps you were the achiever in your crowd, or the caregiver in your family, or the peacemaker wherever you went. Or perhaps you were the practical one or the numbers person. Part of the self-exploration and assessment process consists of reviewing those old specifications, particularly those assigned by other people, and determining to what extent they are *valid for you at this point in your life.*

HOW DID I GET TO WHERE I AM?

My tendency in life has been to stay off the beaten path. To an outsider, my career seems logical and orderly, but it really is not. Thus while most of my HBS peers were gravitating towards Wall Street, I selected retailing, an area generally less well traveled by HBS grads.
                    MANAGEMENT CONSULTANT, CONSUMER PRODUCTS, HBS '59

The first exercise in the *In Transition* process is a guide to help you think about what brought you to your present situation. It enables you to assess your own history, to examine how you have made decisions in your life, and to review how the results reflect on your decision-making process.

THE FORKS IN THE ROAD EXERCISE

STEP 1: Make a retrospective chronological log: take a pad or notebook, and at the top of the first page write "19__" (the current year). On the second page, write "19___–19___" (the preceding two years). Continue back in time, with each page representing a two- to five-year period. The last page should be "My Grade School Years."

STEP 2: Consider the factors that caused you to make the decision at each significant fork in your life path. These might include parental influence or example, input from others such as teachers or older siblings, academic and extracurricular preparation, work experience, economic pressures, the compensation package, or security.

STEP 3: As you recall each factor, make a brief note of it on the appropriate page in your retrospective chronological log. Include enough detail to recall it later but not so much to slow down the process.

STEP 4: Continue working on the log on and off for a week or so. One thing will remind you of another, sometimes with no obvious connection. You'll dry up for awhile, then another influence will come to mind. Keep the log at hand, so you're ready to catch the memories as they drift by.

STEP 5: After you have captured most of the relevant factors, go through the log to look for common threads. How did each which-fork-shall-I-take decision come about? Who made the decision? Where you had a say, what were the primary influences on you? Examples: "Mom insisted that I go to a local college." "I took this because it came along very quickly." "They pursued me!"

STEP 6: Pay particular attention to sections of your career path where you did not do well or did not enjoy your work. Why did you take that path? How quickly did you get off?

STEP 7: Do a written summary of the themes that emerge from your log. Some sample themes include the following:

- Financial achievement and success were powerful draws; conversely, without the prospect of financial gain an option had very little appeal.
- The need for autonomy and a sense of control drove my decisions.
- A strong desire for compelling work or total absorption in work was the hook.
- I preferred fast-paced work, tough deadlines, and full agendas.
- My priority was succeeding on a range of fronts—professional, personal, spiritual, family, health. I took jobs that allowed me that latitude.
- Jobs promising intellectual satisfaction strongly appealed to me.
- The people in the environment made a big difference.
- I've been hooked by certain kinds of bosses.
- I was heavily influenced by other people's preferences for me.
- High-status companies—name brands in their field—were always the draw.

The Forks in the Road Exercise can be very illuminating. Knowing how you arrived at your present situation and being alert to any false positives or other misleading influences at past decision points is your first step toward improved decision making in the future. The exercise also may evoke strong feelings, ranging from affection for the positive influences in your life to anger at how little say you had at key forks in the road. Stay focused on the present; endless speculation about the path you *should* have followed or the very different circumstances you would be in today if only you had done one or two things differently is fruitless.

Another purpose of this first exercise is to consider the question, "Am I on the right road headed toward the right destination?" That question can't be answered easily, so don't rush it; you will have ample opportunity to reflect on it further. If you come out of the Forks in the Road Exercise with a strong realization that you have taken a number of wrong turns along the way, that is very useful good news/bad news/best news information. Becoming aware of being on the wrong road is good news. Realizing that you have expended a great deal of your life headed in the wrong direction is disconcertingly bad news. Discovering the wherewithal to seek and find the correct road is the best news of all.

As a first entry in your product specification file, enter your Forks in the Road Exercise. You've started the self-exploration and self-assessment process. You're on the way to heightened self-awareness, to *knowing you—the product.*

5

LIFE MISSION, PRIORITIES, AND TRADE-OFFS

Your work is only one aspect—although a major one—of your life. The most successful and fulfilling careers are aligned with one's mission in life, with one's ultimate values. Many career difficulties stem from conflicts between the demands of a job and those core values:

> *Figuring out what to do with the rest of my life that can be meaningful is very important to me. Jobs don't fulfill me. I have done well—in terms of money and title—but in the last three years I've had five positions.*
> STRATEGIC PLANNER, INFORMATION SERVICES, HBS '81

The self-awareness exercises in this chapter invite you to return to basics and explore your life mission and priorities.

YOUR LIFE MISSION

The initial exercise in the HBSCNY Career Seminar is occasionally met with puzzled looks and, in extreme cases, outright resistance. It involves imagining that point in time when your life has come to an end and writing your eulogy. What comments would you like made about you and your life by close friends, by the press, and in informal conversations among colleagues?

Note to skimmers: it is highly desirable that you perform each step of the Life Mission Exercise before you read the concluding discussion.

YOUR BEST-CASE EULOGY EXERCISE:
HOW WOULD YOU LIKE TO BE REMEMBERED?

STEP 1: Find a time and place where you can write for fifteen to thirty minutes free from distractions.

STEP 2: At the top of the first page write, "My Eulogy: How I Want to Be Remembered."

STEP 3: Write as detailed an essay as possible. No one need see this exercise. Do not limit yourself to historical data or even current realities. Remember, this is your best-case eulogy; write with the awareness that change is possible, and your future is ahead of you. Strive to get at what is most important to you.

STEP 4: Set your finished essay aside, but add to it over the next few days as additional thoughts come to mind.

STEP 5: After a week, look at your eulogy with a fresh eye, guided by the questions below. Write down your comments and condense the conclusions into your product specification file.

Assessment of Your Best-Case Eulogy

As you review what you wrote, consider the following points.

1. What thoughts came to mind as you wrote your eulogy? Seminar participants have wide-ranging responses, from "I drew a complete blank" to "I have to make a move." Jot down your personal thoughts.

2. On a fresh sheet of paper, make three column headings: "Achievements," "Affiliations," and "Attributes." Assign each point you made in your eulogy to one of these three columns. Achievements are accomplishments signaled by a verb or a noun. Affiliations are family, friends, communities, groups, or causes with which you were associated. Attributes are adjectives that describe your qualities.

3. Which of your three columns is longest? Shortest? Does this distribution accurately reflect your values? Does it motivate you to think about expanding your set of options? Does it suggest a minor course correction? A radical course correction? Some seminar participants have reached conclusions that startled them. For one, how he approached business was more important than what he achieved:

    No wonder I haven't been able to work up much enthusiasm for my search. I've been focusing on companies with a heavy bottom-line orientation. My achievements list clearly shows an overarching theme of service to others.

    VENTURE CAPITALIST, HBS '88

4. For what audience were you writing? Some seminar participants find their lists skewed by the influence of others. What audience is important to you at this stage in life? Whom do you aim to please?

5. Do you feel that some items on your lists are a real stretch? Somewhat dishonest? Someone else's agenda for you? Eliminate those items.
6. Ask yourself one last question: to what extent was my eulogy simply an extrapolation of my present situation? Have I described myself exactly as I am now plus a few years? Have I constricted myself? Start this exercise again if you sense your first essay was self-limiting.
7. When you are satisfied that your achievements, affiliations, and attributes lists capture your core values, staple them together with your eulogy, and place them in your product specification file.

SAMPLE EULOGIES

Samuel McCarver

Samuel McCarver was a devoted father and husband and will be missed by his many friends, who always found his company to be a source of enjoyment. He was a successful business executive who never forgot that there is more to life than business success. He was an active competitor who enjoyed the competition more than winning or losing. He was a man who contributed to his world not through any significant acts of greatness, but through a lifelong commitment to small acts of goodness.

David Richards

David Richards passed away of old age last week at the age of 84. He is survived by his wife Audrey, two daughters, Jill and Rachel, a son Jonathan and many grandchildren. David was well known for his leadership in the Strategic Technology field, in particular in strategic merger and acquisition activity. He was president of ADAPSO for several years and held many other related industry positions. His education and work career spanned several continents and although he lived in New York for the last 45 years of his life, he traveled extensively, particularly to the Orient, for his business.

Although his career was highly successful he was able to combine with it a full family life and a range of civic duties. He adored and was adored by all of his family and was able to spend sufficient time with them to provide the nurturing and support which enabled them to develop to their full potential. His close and enduring relationship with Audrey was particularly fulfilling to him and became the centerpiece of his life.

David was involved in a range of educational organizations. He was president of U.S.O.R.T. and helped that organization through a difficult period. His involvement in South Africa, the land of his birth, took much of his time while he was in his sixties.

He will be badly missed by many friends, his family and business associates.

Pierre Lenoir

Family Life

- Created a very happy and culturally rich household
- He made his children very happy and in charge of their own lives. He was able to teach his children how to develop their own talents. He was very hands off in the way he brought up his children but at the same time he was tough and demanding
- He was able to transfer to his children the richness of his culture, language knowledge, international exposure, leadership abilities and sports talents. He could offer his children the best education available
- He was very respected and listened to among his family members
- He increased the standard of living of his family and was able to give his wife and children more than what he received from his parents. He managed not to "spoil" his children but instead pushed them to secure their own financial security
- Despite his multiple professional responsibilities, he managed to spend a lot of time with his wife and children, being a true family man

Professional Life

- He was a general manager having profit and loss responsibility for a fairly sizeable business. He had great charisma and a special knack for motivating his people and developing them so they would be productive and enjoy their work. He was aiming very high by setting high standards for his group and for himself
- He was able to give his people a clear sense of direction
- He had the vision to move our company from being primarily a U.S. player to become a global player using his international experience
- He pushed his managers to develop and invest in their own people. He stressed the importance of training. He gave his managers the right incentives to constantly generate new ideas to improve the business
- He grew the business and made it profitable by identifying and bringing to market attractive new business opportunities. The business opportunities he pursued were successful because he used his skills to assemble all resources to run the business effectively and was not afraid to stick to his decisions. He would often persuade his superiors to follow his ideas despite initial resistance on their part

- He was not the type of manager limited to small incremental changes but was ready to take a step back and make some bold steps to conduct the business differently. He had tremendous market intelligence: he knew his customers and competitors inside out
- On the cost side of his business he was quick in identifying excessive spending and bringing costs within acceptable limits. He promoted long term investments to remain competitive
- He was a very hands-off manager, delegating a lot. He was very accessible and communicated well with a staff and superiors
- He was a very honest manager with no specific political agenda. The culture he instilled was one of true meritocracy. He also knew how to identify and reward good performance
- He was hard-working but not a workaholic and was able to draw a line between his professional and personal life

Cultural/Social Life
- He was a well-read person in English, French and Dutch literature
- He keenly enjoyed ballet, plays and museums and classical music
- He was involved in community activities promoting the education possibilities of less well-to-do people
- He had a few very loyal friends he knew for years

Sports Life
- Pierre was a top athlete: he excelled at long distance running, tennis, rock climbing, skiing and horseback riding. He also enjoyed soccer, skating and squash

Discussion of the Best-Case Eulogy Exercise

The purpose of this exercise is to broaden your perspective. How Would You Like to Be Remembered? is a "blue sky," "what if" question that asks you to consider the parameters within which you are living your life and your ultimate yardsticks of success. It prompts you to do the big-picture thinking so often neglected at times of career transition. A well-done eulogy exercise delivers a number of benefits:

1. You focus on what you really want to have done with your life.
2. You gain perspective on your current situation: you have accomplished much and have important goals as you look to the future.
3. You have a benchmark against which to measure all that is to follow as you reconsider and reconstitute your career.

ANOTHER SLANT ON YOUR LIFE MISSION

If you found the Best-Case Eulogy Exercise either very difficult or so thought-provoking that you would enjoy a little more of the same, try another exercise. Imagine that at some time in the future, perhaps in five to ten years, you are featured in a magazine article. Choose the magazine, and write (or at least summarize) the article.

FEATURE MAGAZINE ARTICLE EXERCISE

STEP 1:   Find a quiet place where you can write uninterrupted.

STEP 2:   Select the magazine in which you would like to be featured.

STEP 3:   Write the article, or a synopsis of the article, emphasizing those facets of your life you would like covered.

Assessment of the Feature Magazine Article Exercise

On a fresh page record your reactions to the following points:

1. Why did you choose the magazine you did?
2. Who would read the article? What kinds of reactions would they have? Would these reactions affect you in any way—directly or indirectly?
3. What did the article say about you? How were you portrayed? What aspects of your life were described?

Discussion of the Feature Magazine Article Exercise

This exercise offers you a glimpse of the individuals and institutions that influence your life. These internalized influences, operating below conscious levels of awareness, have a powerful impact on all aspects of life. When these influences are negative, they limit life choices, reinforce feelings of inadequacy, and even encourage suboptimal career selections:

> *Then there is the conflict over my personal goals versus parental values . . . so that I have trouble conveying enthusiasm.*
> ASSOCIATE, M&A, INVESTMENT BANKING, HBS '80

EXAMPLES OF THE FEATURE MAGAZINE ARTICLE EXERCISE

Sarah is, of course, known for the wonderful business successes she has had with making small companies very profitable without changing the character of the company. Employees all know her by first name, and staff turnover is rare. Working at XYZ Company is more than just a job to the people there; it's fun. It's being around people that you'd want to have lunch with even if you didn't have the office next door. It's offices that show the personality of the inhabitant. Employees feel free to comment on any part of the business (and often do) and truly care about the books they publish. It's never been a highly paid business, but employees of XYZ enjoy coming into the office every day.

As fulfilling as the company is to Ms. Jones, however, she is as well known for her travels. She spends several months every year shooting the rapids, climbing mountains, or visiting new cities. Her goal—to visit every country before she dies—is part of her wish for a very long life.

DIRECTOR, PUBLISHING, HBS '87
CHOICE OF MAGAZINE: *FORBES*

My article appears in Forbes *magazine. The article covers the successful building of a financial consulting practice in an environment characterized by rapid change. It stresses my ability to recognize opportunity and take advantage of it—to be flexible.*

FINANCIAL CONSULTANT, HBS '58

I chose Inc. *magazine, and the article recounted how I started a company from scratch. It stressed that I do things in an entrepreneurial way—as I have all along—and that that style matters very much to me.*

MANAGING DIRECTOR, STRATEGIC CONSULTING FIRM, HBS '84

Forbes *was my choice. The article features my work as an ethicist within a corporate setting. The article reviews my work helping managers make morally responsible decisions.*

DIRECTOR OF CORPORATE RELATIONS, SMALL LIBERAL ARTS
UNIVERSITY, HBS '79

I have always defined "meaningful" as being involved with the more emotional, humanistic side; being aware of my potential, for example— helping others with that. My father was a therapist, and business is not respected by generations of my family—particularly my father's family, where we have a doctor, an architect and two or three college professors. There is much more respect for those professions.

STRATEGIC PLANNER, INFORMATION SERVICES, HBS '81

Becoming aware of these internal influences and their lingering effects may free you to pursue a number of possibilities.

NUGGET: When old internalized tapes do not coincide with your present goals, turn down the volume or otherwise neutralize those inputs. Be sure the goals you set in your professional life are *yours* and reflect your aspirations and your realities. Trying to live by other peoples' standards or outdated *shoulds* and *oughts* is a no-win situation.

YOUR LIFE MISSION STATEMENT

A helpful way to synthesize your assessments from the eulogy and feature magazine article exercises is to develop a life mission statement. It should concisely encompass broad goals related to all important facets of your life: professional, personal, social, political, avocational. It will be some time, if ever, before you are able to carve this statement in stone, so record it expecting ongoing revision and refinement. The example below is one approach:

Until now too much of my life has been focused on my job. It has been almost an obsession. I am defining my life mission as trying to maintain a balance *between the things most important to me: my wife and children, the job that provides money and gives me the satisfaction of using my skills, and service to my fellow human beings. I also wish to achieve a balance between taking care of others and taking care of* me—*which I have neglected in the past. I believe that if I use my skills at something that satisfies the above criteria, I will earn enough money.*

OPERATIONS MANAGER, SERVICE INDUSTRY, HBS '66

As you continue in the self-assessment process, your enhanced clarity about your attributes, values, and motivations will help you define with increasing detail the direction of your life. Career goals based on your life mission statement will benefit you in a number of ways:

1. You will be fortified against the hollow victory syndrome: achieving your professional goals only to find that they aren't delivering satisfaction in ways you anticipated.
2. You will be less likely to sell out when faced with a tempting possibility that is, in fact, at variance with your life goals.
3. You will make appropriate trade-offs: identifying what you need to do to move toward your life goals makes it easier to make go/no go decisions.
4. You will have a better chance of success: by doing what you believe in, you have greatly enhanced your possibilities of staying the course in professional life with minimum conflict and maximum well-being.

NUGGET: Career planning and management done *without* taking into account your life mission and values is work resting on a weak foundation. Take the time to write and analyze your eulogy: you will reap the benefits for years to come.

As one manager asked succinctly, "Is my work getting harder, or is my work *not closely enough related* to what I want my life to be about?"

YOUR PRIORITIES

In the HBSCNY Career Seminar, the eulogy exercise is followed by an exercise in setting priorities. While commonly done in business, establishing priorities takes on a new significance when the subject under scrutiny is your life. The goals of this exercise are threefold: to identify your most important priorities at this point in your life, to acquaint you with the concept of trade-offs or price tags, and to give you a method for screening fields of interest and specific job opportunities.

Consider one seminar participant's dilemma:

I've been promoted to another position with an additional level of responsibility. The current job is very exciting and challenging, but I feel guilty staying because I have not achieved my monetary goals. I am not building any equity. There is not much room for growth within the organization; my boss isn't moving, so I'm looking at merit increases of 3 to 5 percent. We're about to start a family, and I'd like my wife to be able to work only part-time. Maybe this has been my fling; now I feel I have to step up to earning more. But I'd be giving up a lot in day-to-day satisfaction.

MARKETING MANAGER, ELECTRONICS, HBS '79

The Near-Term Priorities Exercise is designed to help you at just such a crossroads.

THE NEAR-TERM PRIORITIES EXERCISE

STEP 1: Find a place where you can write free from distraction.

STEP 2: Copy the following list in the alphabetical order shown:
Co-workers
Contribution to society
Current income
Equity ownership
Family
Friends
Future income
Geographical location
Health
Influence and power
Intrinsic nature of the work
Leisure time
Personal growth
Prestige and status
Professional growth
Security
Spouse or significant other
Workplace environment

STEP 3: Rank the items according to their importance in your life *at this point in time* to construct your list of near-term priorities. No ties, groupings, or mergers!

Assessment of the Near-Term Priorities Exercise

You may have found it difficult to establish your near-term priorities. It forces trade-off decisions. It requires facing up to the reality that it is not possible to have it all at any one point in professional life:

This is not the whole story. I'm very divided about prestige and status. The reason the bottom six priorities are down there is because they are

*non-job related, and my emphasis is on money, on wealth accumulation.
I feel like I ought to take emphasis off the job . . . but I'm not yet willing
to sacrifice for the touchy-feelies. . . . This does have bearing . . . do I
consider taking the scenic tour?*

DIVISION PRESIDENT, MANUFACTURING, HBS '74

*I got involved with a small investment company. My problem is that I'm
doing well, I'm quite successful, I'm making more money than I ever
wanted. However, it's a deal-oriented shop and I'm doing work at home
nights and weekends—the deal is king. I have refused to stay late at the
office from the beginning; I leave to get home for dinner with the kids.
But the commute is a problem. And lots of travel. I'm not going to be
able to "get away" with my priorities much longer—something will have
to give.*

CFO, SMALL INVESTMENT COMPANY, HBS '67

Understanding your priorities gives you a concrete tool for evaluating
career options. It helps you decide whether your next phase of life will be
an all-out push for income and professional growth, for example, or a time
for the scenic tour. Is this the time to solidify relationships with friends,
family, or spouse—or to take the plunge for equity ownership and buy a
small company that will consume every waking moment?

The "Phantom Spectator" Ranking

While doing the last exercise, you may have realized that you would adjust
your ranking of priorities depending on who was looking over your shoulder. As one HBS graduate said, "I'm going to come out looking like a
jerk!" To whom, we ask? Choose the most influential "phantom spectator" in your life—your boss, your college or graduate school class secretary,
your spouse or significant other, a parent or other influential person—and
rank your priorities to satisfy that observer. What priorities would satisfy
that influential spectator?

Compare your first list and this phantom spectator ranking. If you are
like our seminar participants, you may discover that your priorities shift
markedly if, for example, you consider submitting them to your graduate
school, your class secretary, your spouse or significant other—or even your
employer. Or you may realize that your first ranking was, in fact, not the
"real you" but you in your professional role:

*My first ranking was as a member of the leading management consulting
firm I work for. Frankly, that was pretty straightforward. I didn't even*

realize the phantom spectator was looking over my shoulder! Then I said, "What if I do this as myself?" *That ranking was more difficult, but the results felt much more valid.*

ASSOCIATE, CONSULTING, HBS '83

The "Hired Detective" Ranking

The Priorities Exercise is a reminder that there are only twenty-four hours in a day. No matter how clever or hard-working, you can't do everything. In fact, you're lucky if you can do most of the items at the top of your daily "to do" list. Your priority ranking should determine how you allocate those limited hours. Does it? What would your *apparent* priorities be to an outside observer? Do a ranking imagining that you have been monitored by a hired detective for twenty-four hours a day for the past month. How would the detective's ranking compare with your priorities ranking? Do you detect any inconsistency between how you would like to order your life and how you are actually living it?

The phantom spectator and hired detective rankings give you a preliminary reading on who is influencing your ranking and how significantly you deviate from your professed priorities in daily life. Many managers claim to have one set of priorities but live according to another: they say friends are important, for example, but never make time to build or maintain friendships. Others attempt to live by externally mandated priorities at the expense of personal priorities: they rank income high because that's where it "should" be.

NUGGET: There are no right or wrong rankings, only rankings that are appropriate to an individual at a given time, based on very personal considerations.

To cross-check your initial ranking, under circumstances designed to yield a more valid priorities profile, we recommend the following exercise. You will most likely have the experience this seminar participant did:

Doing my Priorities Exercise during the seminar session I got one answer, but later, using refined definitions and the grid to weigh one priority against the other, my top six were in a different order.

MANAGING DIRECTOR, STRATEGIC CONSULTING, HBS '84

Refining Your Near-Term Priorities Exercise

STEP 1:   Get eighteen index cards, preferably four inches by six inches (three inches by five inches will do).

STEP 2:   From the list provided in step 2 in the Near-Term Priorities Exercise, write one priority at the top of each card, starting with co-workers and ending with workplace environment.

STEP 3:   Take one card at a time, and answer, in one or several phrases, "How do *I* define this priority? How do I know when I'm meeting this priority? What does it mean to *me?*" Here are some sample priority cards:

Current income
• Earning enough not to feel taken advantage of or discounted

---

Professional growth
• Developing a solid professional reputation
• Consolidating and repackaging the skills I've developed
• Strengthening self-esteem

Co-workers
• Enjoying the people I work with
• Respecting the people I work for
• Working in a team
• Being able to play ball with my co-workers

STEP 4:   Review your definitions to be certain you have addressed each priority. No card should read, "Not that important." No card should have the dictionary definition of the word or phrase. No card should have someone *else's* definition. How would *you* satisfy each priority?

STEP 5: Turn to the priorities grid in Appendix A. This grid is designed to facilitate a forced-choice ranking. Look at each possible pair of priorities, and answer the question, "If I could honor only one of these priorities at this time—if I were forced to make a choice—which is more important to me?" Follow the directions included with the grid.

STEP 6: Record your priorities, by number, from your top priority (the one you selected most often in your forced-choice exercise) to your lowest priority.

STEP 7: Take your priorities cards and put them in the order reflecting your grid's results.

Discussion of the Near-Term Priorities Exercise

To summarize this exercise, group your priority cards by thirds into these categories:

- Top third: the Nonnegotiables, the deal breakers
- Middle third: Desirable but not essential
- Bottom third: the Price Tags, things you're willing to give up

Are you comfortable with these groupings for *this stage in your life?* Your bottom six priorities should include those aspects of life you are willing to do without or to compromise at this juncture. They must be expendable: these are the price tags you are willing to pay in order to get your top third.

NUGGET: Copy your bottom third—your price-tag priorities—onto a three-by-five card. Put that card where you will see it often in the coming weeks: when you open your briefcase, look in your mirror, open your desk drawer. Each time you read it, verify your price tags by noting, "I am willing to de-emphasize these facets of my life in order to achieve the six priorities most important to me."

At this suggestion a few HBSCNY Career Seminar participants ask, "What about my spouse's input?" One seminar participant had this experience:

I discussed my priorities with my wife. She gave me what she thought my priorities should be.
VICE PRESIDENT, COMMERCIAL BANKING, HBS '63

Your significant other should not dictate your priorities. But the person most affected by your priorities should have an active voice as you solidify your ranking.

It is so important to share your priorities results with your spouse—not to force his or her agreement but to better understand and talk about priorities that are incompatible.
MANAGING DIRECTOR, STRATEGIC CONSULTING, HBS/PMD '84

Imagine you defined your geographical location priority as follows:

- Continuing to live and work in New York, New Jersey, or Connecticut

If *you* consider geographical location a price-tag priority—one that you are willing to trade for others—then you and your spouse or significant other need to be aware that a move is a strong possibility. Similarly, if relocating is a deal breaker, and if you absolutely will not move, you both should be prepared for a longer search.

Career transitions challenge the closest of relationships. Be sure you and your spouse or significant other agree on the priorities guiding this transition and the price tags that must be paid. Returning to your jointly owned priorities will be invaluable in the weeks ahead.

CASE STUDY ON PRIORITIES

A strong grasp of his priorities influenced one HBSer's process of job selection. Once he did an initial ranking, priority cards, and the priorities grid, his top six priorities emerged as follows:

1. Geographical location
   - Working in New York metropolitan area now, close to family; fiancée also based here
   - Ideal geographical arrangement: job in New Jersey, can drive to job in 10 to 15 minutes

2. Security
   - Feeling that I can pursue my career in the same company for as long as I choose
   - I decide whether to stay or leave: they support my goals

3. Current income
   - Earning $90,000 to $130,000
   - Minimum $80,000

4. Intrinsic nature of the work
   - A business field that interests me as much as computers do—e.g., communications, entertainment
   - Prefer applications of new or advanced technologies

5. Family
   - Spending time with my wife-to-be
   - Staying close to other family members
   - Keeping the stress level at the job down

6. Professional growth
   - Doing new things
   - Breaking out of the mold the headhunters are trying to keep me in
   - Being successful in new areas—or at least being put into them!

When he received strong indications of interest from an aggressive firm, he made a simple checklist to assess how that prospective job rated:

1. Geographical location	Yes
2. Security	No. They have hired 200 people within six months; they could contract just as easily. And how will I make myself indispensable?
3. Current income	Yes
4. Intrinsic nature of the work	Yes
5. Family	Yes
6. Professional growth	Unclear

Two of his nonnegotiables—security and professional growth—were in doubt. Clearly he needed more information. Five days later, he reported back the following information:

They have firmed up the offer—a base of $100,000, a guaranteed bonus of $40,000 this year, $55,000 or more next year based on performance. Net, financially I wouldn't be sacrificing. But my anxiety level is pretty high right now. I have gone hot and cold on the job all along, yet it is a new dimension technologically, and I would be able to deliver results— rather than just write papers.

But as a vice president of systems considering financial services, this HBSer had a lot of concerns about security, number two of his six top priorities:

I asked my future boss how he judges success; that is the best way to tackle the security question. He views success as delivering on what he has promised to the line groups. Fortunately that has always been my long suit.

And professional growth?

I would definitely be in on front-end technology planning and implementation. I like the fact that people volunteered that they like to work in teams; that's where you really get professional growth in my field.

So what were the reservations that made this manager "go hot and cold" on the job?

This boss works ten hours a day and takes work home. He has never taken more than a week at a time on vacation. How can I expect much leisure time in that kind of setup?

Sure enough, leisure time, a middle-third priority—desirable but not essential—was looming large, which forced him to reassess to what degree this concern about leisure time was really important to him. This manager ultimately concluded that he could continue the job search for a long time and not find something as close to his top six as the offer in hand and accepted the job. Good priorities work enabled him to analyze what he had and decide appropriately for the next chapter of professional life.

When we checked in with him several years later, we got a glowing report.

It's a great job. Yes, my boss really does work hard, but I work the hours I'm most comfortable with. He really is one of the nicest people I've ever worked with, and I have great peers and a great staff. I've gotten more done in three years than ever before, and I've become well known in my field.

VP, SYSTEMS, FINANCIAL SERVICES, HBS '75

TRADE-OFFS ARE A PART OF LIFE

The Priorities Exercise is a reminder that trade-offs are an essential part of life and career planning. After you have refined your groupings (which may take some time; don't rush it), enter your top six priorities into your product specification file. These priorities will serve as a benchmark against which to test important decisions in the coming weeks.

A clear rank ordering of your priorities offers other benefits as well:

- *Sturdiness.* In considering alternatives, in dealing with recruiters, in interviewing, and in making your next career choice, you will radiate a strength that comes from knowing what is important to you, what is secondary, and what—as a pragmatic manager—you will trade off for your priorities.
- *Firm foundation and peace of mind.* By keeping in mind the benefits you will gain, you'll spend less time second-guessing yourself and regretting choices made.
- *Expanded options.* Your experience and education should *expand* your career options. However, the combination of societal pressures, group norms, and influential spectators can narrow your perceived options. Unless you have your priorities clear, you will tend to limit your options.

You may find that your priorities list has a major impact on the decisions you make in *all* facets of your life—and not just your job search. Consider this poignant statement:

> *I wish my wife and I had done the Priorities comparison before she died. It would have resolved a lot of friction between us by clarifying that I couldn't both bring home my salary and be home for dinner early. And we probably would have taken some of those trips that she kept talking about and I was putting off until later.*
>
> VP, ADMINISTRATION, HBS '63

Take the work you have done in this chapter seriously, and hold fast to your life goals and near-term priorities. Your thoughtful consideration of the goals for your life will help you withstand the pressures in the days ahead.

6

STYLES, VALUES, AND MOTIVATIONS

This chapter will enhance your awareness of your style of interaction, your method of processing information, and the values and motivations that influence most of your professional interactions. This session of the HBSCNY Career Seminar is full of "aha!" experiences, as participants realize for the first time the full implications of past events in their lives.

> *There are some things I've really blown. I've been too hard driven, and haven't paid enough attention to people. I've made assumptions about the people I worked for. I've never bothered to analyze myself in the past.*
> DIVISION PRESIDENT, MANUFACTURING, HBS '74

THE FALLACY OF THE INFINITELY ADAPTABLE MANAGER

For many, the archetypal ideal manager is incisive, sharp-witted, and articulate, with the ability to handle virtually any situation effectively. Graduates of business schools are steeped in this concept of the infinitely adaptable manager. During their two-year course of study, HBS MBA candidates immerse themselves in hundreds of case studies, assuming the role of one member of the management team in each case. "You are the CFO. What action would you take to resolve the cash flow crisis?" "You are the head of human resources. How would you advise the line managers?" Every class presents a new case, and every case a new role. Every MBA has worn hundreds of different hats in preparing for a business career.

To play the adaptable manager in hypothetical business situations is a worthwhile exercise. To accept the premise of the infinitely adaptable manager in real-life situations, however, is *risky*. It assumes that all a manager needs to succeed are the *functional* skills to do the job. Such a premise underestimates the influence of nonrational, less obvious factors. No doubt you can recall numerous work situations where everything was done right from a logical perspective but the results didn't come out as expected. Factors other than logic and the astute use of traditional business practices were at work, all the more powerful because they were so subtle.

Another reminder of the significance of these subtle factors is a manager's success—or lack of success—in a job. When a manager is involuntarily separated from a job, rarely is it due solely to a lack of technical skill. Problems usually arise over incompatibilities in styles, values, or motivations.

NUGGET: The discharged manager who fails to recognize the importance of *chemistry*—of style, values, and motivation fit—and writes off a firing to "politics," often charges back into the job market ready to fall into a similar trap. Now is the time to learn about your unique style, values hierarchy, and motivational triggers.

Each manager is a unique combination of diverse elements, some obvious and many others subtle and powerful influences on daily thought and action. Despite ample evidence, many managers resist the idea that unquantifiable, imprecise realities such as style can determine the course of their careers. Because the thought that invisible factors might dilute or thwart a manager's control is disconcerting, most people come up with *any* other explanation to explain events. Listen to this manager's account of his struggles on a job:

> *After four months I became Manager of Bids and Proposals. I did very well, but it was easy to do well. I felt I was sitting in this group of accountants while not being one of these guys. I felt it was too limiting— not enough latitude—although there was. I would have overcome this feeling except the guy who hired me was replaced by the original green eyeshade accounting type. He was really stupid—he didn't understand the stuff I was doing—regression analysis, learning curve theory. I tried to explain it to him—he would ask me to stay late and come to his office and use the blackboard. I had no luck, although I think I'm quite a good teacher.* This guy had another person in mind for my job.
>
> MANAGER, DESIGN AND CONSTRUCTION, HBS '66

How receptive are most managers to any suggestion that they might be blaming others for their troubles?

Most managers are well aware of the influence of subtle factors on their performance in, say, their golf or tennis game. They look for the things that interfere with their control of the golf club or tennis racket, accept criticism and suggestions from the golf pro or tennis coach, and adapt or compensate accordingly. On the job, however, or during a job search, it's a different matter: they are reluctant to acknowledge the influence of factors beyond their awareness or direct control.

NUGGET: If you viewed the challenges of being a manager as more of a game, you might improve your effectiveness. You would hire the right coach to get a helpful perspective on your situation. And you would tackle these challenges with renewed vigor. Try it!

ASSESSING YOUR MANAGEMENT "GAME"

A wide variety of techniques are available to help you determine the subtle factors influencing your management "game." Many involve the use of proprietary exercises or instruments and must be administered under controlled situations. The following techniques have been used in the HBSCNY Career Seminar.

Values

Each of us has a set of internalized values that defines what is valid or important in life. One established instrument for gaining greater insight into your value system is the AVL Study of Values, which has been in use for over fifty years. The AVL uses six scales to tell you how you incorporate six values:

Scale	Dominant Value
Theoretical	The discovery of truth
Economic	What is useful and practical
Aesthetic	Form and harmony
Social	Love of people
Political	Power and influence
Religious	Unity, comprehending existence as a whole

Consider a hypothetical committee of six people, each having a different dominant value and therefore a different view of what is *right* in any given situation. Imagine these six committee members trying to decide how to allocate limited assets or implement a ten-year plan to downsize a company. Their diverse values would mean differing perspectives, which could lead to divisiveness irrespective of the competence or best intentions of the participants.

You may be able to come up with a rough idea of what your values preferences are by using the six AVL categories. In all likelihood, however, the environment in which you live and work has obscured a certain amount of self-knowledge, and you would be in for some surprises if you actually took the AVL. If you're a long-term player in the business community, you may just assume that "economic" or "political" is your dominant value. On the other hand, you may be reading this book because your hierarchy of values is out of sync with your environment. Take a hard look at each scale's dominant value, and enter your best guess into your product specification file.[1]

Styles: The Myers-Briggs Type Indicator

The Myers-Briggs Type Indicator (MBTI) is used to determine individual styles and preferences and to enhance group interactions within an organization. The Myers-Briggs instrument focuses on your preferences and how they differ from those of others in four respects: (1) where you prefer to focus your attention, (2) how you prefer to take in information, (3) the way you prefer to make decisions, and (4) the manner in which you prefer to deal with the outer world.

Briefly, the Myers-Briggs technique identifies preferences on four scales:

"Where do you prefer to focus your attention?"

E ◄───────────────────────────────────────► I

EXTRAVERSION   INTROVERSION
Outer world of actions, objects,   *Inner* world of concepts and ideas
and persons

"How do you prefer to take in information?"

S ◄───────────────────────────────────────► N

SENSING PERCEPTION   INTUITIVE PERCEPTION
Attentive to immediate, real,   Oriented toward the *possibilities*,
practical *facts* of experience and   relationships, and meanings of
life   experience

[1]If you want to pursue this more deeply, see G. Allport, *Pattern and Growth in Personality*, 2d ed. (New York: Holt, Rinehart and Winston, 1961), 279–99.

"How do you prefer to make decisions?"

T ◄─────────────────────────────────► F

THINKING JUDGMENT   FEELING JUDGMENT
Objectively, impersonally,   Subjectively and *personally;* weigh
logically; consider causes of   values of choices and how they
events and probable outcomes   matter to others

"How do you prefer to deal with the outer world?"

J ◄─────────────────────────────────► P

JUDGING ATTITUDE   PERCEPTIVE ATTITUDE
In a decisive, planned, and   In a spontaneous, *flexible* way;
orderly way; aim to regulate and   aim to understand life and adapt
control events   to it

Bear in mind that the MBTI deals with your preferences, not abilities or lack thereof. You are *capable* of performing at either end of the preference scales, but you feel more at home at a certain point on each scale and tend to be influenced by this preference most of the time. A useful analogy is left- versus right-handedness: you use both hands but reach first with the preferred hand. One seminar participant had this insight into his preferences:

> *I majored in electrical engineering. I have always liked the really exact rather than the more fluid. I'd prefer to play the clarinet rather than slide trombone, for example.*
>
> VP, INVESTMENT BANKING, HBS '84

In addition to revealing an individual's preferred work style and environment, the research on MBTI results provides valuable insights into career satisfaction, organizational cultures, and management and leadership styles as related to type.

> *The results of the MBTI testing have been compared, culture with culture, profession with profession, education level with education level, and organizational status with organizational status. The results substantiate that different temperaments work best in different situations. No wonder the "good leaders" are not all of one type. Effective leadership can be exercised by very different kinds of people if they capitalize on their strengths, compensate for their weaknesses, and gravitate toward situations where their natural temperament gives them an advantage. There is no such thing as one set of qualities that deserve the title, "Leadership Qualities."*[2]

[2]William Bridges, *Surviving Corporate Transition* (New York: Doubleday, 1988), 125–26.

The Myers-Briggs allows you to find your own "best fit" of management and leadership opportunities.

Your MBTI "type" (a four-letter abbreviation) is determined by your preferences on each of the four scales. Extensive work has been done analyzing the characteristics and interaction of the sixteen MBTI types. There are no "right" or "wrong" types, but each type functions more authentically in some situations than in others. The MBTI is a vivid reminder that not everyone around you thinks and responds as you do. Understanding your MBTI type will yield insights into how you function, as well as how others may perceive you. Awareness of how other types function can help you to be more effective in your day-to-day interactions. Below we provide a brief description of each type:[3]

ISTJ: thorough, painstaking, systematic, hard working, careful with detail

ISTP: adept at managing situations, aware of facts, expedient, realistic, not likely to be convinced by anything but reasoning

ESTP: action-oriented, pragmatic, resourceful, realistic, prefer to take the most efficient route

ESTJ: logical, analytical, decisive, tough-minded, able to organize facts and operations well in advance

ISFJ: sympathetic, loyal, considerate, kind, will go to any amount of trouble to help those in need of support

ISFP: gentle, considerate, compassionate toward those less fortunate, have an open-minded and flexible approach

ESFP: friendly, outgoing, fun-loving, likable, naturally drawn towards people

ESFJ: helpful, tactful, compassionate, orderly, place a high value on harmonious human interaction

INFJ: trust their own vision, quietly exert influence, have deeply felt compassion, are insightful, seek harmony

INFP: open-minded, idealistic, insightful, flexible, want their work to contribute something that matters

[3]Reproduced by special permission of the Publisher, Consulting Psychologists Press, Inc., Palo Alto, CA 94303 from *Introduction to Type in Organizations*, 2nd Ed. by Sandra Krebs Hirsh and Jean M. Kummerow. Copyright *1990* by Consulting Psychologists Press, Inc. All rights reserved. Further reproduction is prohibited without the Publisher's consent.

ENFP: enthusiastic, insightful, innovative, versatile, tireless in pursuit of new possibilities

ENFJ: interpersonally adept, understanding, tolerant, appreciative, facilitators of good communications

INTJ: independent, individualistic, single-minded, determined, trust their vision of possibilities regardless of universal skepticism

INTP: rational, curious, theoretical, abstract, prefer to organize ideas rather than situations or people

ENTP: innovative, individualistic, versatile, analytical, attracted to entrepreneurial ideas

ENTJ: logical, organized, structured, objective, decisive about what they view as conceptually valid

A more detailed summary of the characteristics associated with each of the MBTI types is shown in Table 6.1. If at some point in your career you have taken the MBTI, enter the results in your product specification file. If not, try to guess your type based on the information provided in this chapter.

At the HBSCNY Career Seminar discussions, the value of the MBTI for enhanced understanding of individual and organization situations is evident:

Extraversion versus Introversion

> *I now understand a minor irritation in my dealings with a colleague. I send him a memo about something. Then he calls or drops by to talk about the memo—almost as if he hadn't read it. What a waste of time! My MBTI is a strong I, which means I prefer to communicate in writing. I'm sure he's an E, so he naturally wants to talk things through. Next time I'll write him a summary, inviting him to meet and discuss the details.*
> TECHNICAL MANAGER, MANUFACTURING, HBS '75

Sensing versus Intuiting Perception

> *After the MBTI I understand why my assistant is so helpful to me. I'm on the intuitive side of the scale, so I tend to rely on hunches and be sloppy about all the details. He is clearly an S because he is very practical, keeps things on schedule, and makes sure I don't make things too complicated. It makes a good team.*
> CREATIVE MANAGER, CONSUMER PRODUCTS, HBS '82

TABLE 6.1 CHARACTERISTICS FREQUENTLY ASSOCIATED WITH EACH TYPE[4]

Introverts

	Sensing Types		Intuitive Types	
Introverts	**ISTJ** Serious, quiet, earn success by concentration and thoroughness. Practical, orderly, matter-of-fact, logical, realistic, and dependable. See to it that everything is well organized. Take responsibility. Make up their own minds as to what should be accomplished and work toward it steadily, regardless of protests or distractions.	**ISFJ** Quiet, friendly, responsible, and conscientious. Work devotedly to meet their obligations. Lend stability to any project or group. Thorough, painstaking, accurate. Their interests are usually not technical. Can be patient with necessary details. Loyal, considerate, perceptive, concerned with how other people feel.	**INFJ** Succeed by perseverance, originality, and desire to do whatever is needed or wanted. Put their best efforts into their work. Quietly forceful, conscientious, concerned for others. Respected for their firm principles. Likely to be honored and followed for their clear convictions as to how best to serve the common good.	**INTJ** Usually have original minds and great drive for their own ideas and purposes. In fields that appeal to them, they have a fine power to organize a job and carry it through with or without help. Skeptical, critical, independent, determined, sometimes stubborn. Must learn to yield less important points in order to win the most important.
	ISTP Cool onlookers, quiet, reserved, observing and analyzing life with detached curiosity and unexpected flashes of original humor. Usually interested in cause and effect, how and why mechanical things work, and in organizing facts using logical principles.	**ISFP** Retiring, quietly friendly, sensitive, kind, modest about their abilities. Shun disagreements, do not force their opinions or values on others. Usually do not care to lead but are often loyal followers. Often relaxed about getting things done, because they enjoy the present moment and do not want to spoil it by undue haste or exertion.	**INFP** Full of enthusiasms and loyalties, but seldom talk of these until they know you well. Care about learning, ideas, language, and independent projects of their own. Tend to undertake too much, then somehow get it done. Friendly, but often too absorbed in what they are doing to be sociable. Little concerned with possessions or physical surroundings.	**INTP** Quiet and reserved. Especially enjoy theoretical or scientific pursuits. Like solving problems with logic and analysis. Usually interested mainly in ideas, with little liking for parties or small talk. Tend to have sharply defined interests. Need careers where some strong interest can be used and useful.

TABLE 6.1 continued.

Extraverts

	Sensing Types		Intuitive Types	
	ESTP	ESFP	ENFP	ENTP

Extraverts

Sensing Types		Intuitive Types	

ESTP

Good at on-the-spot problem solving. Do not worry, enjoy whatever comes along. Tend to like mechanical things and sports, with friends on the side. Adaptable, tolerant, generally conservative in values. Dislike long explanations. Are best with real things that can be worked, handled, taken apart, or put together.

ESFP

Outgoing, easygoing, accepting, friendly, enjoy everything and make things more fun for others by their enjoyment. Like sports and making things happen. Know what's going on and join in eagerly. Find remembering facts easier than mastering theories. Are best in situations that need sound common sense and practical ability with people as well as with things.

ENFP

Warmly enthusiastic, high-spirited, ingenious, imaginative. Able to do almost anything that interests them. Quick with a solution for any difficulty and ready to help anyone with a problem. Often rely on their ability to improvise instead of preparing in advance. Can usually find compelling reasons for whatever they want.

ENTP

Quick, ingenious, good at many things. Stimulating company, alert and outspoken. May argue for fun on either side of a question. Resourceful in solving new and challenging problems, but may neglect routine assignments. Apt to turn to one new interest after another. Skillful in finding logical reasons for what they want.

ESTJ

Practical, realistic, matter-of-fact, with a natural head for business or mechanics. Not interested in subjects they see no use for, but can apply themselves when necessary. Like to organize and run activities. May make good administrators, especially if they remember to consider others' feelings and points of view.

ESFJ

Warm-hearted, talkative, popular, conscientious, born cooperators, active committee members. Need harmony and may be good at creating it. Always doing something nice for someone. Work best with encouragement and praise. Main interest is in things that directly and visibly affect people's lives.

ENFJ

Responsive and responsible. Generally feel real concern for what others think or want, and try to handle things with due regard for the other person's feelings. Can present a proposal or lead a group discussion with ease and tact. Sociable, popular, sympathetic. Responsive to praise and criticism.

ENTJ

Hearty, frank, decisive, leaders in activities. Usually good in anything that requires reasoning and intelligent talk, such as public speaking. Are usually well informed and enjoy adding to their fund of knowledge. May sometimes appear more positive and confident than their experience in an area warrants.

ᵃReproduced by special permission of the publisher, Consulting Psychologists Press, Inc., Palo Alto, CA 94303. From *Myers-Briggs Type Indicator Form G Report Form by Katherine C. Briggs and Isabel Briggs Myers*. Copyright 1977 by Consulting Psychologists Press, Inc.
All rights reserved.
Further reproduction is prohibited without the publisher's consent.

Thinking versus Feeling Judgment

Part of my job involved interpreting company policy in personnel and compensation matters. Trouble was, another manager also had a say in these interpretations, and we always disagreed. It used to drive me crazy. The MBTI made me understand what was going on. I am a T, so I tended toward consistency and fairness. Her preference is F, so she had a natural tendency to tailor the policy to the particular person and situation.

VP, ENTERTAINMENT, HBS '63

Judging versus Perceiving Attitude

Having a strong J and a strong P together on that project caused a lot of friction. I was the J—trying to get each phase of the project finished per our timetable; my partner on the project drove me crazy—always wanting more information and questioning decisions we'd already made. But I must admit that she was the one who recognized the significance of some last-minute data that completely altered our report for the better.

DIRECTOR, ADVERTISING, HBS '87

The MBTI is an extremely useful tool in the self-awareness process. This brief description can only suggest the valuable potential it represents. We strongly recommend that you contact one of the many firms or individuals certified to administer this instrument through the Association of Psychological Type. Contact their headquarters at 9140 Ward Parkway, Kansas City, MO 64114 (816-444-3500), for the chapter nearest you. MBTI resources can also be found through college placement offices, psychologists, and other counselors. The insights gained could be your "aha!"—with benefits accruing to your professional life for years to come. Listen to these seminar participants:

I learned a lot about myself at the Seminar session the other night. My Myers-Briggs said, "You should never be an accountant"—my first career! And I have the typology of a marketer—exactly what I want! I've been too caught up in the "shoulds": this was very affirming of who I want to be.

VP SALES, FINANCIAL SERVICES, HBS '82

I was annoyed at having to take the Myers-Briggs at the Seminar because I felt it labeled me, and labels are confining. Some months later I went back over my notes and was amazed at how my Myers-Briggs results explained my satisfactions and difficulties with my present job. In retrospect it was one of the most useful parts of the Seminar.

MARKETING, INFORMATION PROCESSING, HBS '82

I did not believe in the validity of the Myers-Briggs—until I did it honestly. Then I could see why I had felt so out of place in the work I had been doing for so long. Don't underestimate the Myers-Briggs; it is a very perceptive self-awareness technique.

VP, FINANCIAL SERVICES, HBS '73

A number of books are available on the MBTI and its relationship to individual, management, and leadership styles—as well as environmental preferences and behavior. We particularly recommend:

Gifts Differing by Isabel Briggs Myers and Peter Myers, Consulting Psychologists Press, Palo Alto, Calif., 1986 (telephone orders 415-969-8901)

Introduction to Type in Organizational Settings by Jean M. Kummerow and Sandra Krebs Hirsh, Consulting Psychologists Press, Palo Alto, Calif., 1990 (telephone orders 415-969-8901)

Your Motivational Profile

Another manifestation of the subtle inner factors influencing a person's behavior is his or her motivations. David C. McClelland has done extensive work in human motivation[5], which forms the basis for the following exercise:

STEP 1: Draw three vertical lines and label them *craftsman, affiliation,* and *power,* as shown below.

STEP 2: Read the following definitions of the three motivational categories.

• *Craftsman*[6]: A person high in this category is primarily motivated by competition with an internal standard. This person feels strongly about doing things properly as he or she defines that term, rather than as other people—including the boss—define "properly." A master stonecarver working on intricate details tucked in crevices is the consummate craftsman. If your supervisor says, "Your report is fine as it is," but you stay late to polish yet another draft, that's craftsman motivation.

[5]A large body of work exists on David C. McClelland's work including *The Achievement Motive,* David C. McClelland, J. W. Atkinson, R. A. Clark, E. L. Lowell, Appleton Century Croft, N.Y., 1953, and *The Achieving Society,* David C. McClelland, D. Van Nostrand Company, Inc., N.Y., 1961. For further information see *Human Motivation,* David C. McClelland, Irvington Press, N.Y. 1982.

[6]McClelland called this category *achievement,* but this word has come to mean so many things that we have substituted the term *craftsman.*

- *Affiliation:* A person high in this category is primarily moti-vated by concerns about the welfare of people. This person could be snowed under with work and under tight deadline pressures, but if someone said, "I've got a problem; do you have a minute?" his or her answer would be, "Sure, come in," and the work would be put aside.
- *Power:* A person high in this category tends to seek out positions and other means of influence to make things hap-pen. Although *power* may have a negative connotation to some, here the power motivation is neutral: it can be used for positive or negative ends.

STEP 3: Mark each vertical line to indicate your level of motivation in that category. If much of your time, energy, and attention is influenced by a category, put a mark near the top of the line. If it motivates little in your life, mark the vertical line near the bottom.

STEP 4: Do a second set of markings, assuming your total score must be 10. If you've marked each vertical line near the top in step 3, lower the marks on the one or two motivational scales that aren't strong influences in your life. If you marked each vertical line near the bottom in step 3, move up one or two marks.

STEP 5: The three marks you have made (that now add up to 10) define your Motivational Profile. Enter your Motivational Profile (the score for each of the categories) into your product specification file.

Consider the following managers' comments:

I felt I wasn't going to be able to get ahead by working harder. Rather, it was going to be a political matter—having a "good file" of reports even if I hadn't produced the results.
                    PROJECT MANAGER, CONSUMER PRODUCTS, HBS '84

Dave and I were friendly competitors in the sales department. I worked hard, studied the product literature late at night, spent more time worrying about the customers than my family. Dave tended to take long weekends and do just enough to get by, spending hours cultivating the higher-ups in the department rather than selling something to someone! When he got the promotion over me, I was dumbstruck.
                    SALES MANAGER, CHEMICALS, HBS '68

These two men were working in situations at odds with their motivations. The first had no interest in a "good file" if it wasn't backed up with good results; the second had no appetite for the power game. Promotions in an organization will be influenced by the motivational profile valued by the people handing out promotions. In some organizations Dave's style might be seen as lazy and opportunistic, in others, as the way to get ahead.

A FINAL WORD ON STYLES, VALUES, AND MOTIVATIONS

Subtle but powerful factors influence individuals as they work alone or in groups. Enhanced understanding of your values, styles, and motivations equips you to understand past events in your career and to deal more effectively with future events. Appreciating that your unique combination of attributes can work to your advantage in some circumstances and against you in others is half the battle. With this understanding, you can focus on finding opportunities where you will *succeed* as you develop your career plan and marketing campaign.

7

SKILLS

Are you tempted to skip this chapter because you know everything there is to know about your skills? Reconsider! You have devoted time, energy, and other resources to develop skills that make you effective on the job. You are justifiably proud of—and quite possibly very attached to—the "toolbox" of skills you developed through your formal education and the school of hard knocks. But you may have lost sight of an equally powerful skill set that has not been exploited in your recent jobs or required for your meteoric rise.

> *The core question is, What do I really want to be? I'm looked at as a marketer, but my technical skills are really strong. On a scale of one to ten, I'd give myself a nine on technical skill, a seven on market sense, and a six on marketing.*
>
> MANAGING DIRECTOR, INVESTMENT BANKING, HBS '68

NUGGET: Develop one more skill—the ability to sort through your *entire* skills repertoire and appreciate skills you may have overlooked. Once you decide which of your skills best reflect a synthesis of your talents *and* passions, you have taken an essential step toward defining your career possibilities and ultimately selecting your next port of call. And you will become much more effective in all facets of self-marketing, including resumé preparation, networking, and interviewing.

In a tough job market, you have a pragmatic reason to do a skills audit. From your experience on the hiring side of the desk, no doubt you can recall candidates who appeared to have the skills appropriate for the job

Note: To complete the core exercise in this chapter you must have *The New Quick Job-Hunting Map* workbook by Richard N. Bolles. Your bookstore can order it from these distributors: Ingram Book Company or Baker & Taylor Books. Or you may order it from Ten Speed Press, Box 7123, Berkeley, CA 94707 (415-845-8414). Do it now!

but were not able to convince you of that fact. You may also recall (probably with some chagrin) people who interviewed very well but turned out not to be able to deliver on what they had promised. By introducing a technique for auditing your extraordinary skills, we hope to enable you to both sell yourself into the opportunities of your choosing and select a field or function where your skills deliver. Articulating your abilities *and* delivering on your interview pitch need never be at odds. Get a firm grip on your skills and set yourself apart by successfully integrating you-the-product and your promotion, as this seminar participant did:

> *I've done an assessment of the six departments that would be better fits with my skills—preparing 10K/10Q reports, cash management, product cost projections, sales trends analysis, financial analysis, and accounting procedures. In all of these areas the specific work of the department is quite concrete; writing persuasively is not a constant challenge; and the type of work done would utilize my technical training, my facility with numbers, and my orientation to detail.*
>
> STRATEGIC PLANNER, CONSUMER PRODUCTS, HBS '73

As you read this chapter, stretch your thinking about your skills and abilities. Don't limit your perception of your skills to only job- or work-related abilities. Life is more than your job. Certain abilities are used more than others in a particular job, but your proficiency in managing your life is a function of a much broader skill set. Pay particular attention to the skills you enjoy using. To sum up, your *perceived* skill set is likely to be more limited than the skills you actually possess. If you have forgotten that fact, step back and regain your perspective!

SKILLS BECOME MORE SUBTLE TOWARD THE TOP OF AN ORGANIZATION

Identifying the skills required to do a job becomes increasingly challenging as you move up in an organization. At the lower levels, you may have found it relatively simple to define the specific skills required to do outstanding work. Position descriptions were straightforward, and ads relatively self-explanatory. As you advance in an organization, defining the specific skills required to succeed becomes more difficult. And when you try to understand what employers are looking for in higher management positions, you often will encounter a lack of specificity that can seem downright annoying.

A successful manager must have mastered specific technical skills related to his or her area of responsibility and gained experience using those skills in a variety of situations. Far more important, however, is mastering skills related to handling people, making decisions, and self-management. Such abilities are difficult to capture in words but are evident to the interviewer by their presence or absence.

As we mentioned in Chapter 6, a manager who is involuntarily separated from a job seldom loses that job solely because he or she lacks technical business skills. Even when a merger or general downsizing leads to cuts, particular managers often are dismissed because they have a deficit in this second skills category. If dismissed managers are unaware of the importance of such skills, they blame being fired on "politics" or other circumstances beyond their control.

NUGGET: You can include political finesse in your skill set. In fact, if you don't attend to these skills, you quite likely will repeat your mistakes in the next job. Skills in finance, marketing, and production get you hired. The subtle aspects of your management style can either help you apply those skills to maximum personal advantage or cause you to lose your job. Take this opportunity to become the person who knows your skills best.

Reconsider your skills. The approach to skills assessment in this chapter helps you *rediscover lost skills* you may not have used in your present position. It helps you *determine your favorite skills*—the skills that you like to use and that are most important to you. And it helps you *define your transferable skills*—those you can apply in a range of contexts.

SKILLS: ACQUIRED AND INTRINSIC

Our concept of skills is influenced by Richard Bolles's book, *What Color Is Your Parachute?*[1] We recommend this reference for anyone reconsidering his or her career or undertaking a job search. Don't bypass it because of its apparent simplicity. It is full of valuable advice and a treasure-trove of career reference material. *Parachute* is updated frequently (every year as of this writing); we recommend working with the most current edition.

You have a number of intrinsic skills that come as naturally as breathing in and breathing out. When you use one of your intrinsic skills, certain positive things happen:

[1]Bolles, Richard N., *What Color Is Your Parachute?* (Berkeley: Ten Speed Press, 1991).

- You do the task at hand very well.
- You do the task quickly and efficiently.
- You are able to do the task naturally, without special effort.
- You enjoy doing the task.

In an ideal world, each person would be doing work that draws on his or her intrinsic skills.

Your intrinsic skills were evident in some of your very early activities, those things that grandparents bragged about and teachers praised—your ability to read well or play sports or be friends with just about anyone. With formal education you acquired many other skills, some of which enhanced your intrinsic skills. Other newly acquired skills tended to supplant your intrinsic skills. Skills you were *told* were important took on added stature.

NUGGET: Each of your skills has a hidden *weighted value* assigned at the point at which you acquired that skill. That weighted value may relate to the importance of the skill to an influential family member or teacher or to the type of people presumed to have the skill. An important part of any skills analysis is examining the weighted values assigned to your skills to ensure they are consistent with your value system and not simply influenced by the opinions and aspirations of others.

I've always felt that I should have certain skills—particularly negotiator/ persuader skills. Those would help me do well professionally, although not necessarily personally; I could be seen as aggressive and pushy. In fact, my skills audit confirmed that I am expert at communicating. But I'm not tough, I don't think on my feet, and I'm not good at theatrics. I absorb information and then put forth a position.
VP, INVESTMENT BANKING, HBS '87

Education and life experience may have buried many of your intrinsic skills beneath an accumulation of acquired skills. In extreme cases, you have forgotten skills you once treasured. You may have used them in hobbies or other avocational pursuits until more pressing demands on your time and energy seemed to preclude even those activities. In such a scenario, *all* your activities in recent years may have drawn on skills other than your intrinsic skills. And while you are proficient at what you do, you may have a hunch that your work takes more effort than it should and is less enjoyable than it might be:

The current department used to be long-range planning. I would spend half of my time on three-year plans; I oversaw their preparation through-out the company. But department management changed last year. The new push is on strategy rather than more academic analysis. Now things are very unstructured in most ways. I'm putting together presentations for senior management that summarize what their strategy is—in writing. I was always good academically—that is how I've gotten by—I'm a very quantitative person. I'm not strong in interacting with other people. Bottom line, I'm too theoretical for this job, so it's not comfortable anymore.

STRATEGIC PLANNER, CONSUMER PRODUCTS, HBS '73

If this story strikes a familiar note with you, you're a candidate for Dick Bolles's *The New Quick Job-Hunting Map* skills inventory. This inventory provides a fringe benefit, as well: you will develop a data base of achievements to use in drafting your resumé (Chapter 15). As these seminar participants said,

The skills exercise was arduous but very helpful. The systematic approach helped me to dig deeply.

DIRECTOR, CONSULTING, HBS '61

In my career so far I have taken the safe route—*the option with little downside risk. The skills exercise forced me to recognize I've under-utilized many talents that are really important to me. I want to change that.*

ASSOCIATE, CONSULTING, HBS '85

YOUR INTRINSIC SKILLS EXERCISE

STEP 1: Create a retrospective chronological log, as you did in the Forks in the Road Exercise in Chapter 4. At the top of the first page write the current year. Title the following pages in reverse chronology with each page representing a life stage—current position, prior jobs, graduate school, military service, college, high school, elementary school.

STEP 2: Find a quiet place, and recall all of your accomplishments during each life stage. Define *accomplishment* loosely, as something that happened because you were there; you were the one who did it. Write down every accomplishment that comes to mind— big or small, job- or nonjob-related, widely recognized or known only to you, done in a group or alone.

STEP 3: Keep at it! Carry your log with you for at least a week as you continue the exercise. This is not an easy process; when you dry up, take a break, but keep the log nearby for the next recollec- tion. This memory retrieval process has no order or logic; one thought leads to another apparently unrelated recollection. Keep in mind this analogy: creating a good accomplishments inventory is like cleaning out an attic. Everything has been thrown in haphazardly, it's all there, but individual items must be retrieved one at a time.

STEP 4: After a week or so of jotting down accomplishments, you will start to feel that the attic is clean. We recommend working until your inventory has twice the number of accomplishments as your age. If you have trouble meeting that minimum, you may be using too stringent a definition of *accomplishment.* Or you may have accepted someone else's definition of achievement. Or you may be focusing only on job-related accomplishments and overlooking other arenas such as avocations, athletics, community work, hobbies, and personal triumphs. Go back and make sure this is a *whole life* inventory.

STEP 5: Once you are reasonably sure that your accomplishments list reflects all facets and stages of your life, go back and star those accomplishments you *enjoyed in the doing.* This is not an easy task for people who are highly goal or achievement oriented. Ask, "Did I *enjoy* this activity in the *process* of its *becoming* an achievement?" If the process was painful, dull, or tortured in any way but you really enjoyed the recognition you received afterwards, do not star that accomplishment!

STEP 6: Wait at least a day. Then eliminate from your starred list of enjoyable accomplishments those you really didn't enjoy in the doing but that were so noteworthy that you couldn't bear to exclude them. (Don't worry, they won't be lost; you'll work with them later in preparing your resumé.)

STEP 7: Select *twenty* accomplishments that were the *most* enjoyable in the doing. Draw from a variety of stages and situations; select from career- and noncareer-related achievements. Again, this is not easy to determine; enlist the help of a friend to listen to you describe your accomplishments and tell you which ones you make *sound* the most enjoyable.

STEP 8 On a fresh sheet of paper group your achievements by core similarity. You might use a skills category that comes to mind when you think of each, such as organization ability or creative talent or leadership (see Appendix B for a case illustration). Try for no more than ten groups.

STEP 9: In a final paring down, select *seven accomplishments* that vary in time, circumstance, and nature. You may take one from each of your groupings—the one you remember with the greatest pride, fondness, or enthusiasm. If you had more than seven groups, choose the seven accomplishments to which you feel most attached. Again, try to include both job and nonjob achievements.

STEP 10: With your seven diverse enjoyable accomplishments chosen, write a one-page narrative about each. Revisit those achievements in complete detail, noting everything you can remember about the process. These essays should be great reading; see Appendix C for inspiration!

STEP 11: In your copy of *The New Quick Job-Hunting Map* (see the footnote at the beginning of this chapter), turn to page 15. Read Dick Bolles's instructions. Insert a shorthand name for each of your seven accomplishments at the top of pages 17, 19, and 21:

...ge, ur uic uciais of a particular phenomenon or place. centrating; keeping track of details; focusing on minutiae.

, to discover similarities and dissimilarities. Comparing; similarities or dissimilarities; perceiving identities or diver-

ation in the mind or on various materials. Entering (data); ng; recording; memorizing; classifying expertly; protecting; emembering; retrieving; extracting; reproducing; imitating; curately.

r complex arithmetic. Counting; taking inventory; calcu- financial records; reporting; maintaining fiscal controls; ntly with spreadsheets and statistics (and, by exten- ics, and telecommunications).

detecting; surveying; inventorying;

Adapted from *The New Quick Job-Hunting Map*.
© 1979, 1985 Richard Nelson Bolles.

STEP 12: Start by auditing your accomplishment in the *far right* column (column 7). Consider each of Bolles's forty skill sets listed on pages 16, 18, and 20. To what degree was a particular skill set instrumental in the accomplishment you described in your essay?
- If a skill listed was a *major factor,* darken in the square heavily.
- If it was *not applicable* to the accomplishment, leave the square blank.
- If it was *somewhat relevant,* shade in the square lightly.

STEP 13: Use a blank piece of paper to mask the markings from your column 7 accomplishment audit so they will not influence your subsequent entries. Repeat the audit process above for your column 6 accomplishment.

STEP 14: Repeat the audit process for your accomplishments in columns 5, 4, 3, 2, and 1. Cover your previous audits to give yourself every advantage in this self-administered skills inventory.

STEP 15: After you have completed all seven audits, look at the results. Any consistency of shading in the boxes adjacent to a skill set points to an intrinsic skill. Most likely you will not end up with a conclusive pattern. Your results may look something like this:

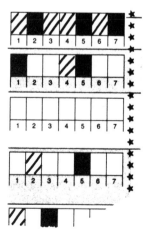

...gc, or the details of a particular *phenomenon or place.* centrating; keeping track of details; focusing on minutiae.

, to discover similarities and dissimilarities. Comparing; similarities or dissimilarities; perceiving identities or diver-

ation in the mind or on various materials. Entering (data); ...g; recording; memorizing; classifying expertly; protecting; ...emembering; retrieving; extracting; reproducing; imitating; ...curately.

v complex arithmetic. Counting; taking inventory; calcu- *financial records;* reporting; maintaining fiscal controls; ...ntly with spreadsheets and statistics (and, by exten- ...ics, and telecommunications).

...- detecting; surveying; inventorying;

Adapted from *The New Quick Job-Hunting Map.*
© 1979, 1985 Richard Nelson Bolles.

Alert: If you have blacked in an *entire row* of squares opposite any of the forty skill groups, you may be forcing the results because of a strong desire to record and retain that particular set of skills. A 100 percent filled-in row should not be your objective!

STEP 16: Your analysis of your intrinsic skills is now complete. Record on a separate sheet of paper those skill groups with four or more shaded boxes on your audit form. Enter these into your product specification file.

STEP 17: Save your entire log of accomplishments; it will be the starting point for the resumé preparation process covered in Chapter 15.

IN A RUSH?

If you don't have the time necessary for the Intrinsic Skills Exercise, you might try this shortcut to determine some of your most natural skills. Ask twenty people who have seen you in action to tell you one thing you do very well. Write down their responses, and note the common threads. This is no substitute for doing your Intrinsic Skills Exercise, but it can be a first step to a new perspective on your skills.

Discussion of the Skills Exercise

Properly done, the skills exercise requires considerable time—at least a week to collect the accomplishments and four to six hours to group your accomplishments by core similarity, select your most enjoyable seven, write your one-page narratives, and complete the skills audit. A superficial attempt at this exercise is worse than not doing it at all. If rushed, the results may give the erroneous impression that the skills you've used most recently on the job are your best bets for the future. Take the time necessary to uncover your buried intrinsic skills, or save this skills audit exercise for another time.

As you proceed with your skills audit, you may become alarmed if it seems to be leading you in disconcerting directions. A person whose entire career has been in investment banking may realize, midway through the exercise, that *none* of his or her most enjoyable accomplishments had anything to do with investment banking. Even more alarming, the intrinsic skills may seem to be best suited to professions with compensation levels far below what he or she is currently earning. As one manager put it, "Will I get a job *using* these skills? Will anyone *pay* me for them?"

Don't let these observations sabotage the exercise. Hang in there! *You need not change careers based on this exercise.* You may factor your intrinsic skills into your search or try to use more of them in your existing job or even seek opportunities to use them in avocational pursuits.

CAREER COURSE CHANGES: TRANSFERABLE SKILLS VERSUS EXPERIENCE

Job changers and interviewers alike have a fantasy: the candidate's background fits the job specifications perfectly, with education, experience, and skills identical to the job's requirements. Needless to say, such an obvious fit is seldom the case. More often, whatever fit exists between your background and the job you're after is not entirely self-evident. And if you are considering a radical course change in your career, it may be even more difficult for prospective employers to see much, if any, connection between your background and the position to be filled.

The Intrinsic Skills Exercise breaks down your accomplishments into transferable skills. You have demonstrated these skills in one arena, but you can use them with equal effectiveness in many other arenas. You need to make a case for the transferability of your skills, as this seminar participant did:

> *I did not have the conventional background for this job, so everyone in the interviewing process had several "skepticism points" they could use to ding me. By raising their concerns at an early stage in the discussion, I could make the points I had honed during my self-assessment as to why the move made sense in terms of my skills and other attributes. I got the job!*
>
> ASSOCIATE, CONSULTING, HBS '79

Skills are not always a substitute for specific industry experience. In general, skills are transferable, but experience is not. Experience involves knowledge of specific technologies and markets, relationships with specific individuals, and familiarity with the mores and idiosyncracies of an industry. But don't jump to premature conclusions. To rule out fields in which you have no experience is to discount the power of your transferable skills set.

BENEFITS OF A GOOD SKILLS AUDIT

Identifying your intrinsic skills and using them to focus your career direction has enormous benefits.

1. You stand a better chance of ending up in a situation in which you will be both *successful and happy.*

> *I like to work with information first—to become the expert before working with people. I never like to go into a meeting unprepared. I like finding out answers and different ways to do things. The Bolles skills audit confirms the way I operate: I'll hear about a deal, listen, take notes, and then go away and come back with fifteen questions.*
>
> VP, INVESTMENT BANKING, HBS '87

Careers that don't draw on your intrinsic skills may appear successful to the onlooker but fail to deliver for you on a daily basis. Unhappiness or lack of fulfillment in professional life are frequently the by-products of a career built on the wrong skill set.

2. Your new career direction will be *based on skills you value,* rather than skills valued by family, friends, educational institutions, or current trends in corporate America.

> *The heart of my discomfort at this consulting firm was the business judgment required of me—after all, I'd only worked for two years, and here I'm supposed to give expert advice to CEOs. I fell down when I had to get a client 80% of the way there on gut and general principles, with nothing buttoned down. It was too intimidating—*yet I took the job knowing that was a weakness, and feeling I should conquer it.
>
> CONSULTANT, HBS '80

Not surprisingly, a career built on skills *you* value is on a firmer base, one that will stand you in good stead in an ever-changing environment.

3. Bringing to mind forgotten experiences and skills you have not used recently gives you a broad data base from which to *generate new directions.*

> *The best job I ever had was working for the purchasing division of a large company in their corporate office. My job was doing all the buying to keep the building going—ordering work pants, planning the ponds at the new group headquarters, getting sealed bids on a million rolls of toilet paper! It was* a far cry from the sophisticated world I work in now!
>
> WALL STREET LAWYER, HBS '76

We'll talk more about using your skills audit to evaluate new options in Chapter 12.

4. Your effectiveness and *credibility in interviewing* will benefit greatly from a well-done skills audit. One of the managers in our seminar described his quandary:

Whatever I've achieved, I don't value. I discount what I have achieved,
instead of recognizing that it is special. So I don't sell myself well.
                                   VP, INVESTMENT BANKING, HBS '81

A clear idea of your skill base, with specific instances in which those skills were applied, will give you a great advantage in needs-benefits selling (see Chapter 16).

5. As mentioned earlier, if you are considering a change in career direction, this exercise is essential preparation for articulating your *transferable skills*. To sell yourself into a new field, you need to convince your network, interviewers, and any other "facilitating agents" in your search that the skills you have used in one arena can be readily used in a new setting.

We hope this chapter brings you the benefits a thorough skills audit has brought to many seminar participants:

Doing the achievements list and the skills exercise was good for me.
Seeing how much I'd done and how many things I'm good at was very
empowering. I said to myself, "I've got options!" The other thing that
amazed me was that some of those achievements could be so small and
yet feel so meaningful to me.
                 MANAGING DIRECTOR, STRATEGIC CONSULTING, HBS/PMD '84

Congratulations to you who have made it through the most time-consuming exercise in the book. For you skimmers, there's still time to go back and reap the rewards!

8

ORGANIZATIONAL FIT
AND POLITICS

No doubt you can recall being in situations in your business career where you felt frustrated—out of place or even set up in some way.

> *To be credible in this company you have to be very politic. First you have to come up with a problem that can be solved by a means known to the company. And the problems must have ready solutions. Then the timing has to be appropriate. Of course you have to take an approach that galvanizes attention. And heaven forbid that you be academic. It's politics all the way.* I resent others not wanting the facts.
>
> STRATEGIC PLANNER, CONSUMER PRODUCTS, HBS '73

> *I was approached by a division vice-president. He had six companies started by entrepreneurs, and wanted to make sense of it. He was looking for a place for me, and good people were involved. But it was a bad fit with another executive who was moved in and to whom I reported. I felt the VP had hired me, and I guess I acted that way. So I was not seen as one of my boss's people—but rather as a spy. I knew it, but I was young, and I thought my record would speak for itself. This guy had such a cold personality! Eventually the VP left and I was fair game for my boss, who asked for my resignation on New Year's Eve.*
>
> CORPORATE PLANNING, PETROCHEMICALS, HBS '66

Examining these situations in detail is an important part of a self-inventory. Equally important are insights into the types of situations in which you thrive—perhaps where you were in sync with the mission of the organization, or selling a product you represented well, or managing a process using your well-honed organizing abilities, or working with just the right partners. Your self-inventory will provide important information about your tolerances; you'll have, at your fingertips, a list of variables to look for in the market assessment phase.

NUGGET: As you move forward in Part 3 to formulate your marketing plan, account for your limitations. Near term, avoid inappropriate markets for you-the-product; longer term, you may elect to work on overcoming some of those limitations.

The following exercise invariably generates animated discussion in the HBSCNY Career Seminar, as participants share humorous and sometimes rueful reminiscences.

ENVIRONMENTAL FIT EXERCISE

STEP 1: Take three sheets of paper. Divide each into two columns labeled *Best Case* and *Worst Case.*

STEP 2: Put one of these headings at the top of each sheet: *Boss, Peers, Environment.*

STEP 3: Go back over your work career and recollect "good" and "bad" supervisors, coworkers, and work environments. Write a brief description of each in your worksheets. *Alert:* Don't rush it! This kind of backtracking takes time. Make sure you have uncovered all relevant memories, particularly the unpleasant ones. Not coming up with any "bad" memories? Red flag! This exercise will be helpful only if you are thorough and honest to yourself.

STEP 4: Review your worksheets, looking for situations that evoke *particularly* strong feelings, positive or negative. Circle these; they indicate dynamics for which you have a very high affinity or low tolerance.

STEP 5: Studying each worksheet in turn, look for *common threads* among the best and worst cases. Note these at the bottom of the list as specifically as possible.

STEP 6: Make an honest assessment: Where are your long suits? Where are your short suits? What configurations do you need to avoid in the future? Where can you commit to getting a better handle on your reactions? Where can you change?

STEP 7: Distill the essential conclusions from this exercise, and enter them into your product specification file.

LOOK FOR WHAT'S BEHIND YOUR HIGH AND LOW TOLERANCES

After years of conducting the above exercise with hundreds of HBS graduates, we have accumulated a long list of best-case and worst-case qualities in a boss, peers, and the environment (see Appendix D). Not surprisingly, in seminar discussions disparities and contradictions abound, reflecting the varied predilections of the different participants. However, when inconsistencies show up within one person's list, these need to be examined.

By looking closely at your preferences you can discover insights about yourself. Review the actual situations that informed your best-case and worst-case lists—the ones in which *you* played a leading role. At the time you may have been too involved in what was going on to fully appreciate the implications. By re-creating these situations, you can see your experiences more objectively and record your insights for ready reference.

NUGGET: As with any self-exploratory exercise, an objective second perspective is invaluable. After you have written down your best-case and worst-case boss/peers/environment recollections, let someone on your board (spouse, close friend, counselor) review your lists with you. Add their comments and insights to your notes.

As you review your worksheets, keep these points in mind:

1. Which of your preferences are *critical* to your success on the job and which are simply *desirable?* When we asked one manager in our seminar for her critical items, she was very clear:

   While I haven't the vaguest idea as to my ideal next job, I know this much: I want to work at my desk, at home. I want to be working with colleagues of similar intellect. And I want to work with people who value my ability to help them. Being in motion—going from one location to another— energizes me. Lastly, I don't want to be involved with details.
   STRATEGIC PLANNER, PUBLISHING, HBS '81

   List your critical preferences and put in your product specification file. Finding those qualities in your next situation will be one of the objectives of the market assessment and interviewing process (see Part 3).

2. Ask yourself, "*Why* do I have these expectations of my co-workers?"

Then I was managing projects, which was the most stressful of all. No one could do the work like I could—it became unbelievably time-consuming as some of our people were very mediocre. I was going to hit a home run for each and every client.
                    PROJECT MANAGER, CONSULTING FIRM, HBS '84

Are your expectations of your co-workers consistent with how they are rewarded by the company? If you traded places with your co-workers could you live up to your expectations? Are you trying to re-create an idealized past situation?

3. Look for inconsistencies or mutually exclusive preferences. Make a conscious trade-off, and write down your selection so you won't forget what you've decided.

4. Be realistic in defining your criteria for a supervisor. Avoid the common trap of looking for an ideal boss:

I'm looking for a boss who shows trust and confidence in my ability and gives me lots of latitude to do what I want. A boss who realizes that I've done a job better than anyone else. A boss who is comfortable with my approach to the job and my follow-through. Someone able to put out of his mind that I may have had a better education. Someone able to look at me as an individual who is nice to work with and brighter than most people assigned to him. Someone willing to train me. Someone sufficiently self-confident to be totally comfortable with everything I do.
                    VP, COMMERCIAL BANKING, HBS '65

Perhaps the boss in the above description should be able to walk on water too! Inevitably, the person you report to will fall short of your, as well as his or her, expectations because of human fallibilities and organizational realities. Your boss has a boss, whose style and standing within the company influence the situation. Other factors—such as the company's financial situation, strategic considerations, the state of markets and the economy—may prevent your boss from playing the role as he or she would prefer. Be considerate of your boss's reality.

5. Many friction points experienced with superiors point to unresolved issues with parents or other early life authority figures.

My worst-case boss list can be summed up in one phrase: forceful father types. Spare me the bosses who scream and yell, who imply I'm stupid, who intimidate me in any way, basically. I've had enough of that from my own father.
                    VP, COMMERCIAL BANKING, HBS '65

If your worst-case examples in the Environmental Fit Exercise indicate that you tend to find yourself in workplace situations reminiscent of earlier negative life experiences, free yourself for a better situation in the next chapter of professional life.

POLITICS IN THE WORKPLACE

In doing the last exercise, you may have recalled one or more instances where your life was complicated by *corporate politics*. In the HBSCNY Career Seminar, a discussion of worst-case environments invariably includes instances of office politics. However, participants have widely varying ideas about what constitutes politics. Quite frequently, a specific instance described with distaste by one seminar participant is regarded by another participant as quite normal—or even as an opportunity for advancing the organization's or the individual's interests.

Dealing effectively with a political situation means recognizing when politics are at work. A major impediment for many high achievers is failing to recognize a political situation, let alone accept this reality of organizational life:

> *Now our group is headed by a guy who told me up front that I wasn't the kind of guy he wanted: he wanted an engineer. I decided I would show him what I could do. Meanwhile the work load for our group was dropping: I often thought of projects but nothing came of them. After some false starts I came up with a new concept to make a project more economical. I received zero credit—yet when a junior analyst showed this guy high net present value calculations for my concept, my boss took over the concept and spent two years developing it! Now I get very little to do, and when I am given something, I can see it has very little chance of working, so I either have to tell him or work on something really foolish. I'm perceived as someone who doesn't care—when in fact I care a lot and am in a tremendous rage most of the time.*
> SCHEDULING AND CONSTRUCTION MANAGER, HBS '66

> *Under the new owners it is not fun. This company has had quarter-to-quarter increases for twenty-six years. The new company head is very crude. He is very arbitrary, and capricious, a what-have-you-done-for-me lately kind of guy. He attempts to control everything. For example, the company will pay for one physical if the results are sent to his office. Also, my old boss has changed like a chameleon since the new owners came along. They're putting tremendous pressure on us. The company is one that has lots of old-line businesses, so we're forced to milk the business.*

We've grown at 20 percent compounded annually since 1946 but not with
this strategy.
VP FINANCE, ELECTRONICS, HBS '60

What is a political situation? How do you recognize when you're in
one? The following two definitions have been useful guidelines to
HBSCNY Career Seminar participants:

Definition A: The degree of politicization in a workplace is a function
of the discrepancy between the stated rules and the way the workplace actually operates—how the game is actually played.

Definition B: A political situation is one I am unable to handle
effectively, in spite of my expertise and training. If I could handle
the situation, it would not strike *me* as political.

Some people, such as the manager quoted below, have an aptitude,
even a talent, for doing well in highly political situations:

Politics in organizations is inevitable. *I think I can play the game pretty*
well; I play honestly, and I can play as roughly as the situation requires.
SENIOR EXECUTIVE, FINANCIAL INDUSTRY, HBS '77

Those not as adept in this area often have strong feelings about politically
savvy co-workers, calling them opportunists, brown-nosers, people who
don't do their homework, who never pull their weight, who let work slip
while they make nice with the boss:

I have been mad in the past for not being rewarded for what I *was taught*
was important. Most companies don't adequately encourage people who
are really good at using their brains—the hard-working, bright ones—to
get promoted, be recognized, even get paid what they're worth! Perhaps
two career paths are needed—one for the manager, one for the brain.
VP, INVESTMENT BANKING, HBS '72

Bottom line? "When they get ahead of me, it's not fair!"

"Conquering" the politics of the workplace requires a radical reorien-
tation in thinking. Stated simply, political skills need to be respected as
much as well-developed financial, marketing, or management skills.
"Those people" mentioned above have a talent for dealing with reality in
the work environment. They do not set themselves up to fail in political
situations by being rigidly self-righteous. They are realistic about their
personal values and those of the corporation for which they work. The
seminar participants quoted below developed the knack of dealing effectively in political situations:

*I have always tended to go "by the book." After the seminar discussion
on political situations, I looked back and recognized that I have gotten
into political difficulties when someone in the organization was playing
with a different book of rules. Since that realization, I have gotten much
better at picking up clues about which book is being followed.*

ASSOCIATE, CONSULTING, HBS '86

*I realized that I approach situations very practically—bluntly might be
more accurate. I tell it like it is and raise issues others are skirting. What
I've started to do when I get into situations that require being indirect or
doing a lot of schmoozing is to latch onto someone who's good at that
and try to keep my mouth shut.*

DIRECTOR OF CUSTOMER SERVICES, MANUFACTURING, HBS '64

Just how nimble are *you* in politicized situations? Does your blood boil
at the very thought of "giving in" to the political realities? Does developing the skills to succeed in a politicized environment feel like compromis-
ing your value system? Does the concept of surviving, let alone thriving,
in a politicized workplace strike you as violating your own moral code?

Or are you at a point in professional life where you're ready for a crash
course in navigating political settings and ready to sign up? Can you
envision the benefits of having a broader range of responses at the ready
when you come up against a political reality? Could you make a project
out of developing a "third eye" or "observing ego" as your ally, to register
your reactions accurately and help you select your response?

NUGGET: *You* make the decision about how much to enhance your
political savvy. Be honest and realistic. Take into account your history,
your knowledge of how you react to situations when you have not
made the rules. You have choices. Like the good manager you are,
make a decision that takes full account of your political skills inventory.

You may elect to upgrade your savvy—and enjoy the benefits this seminar
participant did:

*I was assigned a job that was 90 percent systems and 10 percent projects.
I wasn't using my brains or anything I valued. My work had no relevance
for me, so I developed an attitude problem. I managed to do something
about it—and then I got the most important project in our group. My star
started rising, and now things are better than they have ever been.*

AVP, COMMERCIAL BANKING, HBS '82

AN ANALOGY: "WHAT GAME AM I PLAYING?"

Sean, an avid footballer in England who recently transferred to the United States, misses the game. "Come and play football with us," say some new acquaintances. Sean shows up in shorts, shirt, and shinguards. Play begins. Wham! He is tackled violently by someone in a helmet and full body pads. "You can't do that," says Sean. Next an opponent grabs the ball and runs across the goal, which the official allows—to Sean's dismay. "That's against the rules!" he says. And so the game goes, with Sean becoming increasingly frustrated, bruised, and angry, both at the other team for not playing fair and at the officials who must be taking bribes to permit such illegal goings on.

From a sidelines vantage point it is clear that Sean is in the wrong game. So why is it taking him so long to recognize this fact? Why doesn't he find a *soccer* game where his talents and experience can be used to better effect? Sean is trapped because he is so intent on putting things right—from his point of view—that he has neglected to ask the key question: *"What game am I playing in?"*

When a head-down, diligent, responsible manager gets into a similar situation, it is easy to feel blind-sided, caught in the politics. Don't forget the two questions that will help you spot and deal with political situations: "What game are we playing?" and "Do I want to play that game?"

NUGGET: Don't let dedication and diligence turn into counter-productive rigidity or moralistic self-justification. Recognize that adapting to the circumstances may, in fact, be the appropriate response in certain situations. To deal effectively with political situations, maintain a healthy balance between your internal standards and the realities of the workplace. Address the situation as it exists rather than as you wish it to be.

Enter insights you have gleaned from this chapter into your product specification file, highlighting any "must haves" and "must avoids." To the extent you've tended to misread or misinterpret reality, remind yourself to concentrate more on the facts and less on the "oughta-be's." And keep in mind that political situations are seldom black and white but most often result from differing views of the game and the rules.

9

TO SEE OURSELVES AS OTHERS SEE US

O was some power the giftie gie us
To see oursel's as ithers see us!
—ROBERT BURNS, "TO A LOUSE"

Robert Burns's poem "To a Louse," from which the above lines are taken, is subtitled, "On Seeing One on a Lady's Bonnet at Church." Burns's point, of course, is that the grand lady, in her fine hairdo, bonnet, and dress, sits blissfully unaware of what is obvious to others. Many managers are equally unaware of how they are perceived by others. This inability to see ourselves as others see us can be particularly damaging during the transition process, a time of meeting new contacts and selling to prospective employers.

DANGER SIGNS OF GAPS IN YOUR SELF-PERCEPTION

Be alert to these indicators. They may signal a significant gap between your self-perception and how others perceive you:

- Recruiters send you out on the "wrong" interviews.
- Feedback from your boss, co-workers, or friends dumbfounds you.
- You frequently find yourself dismissing negative feedback about how you come across.
- In explaining unsuccessful situations in your career, you consistently blame factors outside yourself: a string of incompetent bosses, no options, a hopeless political situation.

If any of these sound familiar, you may be in the same unfortunate situation as the lady in the poem—blissfully unaware of something obvious to others. Read on!

Skeptical that others can "read you" so readily? So are many

HBSCNY Career Seminar participants, until they do the First Impressions Exercise. Each participant is matched up with someone he or she has not met before and then given two minutes to briefly describe to his or her partner the publication and topic from the Feature Magazine Article Exercise in Chapter 5. The partners then separate, and each person fills out the following questionnaire on his or her partner, based on what was gleaned in a conversation of less than five minutes.

Unlike the other exercises in this book, you can just read about First Impressions. If you'd like to try out the questionnaire go right ahead.

FIRST IMPRESSIONS QUESTIONNAIRE

Based solely on your (admittedly limited) observations and intuitions about your dyad partner, what perceptions and outright guesses can you venture about him or her? Remember, this is speculation, not fact, so don't worry about incorrect answers. Go with your first reaction; skip over questions where a quick response doesn't occur to you.

1. What are his or her favorite diversions (theater, reading, sports, gardening, travel, work, others)?
2. What were his or her early years like (where, family size, sibling order)?
3. At what kind of social gatherings would you expect to find him or her?
4. What type of work does he or she do (selling, finance, managing, analyzing, production, human resources, other)?
5. At a sporting event, what role do you see him or her in (player, spectator, coach, referee, concessionaire, business manager, owner of the stadium, other)?
6. Does he or she remind you of any notable or famous person?
7. If he or she were in a theatrical production or talent show, what kind of part or role could you visualize?
8. What were his or her favorite subjects in college?
9. Mark on each spectrum where you think he or she is most comfortable:

Works alone	———————	Works on a team
Relishes change	———————	Prefers status quo
Risk taker	———————	Plays it safe
Thrives on pressure	———————	Prefers low key
Small company	———————	Large company
Thinker	———————	Doer
Works with people	———————	Works with data
Loves planning	———————	Prefers seat-of-the-pants management
Competes with others	———————	Competes with self
Start-up type	———————	Operational type

Discussion of the First Impressions Questionnaire

Logic says it would be impossible to accurately fill out this questionnaire about a virtual stranger. However, when dyad partners show their questionnaire responses to each other, the degree of accuracy is unexpectedly *high*. The amount of insight into the other person represented by these admittedly speculative answers never fails to amaze participants. Exclamations of "How did you *know* that?" are common.

NUGGET: You telegraph much more about yourself than you might imagine. To deal more effectively with others, learn more about how others see you.

Never forget that as you meet for a networking breakfast or walk into an interview, you create an impression *before* you say anything. If that impression is not consistent with the "product" that you want to present, you have an uphill sell. For example, if you want to present yourself as an action-oriented line manager but an observer's first impression is, "Here comes a classic thinker-philosopher," you have a credibility problem. And the problem is insidious because many people you meet in this process are unaware of the unconscious judgments they make based on those first impressions.

If you are aware of how you initially come across, you can work to alter or manage your first impression. For example, you can speak directly to any contradictions between your demeanor and your abilities. You can allude to the fact that in a number of situations people have underestimated your abilities *because* of their first impressions. By prompting a contact or interviewer to reassess his or her first impression, you go a long way toward negating a potential liability.

The other lesson to be learned from the First Impressions Questionnaire is that you have gut-level instincts that give you access to data as valuable as any gathered through your five senses. You have intuitive skills that can be used to good advantage in assessing people and situations. Trust these talents and learn to use them even more effectively.

THE COMMUNICATIONS WINDOW

In communicating with another person, both with words and through un-spoken language, the nature of the communication can be conceptualized in a matrix we call the communications window.[1] The four quadrants of the window represent degrees of self-knowledge and self-disclosure in a one-on-one communication situation such as an interview. Each quadrant represents "What is known about me"—by myself and by the other person.

	Things you know about me	Things you don't know about me
Things I know about me	Open	Mask
Things I don't know about me	Blind	Potential

Open area: You know; I know.

The upper left quadrant represents communications where each party is *equally* informed, symbolizing the free and open exchange of information.

Mask area: You don't know; I know.

The upper right quadrant represents communications where I am aware of certain facts or realities but the other person is *not.* It is my choice whether, and when, to share this mask area information with others.

Blind area: You know; I don't know.

The lower left quadrant represents communications where the other person knows things about me of which I am *unaware.* Habit-

[1]Based on the Johari Window in *Of Human Interaction* by Joseph Luft, 1969. This concept is also dealt with in depth in *Group Processes: An Introduction to Group Dynamics* by Joseph Luft. Copyright © 1963, 1970, and 1984 by Joseph Luft. Published by Mayfield Publishing Company.

ual patterns and messages I communicate unconsciously fall into
this blind area.

Potential area: You don't know; I don't know.

The lower right quadrant represents communications where *neither*
party is consciously aware of what is being transmitted. Neverthe-
less, messages are being relayed and may influence the communications, for good or bad. This quadrant is the area of hidden human
potential.

The communications window offers a number of insights into person-
to-person communications related to the career transition process and to
interviewing in particular:

1. The most effective interactions occur when communications fall
   within the open area. Two individuals who feel comfortable with each
   other tend to move much of their respective communications from
   the mask area to the open area. First encounters, such as an interview,
   often start with a *minimum* of communications in the open area.
2. A good interviewer works to move communications from the mask
   area to the open area and thereby create a comfortable situation.
   Similarly, as a candidate in an interview you can obtain more information by acting in a way that prompts the interviewer to move from
   the mask area to the open area.
3. The more you can enlarge the open area during any interaction—a
   meeting of your board, a networking luncheon, an interview—the
   more favorable your impression on others will be. Your openness will
   set you apart from individuals who put little in the open area and thus
   give the impression of trying to hide something.
4. *Communications within the confines of the two lower quadrants—in
   the blind area and potential area—are beyond your control.* This is
   most obvious in the blind area, where an interviewer can see something to which you are oblivious. But it also applies to the potential
   area, since your unconscious inputs and reactions can create impressions that influence the opinions of the interviewer. In any communication, what you don't know about yourself *can* hurt you.

INFLUENCE OF THE SUBCONSCIOUS

The relationship between the conscious and subconscious mind has been
compared with an iceberg, the conscious mind being the small portion of

an iceberg above water. Realizing that 90 percent of day-to-day behavior is controlled by the subconscious can be unnerving to say the least.

NUGGET: Confront your unfinished business. Unresolved issues that lurk in the potential area impair your ability to present yourself and conduct your daily transactions. Unfinished business will interfere with the successful implementation of your marketing campaign. Corrective action is essential.

You can use many approaches to identify and deal with unresolved issues. Quite possibly you will encounter and resolve some issues through this self-assessment process. As the communications window emphasizes, the challenge is to become aware of your blind spots, as these seminar participants did:

I am frequently aware of a semiconscious rebellion on my part—especially when I feel I'm going to be professionally compromised. I strongly resist "going with the program" if it doesn't meet my standards, or conform to my way of doing things.
MANAGER OF SHIP DESIGN AND CONSTRUCTION, HBS '66

After I was let go, I realized that a number of people in the company had tried to give me clues to help me keep my job. Taking advice has always been difficult for me; in this case it lost me a job.
ASSOCIATE, CONSULTING, HBS '86

For a long time I have had difficulty accepting authority. When I lost my job, my reaction was to look for a company I could buy—so I could control everything. It cost me a lot of money and didn't work out, but I learned a lot about myself—that I need to address my own authority and control issues.
MANAGING DIRECTOR, FINANCIAL SERVICES, HBS '80

If you encounter indications that unresolved issues are resulting in self-sabotage, you may want to seek the assistance of a professional. Appropriate professionals include psychiatrists, psychologists, and certified therapists. Some have a behavioral orientation and focus on dealing with immediate symptoms. Others quite profitably probe the early years to unearth those old scripts that inhibit day-to-day functioning or effectiveness. Don't assume you need to take the four-days-a-week-on-the-couch-for-several-decades approach. Finding a suitable professional and successfully working through issues that handicap your transition sometimes can be accomplished within months rather than years. And you'll feel like you've thrown off a heavy pack. Why make the journey harder than it need be?

Whatever approach you choose, improving your ability to see yourself as others see you is a worthwhile endeavor. By addressing unconscious issues that hamper your progress, your interactions with others will be increasingly within your awareness and under your control.

10

CONSTRAINTS TO ACHIEVING YOUR IDEAL JOB A WRAP-UP ON SELF-AWARENESS

In this chapter, you'll develop a definition of the job that would be ideal for you. You'll examine the obstacles you perceive as standing between you and that ideal job as this HBSCNY Career Seminar participant did:

> *This guy who knows me well said, "If you can relax, you'll be everything anyone wants." I get stressed out in any setting where I'll be tested, so I'm putting myself in lesser settings to compensate. That in itself causes frustration because I'm not utilizing my background and training.*
> ASSOCIATE, M&A INVESTMENT BANKING, HBS '80

Finally, you'll assess to what extent each obstacle *in actuality* constrains you as you reach for the goal of your self-marketing campaign.

YOUR IDEAL JOB

Your first reaction may be, "I'm not ready to define my ideal job!" And you're correct; it is too early to define the job that would be a perfect fit for you. But it is not too early to take a first cut at that definition. In your managerial role, you have undoubtedly developed business plans, marketing forecasts, or cash flow projections. Such documents do not foretell the future. But they are valid management tools for testing assumptions, generating projections, and consolidating all currently available data. Further consideration of the projected results and their ramifications then leads to decisions to change certain parameters, which in turn leads to a new set of projections—and so on.

Similarly, your initial definition of an ideal job will represent a *first approximation* that defines various parameters. In the next section of *In Transition,* you'll further modify and polish your definition in the *market assessment* process. When you begin your self-marketing campaign, you'll do so knowing your goal is realistic—attainable and in line with your self-assessment.

NUGGET: In business or your own career, if you don't know where you're going, any road will lead there. Take the time to establish a goal for this transition.

THE IDEAL JOB EXERCISE

STEP 1: Write a complete description of the next ideal job for you. Take your time. Try not to be constrained by limitations that come to mind as you are writing. This is a brainstorming exercise. Put reality aside for the time being.

STEP 2: Did you cover every aspect you would include if your next position were that ideal job? Use this checklist to guide you:

Organization

- Mission
- Location
- Size
- Markets served
- Distinctive competence
- Competitive situation
- Corporate personality
- Economic situation
- Name recognition

Reporting Relationships

- Where you fit in the organization
- Whom you work for
- Who reports to you
- Who works with you
- Whom you influence, and who and what influences you
- The attributes you would most like your boss and coworkers to have

Your Role

- Your specific job responsibilities
- The contributions most critical for your success
- Skills and experience involved in the job
- Prospects for advancement

Compensation

- On starting
- In the future
- Breakout: salary, bonus, equity, benefits

Effect on Your Life

- Hours per week involved in the job
- Travel and other demands on nonworking hours.

GOALS AND OBSTACLES: WHAT STANDS BETWEEN YOU AND YOUR IDEAL JOB?

A key function of any leader in an organization is to set goals and then examine any obstacles that might prevent the organization from reaching those goals. You probably have performed this function in your business or volunteer leadership roles. You are now functioning as CEO of your "corporation," and it's time to identify the obstacles constraining your career.

The organizational leader knows that some obstacles are *real,* while others stem from *perceptions* held by those within the organization. A leader also recognizes that some obstacles are insurmountable, while others can be overcome in a variety of ways—by committing additional resources, by examining old assumptions, by introducing a new kind of expertise to meet current challenges. The leader sets the optimum goal for the organization and moves the organization toward that goal, surmounting or avoiding obstacles as required.

Keep this analogy in mind as you consider the obstacles that stand between you and your goal—your ideal job as you have just defined it. Recognize that one factor is different: you are both the leader and the organization. As the leader you are developing clarity about your optimal direction. As the organization, you may have some perceptions, habits, or ingrained patterns of response that create obstacles. Some of these can be altered; some cannot.

"If you recognize you would be better off in your ideal job, why are you still where you are?" The natural human tendency when confronted with such a question is to come up with some very plausible reasons to justify being *here*. And soon justifications become as limiting as having your feet stuck in cement! Listen to just a sampling:

> *"What if my employer finds out I'm looking? They'll say 'Goodbye'—*
> *with two weeks' pay."*
> *"If I wait long enough, won't it fall in my lap?"*
> *"At sixty-one, I'm not a standard hire."*
> *"I don't want to waste people's time."*
> *"I don't want anyone to suffer because I am making a change."*
> *"I don't know the right buzz words."*

The balance of this chapter is designed to help you flag your personal constraints, examine each, and make a conscious decision about how each will impact your market assessment and ultimately your marketing campaign.

ACTUAL AND ILLUSORY CONSTRAINTS

Constraints you perceive as preventing you from using your unique set of skills, attributes, and values on the job can be divided into two categories—*actual constraints* and *illusory constraints*. *Actual* constraints are insurmountable and force a redefinition of your ideal job or the marketing campaign you design to find that ideal job. *Illusory* constraints are surmountable, but only if you are able to recognize them as such and neutralize their effect.

Illusory constraints are not inconsequential: they are often extremely powerful in an insidious way. They may be part of what defines who you are and, as such, represent deep-seated convictions. These are not easy to uncover and are even more difficult to dislodge. Most have psychological underpinnings. Some constraints masquerade as conventional wisdom. Others you have believed as articles of faith for so long that comprehending their full dimension will prove a real challenge.

Unexamined illusory constraints can lead to cynicism, long-term vocational discontent, and underutilization of talents. They can corrode relationships when they involve others. Shakespeare described the paralyzing and limiting effect of illusory constraints over 300 years ago in Hamlet's "To be, or not to be" soliloquy:

> *Thus conscience does make cowards of us all;*
> *And thus the native hue of resolution*
> *Is sicklied o'er with the pale cast of thought,*
> *And enterprises of great pith and moment*
> *With this regard their currents turn away,*
> *And lose the name of action.*
>   HAMLET, ACT 3, SCENE 2

CONSTRAINTS EXERCISE

STEP 1:   Prepare the worksheets from Appendix E for writing in the matrix.

STEP 2:   Constraints—whether actual or illusory—are divided into two further categories: *internal constraints,* related to you and those close to you, and *external constraints,* related to outside realities such as industry norms and market conditions. Subdivisions within those two categories are listed in column one. Fill in only the relevant portions of the matrix; not all the listed constraints will apply to you. Enter the specific constraints standing between you and your ideal job in column two on the appropriate worksheet. Use several sentences to explain each of your constraints.

STEP 3:   After completing all relevant portions of column two, complete the verification section of the matrix as described at the top of column three. Note that the verification questions differ for internal and external constraints: for the former, the questions are, "How real is this constraint?" and "What would happen if I ignored it?" For the latter, the questions are, "How accurate is my perception?" and "Should I validate it further?" Verify only the constraints you listed in column two.

STEP 4:   For each of your constraints, fill in column four. Be as specific as you can in answering, "How is this constraint modifying my goals and my search?"

STEP 5:   After you have completed your worksheets, determine to what extent each constraint is *actual* versus *illusory.* To make this determination for internal constraints, enlist the help of your board and people who know you well. For external constraints we recommend that you complete the verification process with input from appropriate external sources.

EVALUATING YOUR CONSTRAINTS

Before you enter your constraints in your product specification file, evaluate each for its place in the accompanying pie chart. Determine from the diagram into which of the following five categories each of your constraints falls and determine needed action related to each.

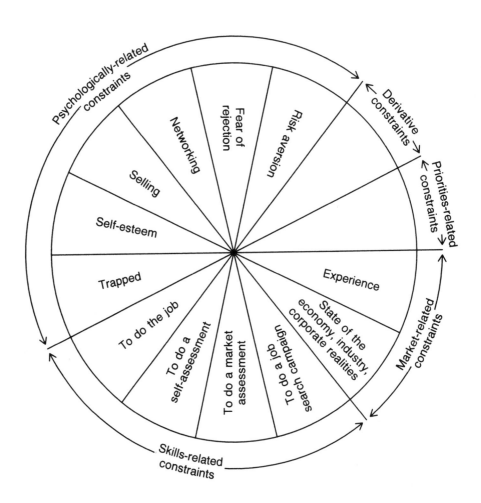

Priorities-Related Constraints

Your priorities-related constraints are actual and legitimate. You have carefully chosen your top six priorities; honor them! Here are some examples of priorities-related constraints:

> *"I want to stay in New York City, Northern New Jersey, or Fairfield County."*
> *"The job won't pay enough for me to live comfortably."*

Market-Related Constraints

Your market-related constraints must be validated. Here's where premature conclusions can limit you unnecessarily. Alternatively, ignoring market constraints can needlessly prolong your transition. Get solid market data from trustworthy sources; don't succumb to your worst fears ("there *are* no marketing jobs in the Northeast") or indulge your fantasies ("selling my background to an advertising agency will be a piece of cake"). Some examples of market-related constraints:

> *"I don't have sufficient industry experience."*
> *"I'm too young."*
> *"I have a 'crooked' career path."*

Skills-Related Constraints

Your skills-related constraints fall into two categories: skills to *do* the job and skills to *get* the job. We firmly believe you can surmount constraints having to do with getting the job, whether they are impeding your self-assessment, market assessment, or job search campaign. Examples of skills-related constraints:

> *"I can't narrow down the options."*
> *"I'm conflicted over fun versus money."*
> *"I don't know how to find where I'm needed."*
> *"I'm daunted by the sheer number of companies; I don't know how to figure out the higher-probability companies."*
> *"I don't have a network. In fact, I have a very small circle of friends."*
> *"I've never done a sell job before."*

Do not buckle under to these constraints!

Psychologically-Related Constraints

Your psychologically-related constraints are best surmounted. Ask yourself, "Could I live with this constraint having kept me from my ideal job?" Examples of psychologically-related constraints:

Trapped

> "I need to do a good job at my current job. I have no time to work on this."
> "I want to develop the ability to stay in one place."
> "Luck is a much larger factor in job hunts than people generally acknowledge."

Self-Esteem

> "I have a sense of total failure at age forty-five."
> "I'm insecure about my abilities."
> "I'm listening to everyone else."

Selling

> "It takes more salesmanship than I'm up to."
> "I don't want to approach people I barely know."
> "I have always changed jobs by being spotted for my good work and being asked to come aboard."

Networking

> "The ideal job requires contacts I don't have."
> "It is hard for me to deal with people I don't know."
> "I don't have the perfect group to build a business with."

Fear of Rejection

> "I might not get anywhere; I might find out I'm not of value."
> "I have difficulty adjusting to new environments—the personalities, the politics."
> "The competition is fierce out there!"

Risk Aversion

> "I don't have the guts."
> "I'm afraid of losing all my net worth."

Derivative Constraints

Your *derivative constraints* are those secondary effects or repercussions caused by giving in to other constraints. We view these as *red-light alerts.* Take them seriously, or these constraints will grind your search to a halt. We recommend, at a minimum, (1) tightening your support system, (2) interjecting an extra level of structure into your search (having to make fewer daily choices, for example), and (3) consulting a competent, qualified expert. See Chapter 9 for further discussion of this point. Examples of derivative constraints:

> *"I have no motivation."*
> *"I'm having real trouble getting up in the morning."*
> *"I'm giving in to diversions and distractions."*

Now you are ready to enter your constraints in your product specification file, by category:

Actual

- Priorities-related
- Market-related, as validated and verified by information interviews
- Skills-related, to *do* the job, as validated and verified by information interviews

Illusory

- Your personal challenges—whether they are *assumptions* about the market that you are using as a convenient out, *skills* you are failing to acquire and use in the transition process, or *psychological blocks* that are as real as a cement wall

SUMMARY

The Constraints Exercise is designed to force you to confront barriers to your progress and to scrutinize each with an eye to eliminating it if possible. *External constraints*—the job market as influenced by the economy, industry norms, and corporate realities—need reexamination. Ask, "Is my assessment of reality *correct?* Or am I working on old, incomplete, or otherwise erroneous data?" Unless you are absolutely sure of the accuracy of your data, reverify it. *Internal constraints*—related to your priorities, your skills, and your psychological makeup—are trickier. Ask, "What would my reaction be, or the reaction of people close to me, if I accept this constraint?"

A thoughtful assessment of your constraints can bring many benefits:

- Naming illusory constraints begins the process of breaking their hold on you.
- Examining your constraints tests the consistency between your life priorities and your career direction, as typified by your ideal job definition.
- Debunking constraints inevitably opens up options and broadens vistas.
- Identifying your actual constraints enhances your understanding of their effect on your career transition. By "owning" the constraints within which you *choose* to operate, you have consciously named your "givens," selected those appropriate to your agenda, and acted consistently with your managerial approach to the transition process.

SOME FINAL WORDS ON SELF-AWARENESS

Congratulations! You've come to the end of the self-awareness section. We trust the past chapters have led you to an increased awareness of your many and diverse attributes. More important, we hope that you have an increased acceptance and admiration for who you are and have established appropriate benchmarks that are of *your* choosing, not those of other people.

PUTTING IT ALL TOGETHER

If you've followed the process, by now your product specification file consists of a variety of lists and notes. Now it's time to pull that file together—to integrate and refine it into a concisely articulated description of who you are. There's no one correct way to do this. You may have a fairly well-integrated picture of who you are. Alternatively, you may be staring in near despair at your file. Go about this integration process in your own way: your approach is part of your individuality.

In this final step use all of your abilities—your logical abilities and your intuitive wisdom. Take advantage of the input of your board to ensure that you are not overlooking something important or harboring any delusions.

Here's one approach to putting it all together:

YOUR PRODUCT SPECIFICATIONS EXERCISE

STEP 1: Read through all of the material you have entered in your product specification file.

STEP 2: On the top of a clean sheet of paper write, "Describe [your name] as a human being." Put yourself in the role of an outside observer whose task is to describe you to someone who has never met you. Cover all aspects of your subject—external appearance, internal aspects, strong suits and short suits, high and low tolerances. Take your time! This should be an enjoyable exercise: you are spending time contemplating someone very special and important to you. After you have finished (presumably your write-up will be several pages in length), lay it aside, but be ready for addenda that come to mind over the subsequent days. Your subconscious needs time to make its contribution to the total picture.

STEP 3: Take some time to celebrate and acknowledge the person described in your write-up. That person has many impressive attributes and has positively affected the world in many ways. That person can and will influence the world in many more ways. The challenge is to select from the many possible options.

You're now ready to begin self-marketing. As you move on to Part 3, make the commitment to continue to grow in self-awareness. Over the past chapters we hope you have gotten in touch with aspects of yourself that you either had lost contact with or to which you had learned to turn a deaf ear.

NUGGET: Don't be like an airline pilot who focuses on only *some* of the instruments on the panel and ignores others because they are not giving the "correct" message. Many people get into hazardous and uncomfortable situations because they have either turned off part of their internal guidance system—or never fully learned how it is supposed to operate.

Now that you have enhanced your self-awareness, use it to good effect! It will help you navigate better and avoid dangerous situations. Best of all, you'll enjoy the journey more because you're aware of what's going on, and you accept and trust the pilot.

III

MARKETING YOURSELF IN THE JOB SEARCH

11

AN INTRODUCTION TO THE MARKETING CAMPAIGN

You have reached the part of the *In Transition* process that many job-changers find the most enjoyable. Your self-assessment work is largely completed; the next chapters are devoted to two additional phases of a transition: market assessment and the self-marketing campaign. In this chapter we set the stage; in Chapter 12 we outline the market assessment process; and in Chapters 13 through 19 we review the elements of a successful self-marketing campaign.

MARKETING: A FAMILIAR CONCEPT

You probably have some exposure to marketing. *Product* marketing focuses first on discovering the *nature* and *needs* of prospective buyers for a product. It does not presume to dictate those needs. The elements of marketing—product, pricing, distribution channels, promotion, sales techniques, and incentives—are determined with an eye to the prospective buyer. Corporate declines often can be traced to losing touch with the market: when companies became "product driven" rather than market sensitive, they failed. Don't let this flaw hinder your job search campaign.

*Self-*marketing begins with the focus on *you*. Part 2 of *In Transition* thoroughly acquainted you with you-the-product. In Part 3 we'll focus first on market assessment—to ensure that you have the most current and accurate reading on the job market. And then we'll turn to the elements of marketing—product (you), pricing (compensation), distribution channels (networking, letter-writing, and job brokers), promotion (resume and pitch). At that point you will *know your market* and be sensitive to its needs.

THE JOB SEARCH: UNFAMILIAR TERRITORY OR JUST UNRECOGNIZED?

A premise of the *In Transition* process is that managers have much more expertise in the market assessment and self-marketing process than they realize. However, if you fail to recognize this, the emotional and psychological shock of being thrown into transition can make job search territory appear strange and ominous. And, in fact, many managers in transition react in strange ways.

Dick recalls an acquaintance who was a successful marketing executive, on a fast track, with an attractive wife and two young children. He was sharp, good-looking, articulate, and competitive in a way that gained the admiration of even his vanquished opponents—a heck of a good salesman. One day, in a power struggle in the division, he was fired. His reaction? He did not tell his wife or any of his friends or acquaintances. Each day he dressed for work and took his customary commuter train, coming home each night at the regular time. He had anticipated that it would be easy to get a new job and imagined coming home and announcing the news to his wife, but as weeks passed he became less confident. One night, arriving home after too many drinks, he let the truth slip. She had known something was wrong and was hurt and angry that he had not confided in her.

Not only did this executive not tell his wife or close friends his circumstances, he suddenly lost the coping skills and well-honed marketing and selling abilities that were his trademark. Why does an expert at managing situations and selling things find it so daunting to manage the job of selling *himself?*

- Many managers, particularly those with sales or marketing specialties, *subordinate themselves to the product* or service they are selling. You marketing executives must reorient yourselves in order to be effective *self-* marketers.
- Many managers approach the job market with a *false sense of entitlement.* They feel they don't have to bother with some of the steps in the process that apply to other individuals. There are classic stories—

NUGGET: Part 2 has enhanced your self-awareness; you should be thoroughly familiar with you-the-product. Now you must become *a superior self-marketer.* Recognize the many ways in which your business skills and experience can be used in the job search arena.

and real-life experiences—about people who believed their products or services to be so superior that they should sell themselves.

As you proceed through this section, you'll realize you have many more tools at your disposal for the job search than you might imagine.

TWO ALTERNATIVE APPROACHES

In the HBSCNY Career Seminar we invite participants to consider two approaches to the job search:

- Using *the mendicant approach,* you go from person to person and from place to place asking for a job. You become, quite literally, someone begging others to come to your rescue. Eventually, you may find a job, but at great cost to your self-esteem. And what kind of managerial job is offered to a mendicant?
- Using *the marketing approach,* you develop a clear idea of the product that you have to offer, define the type of job and environment best suited to that product, mount an effective marketing campaign targeted at prospective users, and present the product as available for a limited time only.

It doesn't require an MBA to choose between the two. The marketing approach is clearly the more effective way to carry out the job search. Being in transition is tough on the ego. Don't compound the problem by taking the mendicant approach; it doesn't do justice to your cause or take advantage of your abilities.

YOUR STATE OF MIND: A KEY PRODUCT ATTRIBUTE

A key determinant of the effectiveness of your job search is your state of mind. A positive state of mind enables you to conduct your job search effectively and energetically. It enhances your credibility in the eyes of prospective employers. Maintain a healthy state of mind by effectively planning and implementing a market assessment and self-marketing campaign. Such a campaign puts you back in familiar territory using familiar skills. It converts the job search from "looking for a job" (with the negative connotations of trying to find something valuable that has been lost) into an active and positive process of self-marketing. Focus on the unique and valuable attributes that characterize you-the-product, evaluate your fields of interest, and then spread the news about this attractive product with all the enthusiasm it deserves.

THE SELF-MARKETING CAMPAIGN

In designing your market assessment and self-marketing campaign, you will use marketing concepts and managerial expertise typical of marketing challenges in business:

- *There is a product. You* are the product. Your values, priorities, skills, experience, even your high and low tolerances represent a combination some prospective buyer will find very attractive. You are the solution to that buyer's needs; you can solve a problem, meet a demand, fill a vacancy.
- *There is a market.* The collection of organizations, clients, and employers who represent prospective buyers of your product make up your market.
- *There are price/performance and supply/demand factors.* These realities of the marketplace must be well researched before you start selling. How many similar products are on the market? What price are the various buyers able to pay?
- *There are product positioning factors.* Just being a "better mousetrap" doesn't cause the world to rush to your door. You-the-product need the proper sales literature (resumé, various types of letters) and presentation (telephone and face-to-face, from initial pitch to final interview).

Your self-marketing campaign includes the following steps:

1. *Characterize you-the-product.* Know the product. Tackle the self-awareness exercises in Part 2 to build a firm foundation for a sound self-marketing campaign (see Chapters 4 to 10).
2. *Do the necessary market research.* Identify prospective buyers, first conceptually (by area, industry, or function). Then investigate your fields or functions of interest to assess your fit with each and the odds of securing a position within your timeframe. Research the price/performance relationship, and establish a price (salary) range for the product. Solidify your learning, culminating with a summary sheet of your markets' primary needs and your specific selling points, acknowledging where a weak link between needs and selling points will reduce

the saleability of you-the-product to that market segment. Rank your prospective markets.

3. *Prepare your product presentation.* Develop a pitch that summarizes your positive attributes in a relevant, credible manner. Identify potential objections and rehearse your responses (see Chapter 16). Design product literature—resumé, letters, appropriate supplements. Test market and refine every facet of your product presentation.

4. *Develop a written action plan.* Based on a reasonable number of hours per day and achievable targets, delineate a phased self-marketing campaign. Avoid unrealistic expectations, both of yourself and of others (your network, recruiters, potential employers). Include specific target dates for contacting prospective buyers, for timely follow-up, and for keeping network contacts alive and informed.

Your self-marketing campaign plan should be in written form. If you balk at this step, you are losing your managerial grip! You have not read this far in *In Transition* to succumb to spaghetti-against-the-wall job hunting tactics. Stay serious and professional about your campaign. The degree of sophistication and detail in your plan should equal that of a marketing campaign you would design for a client or an employer. Make the investment of time and money to do it *properly* as a symbol of the importance you place on it. Moreover, at certain points in your search we suggest you discuss your campaign with your board, your friends, and people in your network. At those times it is to your advantage to have your action plan look professional.

In the following chapters you'll have a chance to consolidate your self-assessment work into a tight line of questioning for your market assessment. You'll have the opportunity to consider fields of real interest: lines of work that could make each day an exciting set of challenges. The investigation process is straightforward and well within a manager's ability to execute. Give yourself the gift of an unobstructed 360 degree view of your many potential options.

12

MARKET ASSESSMENT

The goals of a market assessment are to identify fields and functions of visceral interest to you, to assess those fields for *fit* with your self-assessment results from Part 2, and to determine the *odds* of your securing a position in those fields or functions within your timeframe for this transition. At the end of the market assessment phase, you should have two or three fields that are consistent with your most important priorities, that play to your skills, and that mesh with your high and low tolerances. Similarly, you should know enough about each field to know that you are targeting markets where what you are offering is in demand, ensuring closing on this sale sooner rather than later.

Career counselors are familiar with what we call the crystal ball request: "If I tell you all about me, and I take some tests, can't you tell me what field I should be in?" In an age of sophisticated computers, instruments like the Myers-Briggs Type Indicator (see Chapter 6) and the Strong-Campbell Interest Inventory, it seems that selecting the right job should somehow be a more orderly process. Furthermore, what if the *real* fit is with a field or function totally unknown to the manager in transition?

We firmly believe that *you* are the best qualified person to choose your next field of endeavor. By distilling your self-assessment work into a line of questioning, you can systematically investigate fields or functions of interest and personally determine whether each represents a good opportunity or a poor fit. To *delegate* that selection to anyone else is risky at best and an abdication of your responsibility to yourself as a manager. Any firm or individual purporting to have the market intelligence, personal insight, test instruments, and contacts to "put" you in just the right situation should ring suspect to you (see Chapter 18, "Career Help for Hire"). A well-done market assessment keeps you in the driver's seat of this campaign, making the hard calls and tough choices and doing so with facts and conviction on your side.

If you are well into your career, a part of you may be thinking, "I'm too far along to consider a radical change in fields. That's for the younger set." Not true, as demonstrated by a HBSCNY Career Seminar participant who clearly is not reluctant to consider new areas and accept new challenges:

> *After retiring from the U.S. Navy at forty-seven with the rank of Captain, I went with a large corporation. Not a big change—similar struggles with budgets, people, and programs. Twelve years of this, and I got restless and came to the Career Seminar. Since I enjoyed investing as a hobby, I decided to become a stockbroker. The early stages weren't easy—at fifty-nine, I was the oldest by far in my training group—but I persevered and did well for ten years. Recently I've needed more psychic income, so I got involved avocationally in environmental activities. That was so satisfying that I'll soon convert another hobby into a full-time job: back in the service—this time for Mother Earth instead of Uncle Sam. At age sixty-nine I'm seeing the world through new eyes, and I plan to give it my best shot for many years to come.*
>
> CERTIFIED FINANCIAL PLANNER, HBS '47

PREPARING FOR YOUR MARKET RESEARCH

The first step in the market assessment process involves developing an appropriate line of questioning from your self-assessment. Your goal is to create a screen—a way to measure fields and functions against your life goals, your near-term priorities, your skills, and your work patterns. Begin by systematically revisiting your self-assessment results in your product specification file as described below. The exercises that follow are extensions of work you have already done—the eulogy exercise (Chapter 5), priorities (Chapter 5), skills audit (Chapter 7), and your inventories recorded under Styles, Values, and Motivations (Chapter 6) and Organizational Fit (Chapter 8).

IF I AM TO BE REMEMBERED AS . . . EXERCISE

STEP 1: Take a fresh sheet of paper and make two columns:

| If I Am to Be | Then from This Point |
| Remembered As . . . | Forward I Must . . . |

STEP 2: From your best-case eulogy assessment (Chapter 5), take each item from your achievements, affiliations, and attributes lists, and note in detail *what you need to do* if you are to live consistently with each individual item. You know your life best: remember what has thrown you off course in the past. Note what will keep you moving in the right direction.

STEP 3: Augment your "I Must . . ." column with those items you *didn't write down* because you didn't feel they were relevant to a job search. Or because you were thinking, "I'm already thought of in this way." Or because, "I'd never stop doing that anyway."

STEP 4: Working from the right column of your sheet, develop a line of questioning that captures the implications of each "I must . . . ," *whether you would ask that question or not.* For example:

If I Am to Be Remembered As . . .	Then I Must . . .	Question
Politically involved	Make the time to be active in at least one social justice group	How much latitude would I have for extraprofessional activities? Would the demands of the work day, or heavy travel, make it impossible for me to keep regular commitments?
A good parent	Spend time with and teach my children	Am I going to be perpetually "on call"? Can I plan my activities in advance? Am I so central that others will be waiting on me?
Creative	Avoid a consulting practice where there is not a high intellectual content	Is the work intellectually complex?

STEP 5:   Put your questions into a new file entitled *market assessment file.*

Having solidified your line of questioning to test a field or function for fit with your life goals, now develop questions to test for fit with your near-term, top six priorities. This two-step process parallels what you have just done.

TOP SIX PRIORITY IMPLEMENTATION EXERCISE

STEP 1:   On a fresh sheet of paper, make two columns headed "Must Haves" and "Must Avoids."

STEP 2:   Take your first priority card (see Chapter 5) and read *your* definition. Beneath "Must Haves," note what you need to fully honor this priority. Note as many discrete items as are necessary if you are to live up to your first priority.

STEP 3:   Turning to "Must Avoids," note what you must avoid if you are to honor your first priority. Think about what has prevented you from honoring this priority in the past: it may well do so in the future! Again, be as thorough as possible. For example:

Priority	*Must Have*	*Must Avoid*
Family		
Spending a great deal more time with my kids	Time: a couple nights a week and weekends without professional commitments	Being exhausted by too much juggling
Intrinsic nature of the work		
Doing something interesting with variety to it	Work with analytical content	Work that is completely repetitive
	Work in a complex industry	Work that is intensely fragmented

STEP 4:   Repeat steps 2 and 3 for each of your top six priorities.

STEP 5: Turn each item on your "Must Haves" and "Must Avoid" lists into a question, again whether you would ask that question or not. For example:

Priority	Must Have	Question

Personal growth
  Making people
  around me happy
	The willingness to listen, guide, coach, give frameworks, pay attention, and take seriously my subordinates	How are managers evaluated and rewarded in this field? How much emphasis is placed on developing people? What countervailing pressures exist, if any?

Geographical location
  Living in
  Minneapolis
	A job in
	Minneapolis
		Is the work done substantially in Minneapolis? Are promotions likely to carry me elsewhere? Is the nature of the work such that a job change would mean leaving Minneapolis?

Influence/power
  Having enough
  power to forestall
  anyone's exercising
  inordinant power
  over me
	At least some autonomy on the job	How much autonomy would I have?

STEP 6: Put your questions into your market assessment file.

You now have a thorough list of questions to ask to gauge the fit between your top six priorities and a field or function of interest. Your next set of questions will help you determine how well your skills fit with those fields or functions.

YOUR SKILLS: THE KEY SUCCESS FACTORS EXERCISE

STEP 1: Take out your list of intrinsic skills prepared in step 15 of your skills audit (Chapter 7).

STEP 2: Develop an introduction along these lines: "I have a set of skills that I am eager to use in my next chapter of professional life. I have a demonstrated competence in using these skills, and I enjoy them. I want to review my list to get a sense of how critical these skills are to *succeeding* in this field. I'm not talking about 'nice to have'; I mean really critical to standing out in the field." Prepare questions related to your specific skills.

STEP 3: Put your introduction and questions into your market assessment file.

Your next set of questions should probe the fit between your style, your values, and your motivations—and those of managers in your fields and functions of interest. Again, write out all your questions; you will use some of your questions for your market assessment and others for evaluating specific companies.

STYLE, VALUES, AND MOTIVATIONS PROFILE EXERCISE

STEP 1: Retrieve from your product specification file your best-guess AVL profile, your MBTI type, and your McClelland Motivational Profile.

STEP 2: Develop a concise profile that consolidates your findings from each of these instruments. Then ask, "Is that profile in keeping with what it takes to succeed in this field or function?" For example:

> *I'm the kind of manager who relishes a job well done, according to pretty rigid internal standards. I've spent hours polishing consulting reports, making sure the grammar was perfect, when I know most of the people who will read the thing have never heard of a dangling participle. Is that kind of attention to detail an asset or a liability in this function?*

STEP 3: Put your questions into your market assessment file.

Your last set of questions draws on your organizational fit work in Chapter 8. This is the time to develop questions that examine the specifics in the workplace: your boss, your co-workers, the environment.

FITTING IN EXERCISE

STEP 1: Retrieve from your product specification file the notes you made as you read Chapter 8 on organization fit.

STEP 2: Distill your requirements of a boss, peers, and the environment into a "must haves" list, being particularly attentive to the attributes *critical* to your success.

STEP 3: Describe your requirements and ask, "Is that a likely scenario in this field? Under what circumstances?" For example:

> *I have worked alone in the most recent chapter of my professional life. If I were to have co-workers, I would want those peers to be people with similar values—with a love of people and a respect for people in difficulty. Does that attitude typify people in this field?*

STEP 4: Put your questions into your market assessment file.

Quite a few questions, right? And some you would *never* ask? And others you couldn't get a straight answer to anyway? Consider this analogy. At some point in your life you have undoubtedly considered a number of neighborhoods, looking for the right community for you and your family. You had a big investment ahead of you—in time, in money, and in the realities of daily life you would encounter in your new setting. It was no time to be haphazard or inappropriately circumspect. Many aspects of your life and those close to you depended on your making an informed decision with the best available data. You had to ask the hard questions about housing prices, the school system, community services, and dominant values. You didn't have to make judgments about *other* peoples' choices, but you did need to make a good decision for yourself and your family.

NUGGET: Your market assessment is as important to your future as your choice of a place of residence. As you develop questions to use to sort through fields and functions of interest, don't shy away from addressing the important issues. Good market research at this phase will play a large part in determining your happiness and well-being in the future.

With that analogy in mind, tackle the next exercise as a manager committed to making the most informed and appropriate choice for the next chapter of your professional life. Think back to the times when you didn't ask the key questions and made a decision without good information. You may have traced this theme through your Forks in the Road Exercise (Chapter 4). This is your opportunity to pull together your turning questions—the ones that will validate whether a field or function is a good fit.

YOUR TURNING QUESTIONS EXERCISE

STEP 1: Retrieve the questions you developed in the above five exercises from your market assessment file.

STEP 2: Read each question, and determine whether that question is *industry/function-specific* or *company-specific*. Set aside your company-specific questions to be used at a later stage in the self-marketing campaign.

STEP 3: Consolidate your industry/function-specific questions into a workable list for a thirty- to forty-five-minute conversation with a manager in a field of interest. Keep in mind that your conversation will be prefaced with an opener such as this:

> *As you know, I am in transition and considering a range of options for the next phase of my professional life. I have developed a line of questioning based on what is most important to me at this phase of my life—reflecting my life goals, my near-term priorities, my desire to use a particular skill set, and everything I know about how I approach the workplace. My goal for this phase of the transition is to assess various fields for a good fit—and good enough odds of entry—so as to begin my self-marketing campaign confident that I am headed in the right direction.*

STEP 4: These should be *I*-centered questions; take *you* (the person you will be interviewing) out of every one of your questions.

> *Out:* "Are you using skills you enjoy in this job?"
>
> *In:* "I'd like to use my negotiating skills in my next job. Is that a realistic expectation in this function?"
>
> *Out:* "How much are you earning?"
>
> *In:* "My minimum salary requirement is $150,000. Could I anticipate coming into the field at that level? Under what conditions?"

STEP 5: Reread your consolidated list of questions, and ask yourself, "Would I be comfortable being asked this question?" Rephrase questions as necessary.

STEP 6: Develop the "odds" questions to be asked once you have ascertained that a field or function is a good fit.

> *If I were to set my sights on moving into this field, what would my odds be of breaking in? Within what timeframe? Under what circumstances? Given my background, what are my chances?*

STEP 7: Review your turning questions with your board (see Chapter 3). Add any questions your board suggests are critical to your market research, and delete those that don't pass muster with this group.

So when does the fun start, you're asking? Is this really the most enjoyable part of the *In Transition* process? You're almost there! Your next task is to develop a list of fields, functions, or positions of visceral interest to you. They need pass only one test: "I could get excited about getting up in the morning if I were involved in this field." To develop that list, you have several options; scan the six suggestions below, and use one or two of your choice.

1. Turn to Appendix F and run your eye down the list of fields, functions, and positions. Star the ones of gut-level interest. *Alert:* As you read these lists, do not self-edit by saying, "That is totally impractical," or "I'm much too old for that," or "I can tell you right now I can't earn a living wage in that field." Review Chapter 10 on "Constraints to Achieving Your Ideal Job" if you have any doubts about this instruction.

2. Reread your list of enjoyable accomplishments from your skills audit work (see Chapter 7). Is this the time to reconsider fields or functions you left behind, under some sort of mandate to "set aside childish things"? This seminar participant thought so:

> *The time has come for me to seriously consider a career in sports. I was the manager of every sport in high school; I ended up with six letters! I was on the board that ran the athletic program at one of the Big Ten. I now have great merchandising training under my belt and financial skills from getting my CPA and my MBA. I want to look at the agent and promotion area, the licensing area, maybe even media. This is a real passion. If I could work in this field, it would be a dream come true.*

> VP SALES, FINANCIAL SERVICES, HBS '82

3. Take out your intrinsic skills list, and circulate it in advance of a meeting of your board. Do a group brainstorming, with board mem-

bers pitching in every field or function that comes to mind when you pose the question, "In which fields or functions is this skill set critical?" Write down the entire list, and then extract from that list the fields of genuine interest to you.

4. Scan an expanded group of periodicals, beyond your usual reading list. Pay special attention to write-ups of managers: personal profiles, autobiographical accounts, even accounts of classmates. Possibilities: (a) your college or graduate school alumni/ae magazine; (b) the style or living section of your daily paper; (c) magazines in fields of interest— *Inc.* if you're considering the small business route, the "industry gossip sheets" for other fields. For example, the Wall Street crowd reads *Corporate Financing Week, Wall Street Letter, Bond Week,* and *Mortgage-Backed Securities Letter.*

5. Look at where you spend discretionary time. What do you find intrinsically fascinating? Where do you give your volunteer time? What activities in your weekly regimen are really a joy to you? Any career ideas there?

> *It's not lost on me that no matter how large others might view the task, I am absolutely in my element when I head some effort connected with my alma mater. I have consistently been a class officer; I think of all sorts of things to do to build class connections, like calling classmates when I am on business trips; I bang out letters and organize committees, and it really doesn't feel like work. It dawns on me that strengthening local alumnae clubs—supporting other classes—even doing this sort of thing headquartered at the college might be just the kind of work I should consider.*
>
> SMALL BUSINESS PROPRIETOR, HBS '71

6. As a last resort, if you can't do this without being more comprehensive, there is a list—from able seaman to zoologist—for you. Get a copy of the *Dictionary of Holland Occupational Codes,* Second Edition, coauthored by Gary D. Gottfredson and John L. Holland and published in 1989 by Psychological Assessment Resources, Inc. (Odessa, FL 33445, 800-331-TEST). On pages 278–540—in small print—is an alphabetical list of job titles.

Remember, the idea is *not* to have considered in detail the entire universe of possibilities, any more than in making a move to a new neighborhood you consider every community nationwide! Trust your instincts. If you have never understood how a commodities trader makes it through the day, you're unlikely to do a 180-degree switch by going out to investigate the field.

INVESTIGATIVE INTERVIEWING

You are now ready to begin your investigative interviews. Your goal is to set up an appointment with a professional in each of your fields and functions of interest, and during the conversation to ask your turning questions. Your objective, at the end of this process, is to have a pared down list of fields and functions that *fit* you-the-product, where the *odds* of moving into the field within your time frame are great.

Below is our list of do's and don'ts for this process, followed by the questions you are undoubtedly asking yourself even as you read this section.

Investigative Interviewing Do's and Don'ts

Do:

1. Set a clear, finite agenda for your conversation, having completed your Self-Assessment and distilled from it a line of questioning designed to answer two broad questions:
   - Is this field or function a good *fit* with my long-range goals, my near-term priorities, my skills, and my long and short suits?
   - Am I comfortable with the *odds* of securing employment in this field or function?

2. Set up your investigative interview. State your agenda and offer arrangements convenient to your resource. For example:

   > *Jack, my name is Sara Jones. I was a few years behind you at the University of Minnesota. I am making a career change and thinking seriously about several fields, including association administration. I know what I am looking for, and I am doing some reality checking with people in my areas of interest. Could I take you to breakfast or to lunch (or meet with you at your office or get a time on your calendar) to get your thoughts on the field?*

3. Confirm those plans the day before or the morning of your appointment.

4. Be prompt, note the time your meeting begins and when your allotted time will be up, and end on schedule.

5. At the end of your appointment, thank your contact for the time given to you in a busy day. Confirm that investigative interviewing is playing a key role in your selecting just the right field or function for

you. Establish how and why you might be in contact in the future. For example:

> *Jack, this has been invaluable. As you know, I'm evaluating a range of options, and to be able to talk to someone with so much experience in association management has certainly been helpful. If I do decide to pursue this field, my next steps will include building a list of associations to target for my campaign. May I run that list by you in that event?*

6. Find a quiet place (your car or a coffee shop) where you can *immediately* make notes about your conversation. Record your learnings and your reactions, and take special note of any "red alerts" that suggest the field or function is a no go.

Don't:

1. Make an appointment before you are ready.
2. Discuss industry trends, management shake-ups, stock plays—anything unrelated to your twin goals: ascertaining fit and odds.
3. Ask questions you could easily research by reading about the industry.
4. Overstay your welcome!

Questions about Investigative Interviewing

1. "What if I don't know a soul in one of my fields of interest?"
   Fast-forward to Chapter 14 on Networking, where you learn how to network your way to resources for investigative interviewing.
2. "What if I have *thirty* fields on my list?"
   First decide how much time you want to spend in the market assessment phase. Some managers in transition spend a year on this phase; as professionals closing out one chapter of career life, they stay in their current jobs or work part-time so as to thoroughly assess the world of work. Others have compressed the process into a month. Reread Chapter 10 on "Constraints to Achieving Your Ideal Job" to be sure you don't artificially limit yourself. If your time is restricted, try the following. Pull from your turning questions the one "litmus test" question a field or function of interest is most likely to *fail*. Rather than having an extended conversation with a resource in the field, ask that one question right up front over the phone or in another casual setting. For example, "Sam, one of my near-term priorities is not having to relocate for at least five years. Are enough positions going to come up in the next six months for me to target this field—or would I really need to

conduct a national search?" Or, "Alice, I have run the numbers, and I am not willing to go below $75,000 at this stage. Is that realistic in this field, given what I am bringing to the table?"

3. "This really doesn't strike me as very scientific."
   Scientific is not the objective. Rather, your goal is to evaluate fields and functions for compatibility with what you want to have done with your life, your near-term priorities, your intrinsic skills, and your style. Your data gathering during a market assessment will be well grounded, structured, and systematic. You will be making the decisions. Don't delegate this function!

4. "Won't anyone I talk to have a bias?"
   Absolutely. Feel free to do a follow-up investigative interview in a field of interest if you want a second opinion. Bring the conversation back to your question script if your resource wanders; your goal is to gather important information for your selection process, not to hear tales of daring-do.

5. "Why would someone take the time to do this for me?"
   Like every facet of the *In Transition* process, you are tackling this one like a manager. You are not asking a resource, "What would you do with my life if you were me?" You are not arriving in someone's office without an agenda or with a hidden agenda. Surprisingly enough, as we discuss in Chapter 13, most people make time to assist others if the demands are specific, the time requirements reasonable, and the pressures of daily life make it possible.

ADDITIONAL RESEARCH

During this market assessment phase, make a point of attending seminars, breakfasts, chapter meetings, and other open gatherings of professionals in your fields of interest. Note the number of professional organizations Mary keeps in her files for her women clients:

Advertising Women of New York, Inc.
American Society of Women Accountants
American Women in Radio and Television
Association for Women in Computing
Association for Women in Psychology
Association of Black Women Attorneys, Inc.
Association of Black Women in Higher Education, Inc.
Association of Real Estate Women

Black Women in Publishing
Bridgeport Venture Group
Cosmetic Executive Women
Danbury Venture Group
Decorators Club
Executive Women in Human Services
Financial Women's Association of New York
Legal Association for Women
MIT Entrepreneurs Group
National Association of Insurance Women
National Association of Media Women
National Association of Social Workers
National Council on Women in Medicine
New York Venture Group
Newswomen's Club of New York
Society of Women Engineers
Women Executives in Public Relations
Women in Communications, Inc.
Women in Film
Women in Housing and Finance, Inc.
Women in Production, Inc.
Women in Sales Association, Inc.

Make it your business to read the trade journals serving your fields of interest. Use your network to secure securities analysts' reports on those industries. Peruse your local business library, or spend a day at the career center of a nearby college or graduate school. Scan the biographical books index in *Books in Print* at your bookstore or library; the vocational index may have titles that intrigue you and give you insight into one person's experience in a field.

SELECTING APPROPRIATE MARKETS

At the culmination of your market assessment, you should have copious notes taken after each of your investigative interviews. Quite possibly you will have gleaned additional information from gatherings of other managers in the field, your reading, and briefings from other sources. Your next task is to winnow your original list of fields and functions of interest to *reasonable targets* for your self-marketing campaign. You may have been doing this as you went along, when the information from an investigative interview was fresh. If not, now is the time to revisit your notes and eliminate fields that don't meet your specifications. Consider setting up a matrix to make this distillation easier. One possibility is shown below:

FIELD EVALUATION SHEET

Field or Function: _____

	Yes	No	Unclear
Life goals			
Achievements			
Attributes			
Affiliations			
Near-term priorities			
Priority 1			
Priority 2			
Priority 3			
Priority 4			
Priority 5			
Priority 6			
Skills			
Set 1			
Set 2			
Set 3			
Set 4			
Set 5			
Set 6			
Style			
AVL			
MBTI			
McClelland			
Organizational fit			
Boss			
Peers			
Environment			

Conclusion		
	Go	No go

Keep in mind that the operative concepts here are *fit* and *odds*. Of two managers who conclude a field is a good fit, only one might decide that field is a reasonable target given personal time-line issues. An employed manager who needs to wage a low-level campaign for thirty-six months to secure a position in the foundation world may decide to do just that. Another manager would select a field that has enough to offer *and* opportunities immediately available. Two managers might have equivalent financial resources, but one elects to eliminate a field because his or her psyche couldn't manage an eighteen-month transition period.

NUGGET: Select your target markets based on self-understanding. Factor into your well-researched field evaluation sheet a realistic reading of your personal resources for the self-marketing campaign ahead.

We hope you enjoy investigative interviewing, as so many HBSCNY Career Seminar participants do. While this market assessment phase of the *In Transition* process is covered in just one chapter, it should be as robust and thorough a process as both your self-assessment done in Part 1 and your self-marketing campaign to come in the following chapters. Don't fall prey to the forever-investigating-never-selling syndrome—but don't skip this critical market research.

13

REALITIES OF THE JOB SEARCH

Most managers do not have extensive experience in conducting job searches. This chapter covers the realities of being between jobs and the techniques you need to succeed with your upcoming self-marketing campaign. The realities of the job search may already be familiar to you or, like many truths, once recognized they may seem self-evident. At every HBSCNY Career Seminar we go over these facts of life in the job search.

THE FACTS OF LIFE

It Is Up to You to Get a Job

An amazing number of people between jobs, including well-educated, skilled managers, seem to be counting on someone else to find them work. They lose their "can do" attitude, abdicate their managerial role, and count on happenstance. The responsibility for finding the right job rests solely on *your* shoulders.

- *You* must plan and direct the search, using a marketing campaign that incorporates all your skills and experience, and the CEO concept (see Chapter 3) to maintain objectivity, gain information, and access needed support.
- *You* must find and use all possible resources needed to carry out your self-marketing campaign.
- *You* must ensure that during the ups and downs that are an inevitable part of the job search your physical, mental, and emotional well-being is maintained. Exercise and daily discipline help. Support systems are vital and must be established in advance. The biggest factor in the success or failure of your job search is your state of mind.

Your Job Search Will Take More Time and Energy Than You Expect

This reality is often overlooked or minimized by the manager who has not been in the job market in many years. Convinced that a new position will come up very soon, he or she starts a job search like a sprinter rather than a long-distance runner.

- Don't be a dilettante, a tire kicker only *partially* committed to the job search. There is no surer way to protract your time between jobs.
- Be *realistic* about the time and money required to get to your destination. Think of the job search as analogous to a trip across the desert: to start out without adequate planning and sufficient provisions would be irresponsible. Don't start a job search thinking that it will be only a matter of weeks before you are comfortably situated. Unrealistic expectations take their toll on self-esteem and self-confidence. Do your financial planning up front: develop a budget, establish lines of credit, and gain the cooperation of your family and friends.
- Be careful not to *overextend* yourself during the job search. Quite likely you are accustomed to holding yourself to high standards of productivity. Be sure to factor in the realities of your job search: unlike your past management situations, you may not have staff services, you must do more hands-on work, and circumstances are much less under your control. Be *realistic.* Consider cutting back on volunteer commitments. Limit your availability for household projects. Shepherd your energy. Listen to this veteran of the search:

The job search became totally absorbing for me. I was at it sixteen hours a day, seven days a week—working the phones, planning, and following up. Thanks to the help of some caring people I realized what I was doing. I started exercising and doing prayer and meditation.

PARTNER, INVESTMENT BANK, HBS/AMP '78

The World Is Not Fair

Many experienced managers jeopardize their job searches by not resolving feelings of resentment about the unfairness of their circumstances. Sometimes these resentments are related to specific events or situations: what got them into this transition period; missing the ideal position by just a few weeks; being smarter and more competent than the person who got the job. Or a preoccupation with fairness may stem from a strong belief in how things ought to be.

Some people, consciously or unconsciously, look for a "rescuer" to help them out of a jam and become resentful when that doesn't happen. This may be an actual parent or a surrogate—a local banker, an old boss, a trusted rabbi, minister, or mentor. Or it may take the form of a belief system that promises outside intervention on their behalf.[1]

A simple way to avoid getting bogged down is to assume that the world is *not* fair. When hard work *does* produce results, it then comes as a pleasant surprise. When it doesn't, you don't waste time and energy fretting.

Timing Is Everything

Many frustrations of the job search are time related. Learn to deal with the psychological impact of time's passing. In the short term, you have very little control over time. Be reasonable in your efforts at time management; everything takes longer than expected. If you find yourself getting frustrated, reexamine your expectations. Working with realistic expectations will improve your state of mind, your efficiency, and your demeanor during interviews.

During a job search, time is one of your most precious resources. When you are receiving a salary, the way you allocate your time is one thing. During the job search, your use of time must change.

> *After I lost my job, many of my friends took me out to lunch. Then, one day, a realization came to me: unless I have a specific agenda, these lunches are wasting my time! My lunch host is on salary, so those two hours for lunch are much more precious to me than to him. Besides, after some of these lunches I feel like a charity case. From now on I'll take a rain check and have the lunch when I need some specific information or a boost. That awareness put me back in the driver's seat.*
> Divisional Manager, computer services, HBS '65

One of your primary responsibilities during the job search is to budget your time carefully.

---

[1]The authors, both from a personal and a professional perspective, value a strong spiritual dimension to life—during the job search and thereafter. Our concern here is with people who "bargain with God" or sideline their talents and initiative by waiting for some other person or force to bring about a miracle. We believe that the job search involves a *balance* of faith and action.

Your Other Primary Resource during the Job Search Is People

Just as your attitude toward time changes in the job search, so should your perception of other people. You may have some strong feelings about "using people," or you may be reluctant to ask for help. After you complete your job search, however, you will realize that the majority of the information that led you to your final destination came from *people.*

NUGGET: Using people as resources is distinct from taking inappropriate advantage of others. Using people *effectively* is the key to your finding a new situation in the most expeditious fashion.

Keep in mind the following realities:

No One Owes You Anything

Don't act as if you are entitled to help. When you are seeking free advice, take care not to inadvertently act as if you think, "People owe it to me."

Every Person You Approach Has Preoccupations and Worries

Be sensitive to others. If their response is not what you expect, it may have nothing to do with you:

Remember that VP I interviewed last month? The one that I said should be my role model? I just learned that he's been fired and his wife has cancer. Just think, while I was sitting there envying him "having it all," his world was falling apart. No wonder he didn't give me any networking referrals; his mind must have been miles away. And I kicked myself for screwing up the interview. It's a strange world.

ANALYST, FINANCIAL SERVICES, HBS '73

Most People Want to Help

Despite not owing you anything and personal preoccupations, most people will go out of their way to be of assistance. Your responsibility is to approach them in the appropriate manner and *assist them in helping you.*

- Approach people in a way that acknowledges that their time is limited; seek an appointment at a time and location best for them.
- Establish the length of your meeting in advance and hold to it. To dramatize the point, one HBSer took out a pocket timer at the

beginning of each meeting and set it to the agreed time. When it rang, he was prepared to leave. He was often invited to stay longer, but his willingness to end appointments at a specific hour demonstrated his respect for other peoples' schedules.

- Use your time with people well. Be prepared with questions that indicate you have done your homework (see Chapter 12). Ask questions appropriate to each person: your questions of a peer as you explore a field should differ markedly from those of a well-placed contact who could open doors for you. Take the lead in expressing what you need.

- Be sensitive to peoples' reactions. If you sense a reluctance to respond to a particular line of questioning, back off. If it happens more than once, discuss your questions with your board (Chapter 3); you may be asking inappropriate questions or phrasing your questions poorly.

THE HIDDEN ENEMIES OF YOUR JOB SEARCH

Over the years we have observed that job changers encounter some common difficulties. Keep this list in mind to ensure that you don't get tripped up by one or more of these hidden enemies.

Anger

Some job searchers deny having this problem, but virtually *everyone* between jobs has some degree of anger. Unaware of this feeling, you handicap your job search:

> *The layoff had nothing to do with me personally; the whole department was shut down. And still I felt so much anger—at the company and myself. I kept replaying scenarios, thinking, "Why didn't I ask for a transfer?" and "What if I had handled that situation differently?" and so on. Until I got those feelings sorted out, I was too confused and dysfunctional to think clearly.*
>
> CORPORATE STAFF, PUBLISHING, HBS '85

> *I blew the interview. Things were going well; I was really on a roll. Then she asked me how I left my last job. I started unloading on my ex-boss and how I got really screwed. I couldn't stop myself. I got myself reined in eventually, but the damage was done.*
>
> ACCOUNT MANAGER, ADVERTISING, HBS '81

Unresolved emotions can surface at the worst times, seemingly beyond your control and often unbeknownst to you. They can cause you to behave inappropriately, to make bad judgment calls, and to unnecessarily threaten your candidacy. Don't pretend it can't happen to you. Spend some time, by yourself or with a friend or professional, unearthing feelings of anger and resolving them. Until you do, they represent a ticking time bomb that may go off at the most inopportune point in your job search.

Hidden anger also manifests itself through *depression,* which robs you of your energy and initiative. Depression can be even more detrimental to a job search than occasional inappropriate anger:

> *You may have difficulty believing this now, but I was virtually paralyzed— no energy, no motivation. I just wanted to crawl into a cave and roll a stone in front. Depression is* powerful*. You can't function; you can't even think straight. Your decision-making ability is so warped: the glass is not just half empty, it's bone dry and broken in little pieces.*
>
> SVP, FINANCIAL SERVICES, HBS '61

If you are having difficulty operating at your normal level of effectiveness, talk with a professional trained in treating depression.

Lack of Objectivity or Realism in Assessing Situations

It is difficult to maintain objectivity during the job search when you are deeply invested in the process and experiencing a certain amount of rejection:

> *Even though I've been successful at sales and marketing, the rejection in my job search hit me a lot harder than a rejection by a business client. My* head *knows it's a specifications/fit game, but it is very painful and demoralizing at a deeper level.*
>
> MARKETING EXECUTIVE, MANUFACTURING, HBS '64

Your defense against lack of objectivity is to call on the judgment and advice of others, preferably your board or another group you can contact regularly and comfortably.

Not Enough Hours in a Day

A common trap in the job search is setting an overly ambitious agenda— an impossible list of things to be accomplished. At the close of the day, rather than giving yourself credit for the things you did get done, you criticize yourself for failing to get through your entire list:

> *A friend referred me to Dr. Smith. I'd never worked with a therapist before, but she was great—she helped me understand how I was setting myself up. A part of me was seeing myself as a failure for not having a job, and to reinforce that—in some kind of weird way—I was making sure that I* failed *at something* regularly, *so I could criticize myself for it. I don't fully understand all the "whys," but I sure feel better now that I've got a handle on it.*
>
> MANAGER, PRODUCTION SERVICES, HBS '74

Reconsider one of the facts of life discussed earlier in this chapter: timing is everything. You can make better use of time by being realistic about the actual number of hours at your disposal.

Low Self-Esteem

Your credibility as a candidate is strongly influenced by how you feel about yourself. Sterling credentials, an impressive resumé, and top-drawer referrals are of little value if your in-the-flesh presentation communicates low self-esteem. Have you ever dealt with a salesperson who did not seem to believe in the product or service he or she was selling? When you're waging a job campaign, you are presenting yourself constantly to prospective employers and to individuals who might refer you to prospective employers. If you don't believe in yourself, why should they?

> *The nagging question is always in my head: "Can I still deliver the goods? Am I ever going to get back in?"*
>
> CEO, SMALL BUSINESS, HBS '66

> *My self-confidence was in shreds. I blamed myself for being jobless, and even the smallest incident got distorted. My wife would ask whether we could afford to buy something or go out to dinner, and I'd hear it as a criticism of my inability as a provider. It was the pits!*
>
> PRESIDENT, MANUFACTURING, HBS '54

If you're having trouble along these lines, review the self-awareness section to better appreciate your many positive attributes. The ultimate benefit of the self-awareness process is self-acceptance. Until you have accepted yourself for who you are (rather than what someone else would like you to be), you will be limited in your ability to sell yourself.

Impatience

In your management role you may have gotten a lot of mileage out of impatience and unrealistic expectations, since those reporting to you carried much of the weight of those expectations. Now that you are *both the manager and the implementation staff,* consider any such patterns suspect. If they increase your frustration level, decrease your efficiency, or undermine your friendship with yourself, they must go!

Secretiveness: Unwillingness to Seek Assistance

Many managers needlessly prolong their job searches by being secretive. This natural inclination is rationalized in many ways:

> *"It feels demeaning to have to ask for help."*
> *"I'm unaccustomed to admitting I need help. Being able to do things myself is important to me."*
> *"My friends will think poorly of me: first I lose my job, and then I have to beg for help."*
> *"A good manager should be able to get a job without help."*
> *"Life is competitive; if you show you're vulnerable, people will take advantage of you. "*
> *"I'm ashamed to let my friends know that I'm out of work."*

The entire *In Transition* process, from self-awareness to self-marketing, requires a willingness to be open to the assistance and support of others. If you can't discuss your situation, you have not gotten to the point where you *accept* it. Examine the source of those internal messages that say you are less of a person than you were before you were disconnected from your job. You can't sell yourself until you believe in you-the-product and can enthusiastically recommend yourself to others.

A False Sense of Entitlement

People who are tripped up by this enemy say something like, *"Other* people may have to do self-assessment, market research or marketing campaign planning, but as a [successful executive, former CEO, Harvard Business School graduate—you fill in the blank] I don't have to work this hard. I'm entitled."

You, like everyone, have people to whom you have access, clubs and associations to which you belong, and other such connections. These can and should be used to good advantage in your job search. Problems arise when your actions are influenced by a feeling of entitlement:

> *"No, I don't have a resumé. I suppose I could put something together if it's necessary."*
> *"I naturally had assumed that my interview would be with the head of your department."*

A false sense of entitlement prompts a poor judgment call: "It is OK for me not to follow protocol." The reason behind such a bad call may be poor time management or ill-considered advice; most often, it's self-importance overcompensating for low self-esteem.

The above facts of life and job search enemies are obvious to most managers, once called to their attention. Don't dismiss them lightly; they are played out in actual incidents every day. Review this chapter occasionally during your self-marketing campaign to ensure that you understand job search realities and steer well clear of the pitfalls.

14

NETWORKING: A TRIED AND TRUE TECHNIQUE

You've probably heard the expression "the hidden job market." Most job openings are *not* advertised or placed with recruiters. Most job openings are not filled following an exhaustive search for every available candidate, a thorough evaluation of each resumé tendered, and a totally impartial selection process. Without an aggressive effort to contact people, many job openings will remain hidden to you. Most job seekers secure their jobs through *people contacts*:

> *After I finally came up with a concise description of my ideal job, I spent months networking—in person, by phone, by letter—trying to leave each person with a clear idea of the job I was looking for (as well as the impression I'd be good at it). After a time, one of the people I had networked with was talking to someone who mentioned that his company needed such-and-such, and it rang a bell. He suggested they call me, and I ended up in my ideal job. You don't have to convince me networking works: I know it does!*
>
> VP, SERVICE INDUSTRY, HBS '65

In this chapter we'll discuss *networking*—a technique for increasing the efficiency of your job search campaign, in both the research and selling phases. You undoubtedly have some ideas about networking. You may have tried it, with greater or lesser degrees of success. Some HBSCNY Career Seminar participants report having tried networking, only to find it doesn't work:

> *I contacted a lot of people without much success. Then I hit the networking session of the Career Seminar and realized I'd made a lot of mistakes—like not being specific enough with people about how they might help. I got my act together and started networking* properly, *and the improvement was dramatic.*
>
> MANAGER, RETAIL PRODUCTS, HBS '82

Others find it difficult to *begin* the networking process:

> *In my job, I never had to initiate contacts: people came to me! So when*
> *I started the job search, while I understood the validity of the networking*
> *concept, it was not easy for me to do. Gradually I have gotten better—and*
> *the more I do it, the easier it gets. Without doubt it is much more effective*
> *than waiting for someone to call me!*
>
> DIRECTOR, FINANCIAL SERVICES, HBS '82

N U G G E T : Effective networking *does* work. What most people *term* "networking" is a pale approximation of the real thing. Put aside any preconceptions and past experiences, and learn how to make networking pay off for you.

Networking is a technique, a means of achieving a purpose. Like speaking or writing, in networking what you say, how you say it, and the way in which you present yourself can vary widely depending on your goals. Consider these different ways of networking:

- During the *market assessment phase* of your campaign you explore industries and functions that seem to be potential fits for you-the-product. Through networking you arrange investigative interviews with individuals working in those fields and functions, and gauge to what extent your attributes fit with the nature of each field, the character and current situation of organizations within each, and the requirements for specific functions.
- Once you move into the *self-marketing phase,* you may want to send customized letters to specific division heads in companies high on your target market list. The best way to get that letter read is to begin it with, "[A person known to the addressee] suggested I write you." Using your existing contacts list as a starting point, you network to locate someone affiliated with the company. Your goal is to work your way to someone willing to make that critical personal introduction.
- One of your goals is to *spread the word* of your availability to as many people connected with your targeted market segment as possible. Through energetic networking, you put the news of your candidacy into as many people's minds as possible, thereby increasing the chances of hearing about open positions.
- When your marketing campaign locates a position that seems to be a good fit, you'll want to *check out the reputation* of the company, its product, its financial stability, or even your prospective boss. Good networking expedites your ability to gather valuable input.

While networking is a tool that can be used to achieve a variety of purposes, the key aspects of effective networking are the same for each. Be clear about what you seek, and be considerate of the person with whom you're dealing. For those of you thinking, "I don't have ten people in my network," prepare to stretch your limits.

NETWORKING HOW-TO'S

1. List Your Contacts

Make a list of everyone you know. Yes, everyone! That's not an easy task, but it's a necessary one. Start with the people with whom you are in current contact; then review your Forks in the Road Exercise (see Chapter 4) or your achievements list (see Chapter 7) to recall people with whom you've lost touch. Include people from all facets of your life: business, professional, and voluntary associations; social, community, and religious organizations; college and other educational affiliations; military service. Don't forget customers (past and present), suppliers, lawyers, accountants, bankers, local merchants, and relatives. You may wish to organize the list in some way, but don't leave out someone because you assume he or she wouldn't be useful. You never know who might be useful. This list forms the foundation for your networking. Keep it handy.

2. List Your Objectives

When a need arises that requires networking, first *write down your objective.* You may be looking for specific knowledge about an industry, tactical advice about approaching a company, or an introduction to a specific person. Once you are clear about your objective, develop a very explicit question that gets at just what you're after, such as, "Which companies in the pulp and paper industry are most environmentally aware?" Next, note who on your list might have that information or be able to recommend you to someone who does.

3. Polish Your Script

Write and *polish a networking script.* State your need clearly and concisely. Request the type of assistance you're hoping for from your contact, whether information or a referral to someone a step closer to the information. Stress that you're willing to work through a long chain of referrals to find what you're after; emphasize that even a remote or peripheral suggestion would be helpful.

4. Telephone Your Contacts

Once you're satisfied with your networking script, *pick up the phone.* Begin with people you feel comfortable calling. Explain your reason for calling. Do your best to obtain at least one new name from each contact, an additional link in your network chain. Ask whether you may use your contact's name when you call his or her connections. Most important, never back your contact into a corner.

5. Facilitate the Networking Conversation

- Help your contact think about your request in broad terms. If your contact's first words are, "I don't know anyone who fits that description," make it clear that you'd value any kind of suggestion, however tangential. Cite examples of where someone led you to someone, who in turn knew of someone else who had the information you desired. Intrigue them with the process in order to stretch their thinking.
- If appropriate, briefly describe your marketing campaign and how networking fits in. Demonstrate how much preparation has preceded your call so your contact can see that this is not an idle inquiry.
- If no immediate ideas are forthcoming, forestall a negative response by suggesting your contact mull over your request for a day or two. Make specific arrangements to follow up your call, in a way that leaves no doubt that you will. And do it!
- Be considerate of each person with whom you network. Be organized, be concise, and don't waste anyone's time. Be honest about your needs and sensitive to your contact's relationship with his or her network. Don't expect your contact to share information if you convey the feeling that you might not handle it appropriately.
- Mention early in the conversation that you would like to get one or more names. This gives your contact more time to think of possible names and reduces your need for call-backs.
- For certain networking tasks, face-to-face meetings are the most effective; in many cases, however, less time-consuming telephone contacts can yield equal benefits. Seeking in-depth industry or company information and selling yourself are best done in person. Finding a particular piece of information may be done more expeditiously

by phone. Always be prepared to accommodate your contact's preference: if he or she would prefer that you schedule a face-to-face meeting before sharing contacts, for example, by all means be prepared to meet. Use the tool to fit the task.

6. Cross-Reference Your Contacts

If you are networking effectively, you should be able to create as wide a network as you require to achieve the task. The process generates an increasingly large number of referrals and contacts. *Set up a ready cross-reference system* to track who referred whom and *a follow-up system* to ensure that you call contacts who promised to think about your request or who were unavailable when you first called.

7. Trouble-Shooting

What if your networking efforts are *not* generating referrals? Listen to these seminar participants:

> *I call it "bogus networking." A friend of a friend contacts me, says, "I'm out of work," and acts as if I ought to have a job to hand him. Even if I were CEO of our firm I couldn't do that, but these people don't seem to understand.*
>
> MARKET SUPPORT, INFORMATION SYSTEMS, HBS '82

> *Networking is practical problem solving, but it's important to be working on the right problem. When I started networking, it was difficult. Then I realized that I was headed in the wrong direction. When I started networking for the correct goal, rather than trying to be someone I'm not, the networking process started producing magical results. It was enjoyable, and it led to a wonderful outcome.*
>
> VP, FINANCIAL SERVICES, HBS '71

Check to see what you may be doing wrong by role-playing with members of your board. Return to some of your early network contacts, and ask them for candid feedback. Put yourself in your contact's place:

- Would you be comfortable being approached the way you are approaching others? Would you be likely to want to help, if you could?
- Does your story come across as plausible?
- Are you clear about what you expect from your contacts?
- Are you expecting too much, making your contact feel ill at ease?

- Are you using the time of each network contact to best advantage?
- Are you someone others are comfortable referring to their connections? If you are long-winded, if you overstay your welcome, or if you signal, "Rescue me," go back to the drawing board.
- Are you networking under false pretenses? If you're at the selling stage, don't ask for an appointment under the pretext of an investigative interview (see Chapter 12). Word travels quickly, and no one appreciates being hoodwinked.

Networking is your best vehicle for securing a new position, as many HBSCNY Career Seminar participants attest:

Networking is the heart *of any job search. It got me to the very happy place I am today. When someone I know loses a job or gets in career difficulty, I counsel, "Network, network, network."*

SENIOR VP, FINANCIAL SERVICES, HBS '74

To succumb to any reluctance to pick up the phone or tell your story to an acquaintance or otherwise advertise your availability is to needlessly prolong your marketing campaign. Reread Chapter 10 on constraints if you still experience any qualms about networking. And then take the plunge. You'll be glad you did.

15

RESUMÉS, LETTERS, AND ADS

Resumés, letters, and responses to ads are often your initial contacts with prospective buyers. This sales literature doesn't *get* you a job; no one has ever been hired from a resumé or letter alone. The function of your sales literature is to catch the buyer's attention and to get you in the door for a face-to-face interview. But what's the "proper way" to do a resumé, or write a good cover letter, or answer the ad for the job of your dreams? Whole books have been written on the subject. Service firms earn fees for preparing "high impact" resumés and letters. Everyone has an opinion; ask any group of people for comments on your sales literature, and you'll get a variety of differing opinions, many contradictory.

Forget the conventional do's and don'ts. At the HBSCNY Career Seminar our concept is simple and straightforward. Since your resumé and the letters you write are the sales literature of your self-marketing campaign, the principles of marketing apply: your sales literature should position the attributes of you-the-product in a way that speaks to the needs of prospective buyers.

NUGGET: Don't do any significant work on your resumé until you have fully defined you-the-product via the self-assessment process (see Part 2) and identified and characterized your target market segments via the market assessment process (see Chapter 12).

YOUR RESUMÉ

The test of your resumé is whether it helps you reach your target audience. Begin by drafting as effective a piece of product literature as possible, giving the reader a clear, consistent, and credible image of you-the-product. If your resumé succeeds in projecting that image, you are on the way to an effective sales document. If not, your resumé will hamper your marketing campaign.

Characteristics of Effective Resumés

There are no hard and fast rules for resumés, but some guidelines apply in most situations. The following characteristics describe any effective resumé:

- The resumé demonstrates a manager's skill at *concise communications*—an ability to distill a long and varied career to the essentials. In most cases this means *two pages* maximum. In some cases it is appropriate to attach supplementary information, but keep the basic resumé lean.
- The resumé *skims well* because of varied type styles, underlining, and lots of white space.
- The resumé bullets *representative accomplishments*. It does not obscure the picture with too many accomplishments. Wherever possible, it *quantifies* accomplishments.
- The resumé *helps the reader* understand the underlying message. Without distorting the facts, it minimizes or omits anything tangential, irrelevant, or distracting.
- The resumé has a *focus:* the reader has no trouble divining what you-the-product do very well. It is not a rambling description of someone trying to be all things to all people.
- The resumé communicates the *quality* and sophistication of you-the-product in subtle aspects: paper quality, type choice, layout, grammar, spelling, and appropriate use of words.

Why not simply update your old resumé? The best reason for starting afresh is to avoid old ruts. Reviewing your accomplishments prior to drafting your resumé will help you examine your career objectively and put many elements in better perspective. As an added benefit, if recent events have been unsettling or downright unpleasant, a reminder of the many things you have accomplished does wonders for lifting your spirits and your self-confidence.

You established a data base of accomplishments when you prepared your list for the Skills Exercise in Chapter 7. If you skipped that chapter, we strongly recommend doing steps 2, 3, and 4 as the initial phase in preparing a resumé.

Testing Your Resumé

Who is best suited to decide what information should and should not be included in your resumé? *You* are too close to the situation; in a very real sense the resumé is part of yourself. Enlist the input of others who can bring needed objectivity. Most people test their resumés on friends and acquaintances. This is not a bad place to start, but beware of these flaws: friends may be incapable of looking at your resumé with a fresh, objective eye, and they may hesitate to be candid. Most important, their comments are unlikely to reflect the perspective of a recruiter or potential employer in your target fields.

The one sure way to get an objective assessment of your resumé is from a person who doesn't know you. Here's how:

1. Give your draft resumé to a friend, with the request that he or she test it on someone who hires people at your level but knows nothing about you. Have your friend pass on a thumbnail description of what kind of position you are seeking.

2. That third-party tester should read your resumé and describe to your friend the individual he or she sees in the resumé. What strengths and short suits come through? Is the chronology clear? Does your resumé raise concerns that the tester would check out further if you were an actual candidate? If you specified your target job or field in a job objective, does the tester see a good fit between your objective and the data on the resumé? Ask your friend to take ample notes on the tester's feedback.

3. Ask your friend for oral and written feedback. Reassure your friend that you want all comments, good and bad, especially the negatives.

Do this with half a dozen people. If most testers see an integrity to your resumé—a clear articulation of you-the-product with special attributes of greatest interest to your target markets highlighted—you have an effective resumé. If not, modify your resumé to reflect their comments, and run the test again.

NUGGET: The reader of your resumé has many demands on his or her time and probably goes on automatic pilot when reading resumés. Your resumé will most likely be skimmed rather than studied. The careful, thoughtful consideration you would prefer it receive is out of your control. If you make the first cut, however, your resumé will be examined more thoroughly. Be guided by the function your resumé performs: it's a sales document.

Frequently Encountered Resumé Questions

Numerous participants in the HBSCNY Career Seminar have submitted their resumés for group critique. In those discussions, the following aspects of resumé writing are frequently debated:

Should I Use a Functional or a Chronological Format?

By far the most common resumé format is the *chronological,* describing your career in reverse chronological order with accomplishments listed by company and position. A *functional* resumé, in contrast, groups your accomplishments by area of expertise.

For individuals who have had nonlinear career tracks or who wish to make a radical change in careers, a functional resumé stressing your "transferable skills" (see Chapter 7) may be most effective. Rather than call the reader's attention to your places of employment, it communicates your success at using a skill in various environments. This transferability may not be immediately obvious from a chronological resumé. A functional resumé does the work for the reader—highlighting the skills you wish to use on your next job.

You may have encountered a functional-type resumé on the hiring side of the desk and asked, "What is this person trying to hide?" That's a problem: readers tend to view functional resumés with suspicion. If you are considering a functional format to conceal gaps in your work history or to otherwise obfuscate the problems of a chronological resumé, you are considering a functional resumé for the wrong reasons. Time gaps on a chronological resumé may be appropriate—a sabbatical, a break to write a book, a necessary breather to regain perspective, a time to tackle substance abuse. A functional resumé should be your choice *only* when it is a *better* sales tool for you than the more commonly used chronological resumé.

NUGGET: If you and your advisers understand the potential negatives of a functional resumé but still feel it is the best way to present you-the-product, include *a brief chronological history* right up front, in addition to your educational history, before the functional presentation of your skills and experience.

Why Not Use Several Different Resumés?

Many managers consider using several different resumés; it may or may not be valid for you. Consider your motives for having more than one resumé:

- You may choose to have one version that gives an effective overview of your career, with a second expanded resumé or supplements giving more details to be used as follow-up after a face-to-face contact. This makes good marketing sense: you have several pieces of product literature to fit varied situations.
- The more questionable multiple resumé approach is developing different resumés for significantly different products. You fit into this chameleon category when you find yourself thinking, "Which shall I send them—my marketing resumé, my finance resumé, or my purchasing agent resumé?" This may be a symptom of not having done sufficient product or market research to arrive at a clear definition of you-the-product and the best targets for your search. If you're playing the "if-it's-Tuesday-it-must-be-banking" game, you will be less convincing about your merits in face-to-face contacts, be it with network links or with potential buyers.
- You may have a clear understanding of you-the-product, but at the end of your market assessment conclude that several *distinctly different market segments* are equally attractive to you. In this case, prepare several different versions of your resumé, each oriented toward one market segment. After test marketing, you may consolidate to one or you may conclude that each segment requires distinct product literature.

All in all, we are convinced that *one* resumé, brief in nature, augmented by a well-focused letter or carefully prepared supplements, is the best way to present you-the-product.

Shall I Start My Resumé with a Job Objective?

If you have selected a narrow target for your job search, it might be appropriate to express that focus in just a few lines. Function, field, unique specialty, and geographical limitation might all be in a brief Job Objective. But don't try the reader's patience with vague and gratuitous phrases such as "well-seasoned manager," "strong interpersonal skills," or "bottom-line orientation." An alternative is to head your resumé with a brief summary (two or three lines) of you-the-product to help shape the reader's impression.

The best rationale for making any statement at the beginning of a resumé is to screen *out* potential buyers. You're saying, in effect, "You're busy, and I'm busy. If we have a mutual interest, let's explore it; if not, let's not waste one another's time." Two examples that pass this test:

> *OBJECTIVE: Management position in the health care industry that utilizes experience in health care technology finance, Harvard MBA, and master's degree in cardiovascular science.*

> *OBJECTIVE: Developing international opportunities for investors, innovative companies, or development organizations, particularly those involved in science, agribusiness, or services. Adept at financial structuring and risk management.*

If your opening statement is not explicit enough to cause your resumé to be rejected from "no fit" situations, it is not an effective statement.

How Do I Handle the Age Issue?

First of all, determine whether the age issue is *your* issue or the prospective employer's. In the HBSCNY Career Seminar, attended by graduates from one to forty-five years out of business school, participants rarely have their concern about age validated by other attendees. You've seen resumés written to conceal the writer's age: no date given for degrees or military service, early jobs omitted from the chronology. What was your reaction? Trying to conceal age does not make a positive impression.

If you have thoroughly assessed you-the-product, you should regard your length and breadth of experience as an asset, not a liability. An old recruiters' joke goes, "My client wants a thirty-year-old with forty years of experience." Don't let a preoccupation with youth lead you to undervalue your experience. If you are a mature, well-seasoned executive, the last thing in the world you want is to get into a hiring line with a bunch of youngsters—where the buyer is looking for something other than *your* strong suits.

How should you handle your age if you are well along in your career? Don't apologize or obscure your age. Let the prospective buyer appreciate the wealth of skills and experience your years have given you.

What Other Data Should I Include?

- *References available on request.* This is assumed and does not belong on a manager's resumé.
- *Age.* If the reader can infer your age from your degree dates, there is no need to list it. If you received your degree later in your career

or if there is any possibility of misinterpretation, state your age (not your date of birth).

- *Clubs, activities, outside interests.* Any data you include should be consistent with the image you want to project. Extended lists of many outside activities are impressive to employers who value outside involvements—but may raise questions if a firm wants total dedication to the job. Know your market!
- *Single/Married/Family.* This is not required. Whether you list your marital or family status depends on the kind of image you are trying to project.
- *Military.* Include basic information, but don't raise questions about whether you are living in the past.
- *Education.* Give institution, degree, and year. Unless you are a recent graduate, educational credentials belong near the *end* of the resumé. The further you have progressed in your career, the less additional detail (extracurricular activities, obscure awards, minors) should be given. Graduating with honors and being elected to Phi Beta Kappa are always appropriate to mention, but be wary of appearing to pad your resumé with past laurels. Mention any national affiliations that might establish a common bond with an interviewer.

Your Resumé Should Be Your Tool, Not Your Identity

Most of the difficulty managers have with their resumés stems from not recognizing that the resumé is a sales tool to further the progress of a marketing campaign. The ability to divorce one's resumé from one's identity and then objectively look at that resumé for its sales effectiveness is critical. If you are having any difficulty doing this, go back over the self-assessment section.

LETTERS: ANOTHER SALES TOOL

A powerful factor in the effectiveness of your marketing campaign is your use of letters. Unfortunately, even managers whose jobs have involved writing good letters tend to underestimate both the importance of letters to a marketing campaign and the burden of their preparation. Writing a letter is no longer as easy as dictating some thoughts or phrases to your secretary and signing the finished product. Now you may be the drafter, editor, typist, and proofreader combined. Or you may be working with a faceless secretarial service that can't interpret your handwriting or your instructions, let alone clean up your grammar.

Even if letter writing is inconvenient, it cannot be neglected.

NUGGET: One of the vital parts of your marketing campaign is an effective means of producing letters that are articulate, well presented, and timely. Be wary of relying solely on yourself or one other person to get out your letters. Don't start your campaign until you have an effective outside secretarial service in place *and* a hassle-free way of getting material back and forth.

Precisely because letter writing takes more time and effort than it did when you were in the office, you need to take time to differentiate between the various kinds of letters you must generate. The amount of time and energy you put into a letter should be in direct proportion to its importance in your marketing campaign. Performing this kind of cost/benefit analysis should become second nature to you. Use these guidelines:

"Rifle Shot" Letters

When you write letters to *key prospects,* the potential return on each letter is great. A large investment of your time to ensure that each is done perfectly is therefore justified. You may take weeks to research the name of the right person to address in your letter and then spend additional time using your network to locate someone who agrees to be mentioned in the first sentence. At the same time, you are polishing the text, testing it on your board, even running it by several advisers with particular knowledge of the company. Finally, the letter is prepared, proofed, and mailed. You call the addressee's secretary several days later to ensure that the letter arrived safely and to find out the best time to make your official follow-up call.

Shotgun Letters

If you are sending letters to a broader range of targets, where no one company is a key prospect, the amount of time you spend on any one letter should be limited. At a minimum, make a reasonable effort to verify that each letter is addressed to the appropriate person; aim high when in doubt.

Broadcast Letters

In today's market, broadcast letters are seldom, if ever, productive. Akin to a mass mailing, using mailing lists, preaddressed labels, and little or no individualization, they can downgrade the image of the sender and are likely to be lost in the flood of junk mail. However, you may have the special situation calling for a broadcast letter. We know of one such successful campaign: a manager looking for a small company to buy sent 800 letters to manufacturing firms nationwide that met his criteria. He is now owner and chief operating officer of one of those companies.

Thank-You Letters

The letter to thank someone who spent time advancing your campaign by giving you strategic pointers or providing a useful referral may be a short note, but it is very important to send. In a thank-you letter to a contact who made an interview possible, consider enclosing a blind copy of your interview follow-up letter. Keep on top of thank-you letters, so they won't be forgotten or overlooked. Too many people neglect this essential. We know a manager who over the course of a year spent an hour helping each of about 100 people in transition. Having received thank-you notes from only 15, he contacted his alma mater and asked to be removed from their resource file. Thank-you letters matter.

Interview Follow-Up Letters

If you are very interested in a position and the fit looks good, the interview follow-up letter is vitally important. Immediately after the interview, put aside everything and write a strong letter summarizing your qualifications for the position. Add any points that have come to mind since the interview that would strengthen your candidacy. Do this letter in a timely fashion, so that it arrives in the interviewer's hands within several days. *These letters can make all the difference.* If you want the job, don't fail to write the letter!

If after an interview your prospects don't appear as promising, get your follow-up letter out promptly but don't spend as much time on it. Have a standard form with mix-and-match paragraphs ready for these occasions.

Campaign Status Update Letters

Update letters are an ideal way to keep your candidacy fresh in the minds of the many people you have contacted. Using your network mailing list, send out a standard letter with individualized salutations.

NUGGET: Keep the cost/benefit concept in mind. Put into each letter the effort appropriate to what you may realistically get out of it.

Other Letter Pointers

1. Recognize you must get through the defense system that each organization maintains to keep out the type of marketing letter you are sending. A good executive secretary keeps paper *off* a manager's desk, aiming to reduce the morning mail to only the items the manager must see. Part of that defense system is the personnel department, to which letters without any referring contact are forwarded. One sure way to get through the defenses is to use your network to *locate someone whose name will be recognized by the addressee.* Start the letter with, "Nancy Lane suggested I contact you." Do your homework! By getting a name you can use in the *first sentence*, you have greatly increased the probability that your letter will get through to a busy manager.

2. *Send your letter to the line manager* directly responsible for the position or to that manager's superior. A network contact with an understanding of the situation is helpful here. Speak to that manager's needs if possible: sell solutions you can bring into the division or department. For example:

My business background would permit me to cultivate corporate interest in Adams College with imagination and understanding. As a student of business trained in the humanities, I understand the great, if often dimly perceived, value of the liberal arts to the corporate world. My previous solicitation of company funds for an international education foundation—an effort that ultimately raised $15 million from fewer than 100 donors—is one example of my success in obtaining financial support from the business community.

---

3. In cases where you have exhausted your network but very much want to have your letter read by a pivotal manager, call and explain your purpose to his or her secretary. Ask for the best time to direct a letter to the manager's attention. Use this strategy only in low-priority situations; for top-priority prospects, keep networking until you have a better option.

4. "To enclose a resumé or not to enclose a resumé?" Play this according to your situation. If your resumé is not a glove fit with the job or the norms of the environment, the safest bet is to send a stand-alone letter outlining your credentials and expressing interest. Follow up with a resumé and cover note several days later.

5. Maintain the initiative. In your letter's closing, say that *you* will follow up with a telephone call in about a week's time. Call when you indicate. Whether the phone is picked up by the manager or his or her secretary, signal clearly that you are aware the boss's time is very limited. Stress that you would welcome an opportunity to meet at any time convenient to the manager.

6. Secretaries can be influential in determining the results of your follow-up calls. They probably schedule the manager's calendar in addition to screening the mail. Treat them with respect and consideration.

7. Don't fax your letter or resumé unless you are already a "known commodity" or specifically requested to do so. The appearance of your communications exerts a subtle influence on how you are perceived. Why risk a weak initial impression due to a malfunctioning fax machine?

Remember Who You Aren't

Many executives handle most of their communications by telephone, fax, or memo. Their letter-writing skills may have atrophied due to over-reliance on a good secretary. If you fit into this category, remember that during your marketing campaign you are on the outside trying to get in. Effective letters augmented by skillful telephone follow-up are key factors in a successful marketing campaign. Don't be above testing your letters on your board (see Chapter 3), getting pointers from a career counselor (see Chapter 18), or checking with a friend who majored in English!

We'll close this section with a true story to illustrate how powerful a good letter can be. One seminar participant found his ideal job through one letter—a meticulously crafted letter. Having defined his target area, he identified one key person at the top firm on his list. With the assistance of his board he drafted and redrafted until he came up with a letter everyone agreed was to the point and highly credible. The result? He was invited in for an interview, negotiated a good deal on a wonderful job, and has been at the firm ever since. Here is his letter:

Dear Mr. Simpkins:

    I am a Harvard Business School graduate with over twenty years business and manufacturing experience. For the past seven years I have run my own manufacturing company where we initiated computerized control of many of the manufacturing operations. We were one of the first of our size to successfully undertake the process.

    Now I want to use my manufacturing and computer experience to help smaller manufacturers gain better control of their operations. My manufacturing background will gain me access to these companies, including many of my former customers and suppliers, who have yet to use computers to run their operations efficiently.

    [Network contact known to Mr. Simpkins] and I recently conferred about possible opportunities, and we talked about your reported expansion plans for ABC Corporation. He suggested that I contact you about how I might be able to help ABC increase sales of computer systems to manufacturing companies. I would like to meet you to discuss these ideas. I will call you in a few days to set up an appointment.

    Looking forward to meeting you.

Sincerely yours,
Thomas P. Straus

RESPONSES TO ADS

Some managers in transition feel that responding to ads is beneath their dignity. Admittedly, writing to a post office box number has less appeal for many than meeting with an executive search consultant in a well-appointed office. And responding to ads, especially blind ads, is a reminder that you don't have much control over the process: most likely you won't *get* a response *unless* the hiring firm (or recruiter) believes you might be an appropriate candidate. Small wonder that managers too often disregard the ad route.

    Behind each ad, however, is a job. The perception that ads are placed by recruiters just to collect resumés may be true for some specialized recruiters seeking "inventory" for lower-level positions. However, when you see a more costly display ad for an executive or professional position, assume it represents an assignment to be filled.

Pointers for Working with Ads

- If the ad describes a position close to what you're seeking, clip it. It doesn't matter whether it was placed by the employer or by an intermediary, whether the contact is a company or a box number.
- Reconstruct the job specification or position description from the ad. Read between the lines. Which criteria are the most essential? What is unmentioned but likely to be relevant?
- Make a list of your skills and experience that match the job specification. Summarize this list in a one-page letter that establishes your fit with the job. Don't put too much in; your resumé, attached to the letter, will tell the rest of the story.
- If the ad asks for salary information, your letter must say *something* about compensation. Your letter may be opened by someone who lacks the ability to understand your superb qualifications but is quite capable of discarding any responses that do not contain numbers and a dollar sign. *What* you say about salary can vary: you can indicate your present salary; you may allude to your target salary range; you may include qualifiers such as "depending on the nature and prospects of the position." If your qualifications appear to fit the position, the recruiter needs only enough information to know that the salary you're looking for and the compensation available are not totally out of line.
- Don't waste your time on ads that describe tantalizing positions that are *not* a good fit with your skills, experience, or other attributes. If you have placed ads for positions, no doubt you have been mystified at why some respondents wasted the postage to send in a resumé so far off the mark.
- Take your time. Typically, an ad generates a flood of responses in the first week. A letter arriving a bit later, well-crafted and standing out from the others, may hit at a time when the recruiter or hiring manager is starting to despair at the lack of strong prospective candidates. Don't waste the money on overnight delivery for responses to ads; you have a window—usually at least two weeks—before any resumé deadline.

Sample Ad Response

SERVICE QUALITY

This key position calls for you to identify, define, and measure the service quality of our health care products and to report trackable results to product managers, customers, and providers. Based on your findings, you will be responsible for initiating and implementing strategies for improvement.

To qualify, you must possess five or more years' prior experience in a corporate customer service or service quality position with the ability to communicate a vision for how top-notch service quality can be established and maintained. Strong communication skills to establish effective working relations with our MIS department, product managers, and health care providers are essential. In addition, you must be computer savvy, using technology as a strategic business tool in response to customer and management needs. A health care background is helpful but not necessary, and qualified candidates from other sectors are encouraged to apply.

Over 300 people responded to the above ad. Only three were invited for an interview. One, an HBSCNY Career Seminar participant, wrote the following letter:

Ms. Susan Saunders
Family Pharmaceuticals
Miami, Florida

Dear Ms. Saunders:

Enclosed you will find my resumé in response to your recent advertisement in the *Wall Street Journal.* The service quality position sounds challenging and exciting, and I would welcome the opportunity to discuss it with you.

As Manager of Quality Control in the headquarters group at Mammoth Corporation, I have conducted quality reviews of eleven customer service operations and worked with local management to implement improved measurements and higher standards. Three of these were insurance programs administered by outside vendors. It was particularly satisfying to design and put in place state-of-the-art quality programs for claims adjusting environments and to observe the measurable increase in service quality that occurred.

I have worked closely with software vendors, in-house MIS groups, quality personnel, and line management to design more effective ways of measuring and reporting quality results utilizing strategic computer applications. My strong oral and written communications skills and ability to get along with employees at all levels of the organization have been recognized and commended by HQ and local management.

My salary requirement is in the $70,000 to $80,000 range, with some flexibility depending on the responsibilities and scope of the position.

I can be reached during the day on a confidential basis at my office (see enclosed resumé). Or you can leave a message for me at my home.

Thank you for your consideration, and I look forward to hearing from you.

Sincerely,

Don't look down on answering ads. That may be your next job they're describing.

16

INTERVIEWING

KING LEAR: What dost thou profess? What wouldst thou with us?

KENT: I do profess to be no less than I seem, to serve him truly that will put me in trust, to love him that is honest, to converse with him that is wise and says little, to fear judgment, to fight when I cannot choose, and to eat no fish.

KING LEAR: What wouldst thou?

KENT: Service.

KING LEAR: What services canst thou do?

KENT: I can keep honest counsel, ride, run, mar a curious tale in telling it and deliver a plain message bluntly. That which ordinary men are fit for, I am qualified in, and the best of me is diligence.

KING LEAR: How old art thou?

KENT: Not so young, sir, to love a woman for singing, nor so old to dote on her for anything. I have years on my back forty eight.

KING LEAR: Follow me; thou shall serve me.
　　　　　　—WILLIAM SHAKESPEARE, *KING LEAR*, ACT 1, SCENE 4

The loyal Kent handled that interview well, including the delicate question (illegal in today's job market) regarding age. He got the job!

MARKETER OR MENDICANT?

Return to Chapter 11 and review the discussion on the two approaches to the job search—the marketing approach and the mendicant approach. Nowhere in your marketing campaign will this difference in attitude be more critical than when you begin interviewing, usually the first substantive contact with prospective buyers of you-the-product. A salesperson who believes in his or her product makes a powerful impression. In your interviews you must exude a strong belief both in you-the-product and you the salesperson.

Too often applicants hope a confident façade will hide self-doubt and deep apprehension. They risk being mendicants in a business suit. The many aspects of the interviewing process discussed in this chapter are of little value without a strong sense of self-confidence and a healthy degree of self-acceptance. Both will benefit from the self-awareness process discussed in Part 2. Self-confidence built on self-understanding and *acceptance* of yourself for what you are rather than for what others would have you be are critical to clearly articulating your key attributes and the types of situations in which you function best.

NUGGET: The self-assessment process in Part 2 is the first and most fundamental preparation for the interview process.

MANAGERIAL EXPERIENCE DOES NOT EQUAL INTERVIEWING SKILLS

Many managers are poor interviewers. Some assume interviewing is just a variation of what they've been accustomed to doing on the job. "Why should I have to prepare for an interview? I do this kind of thing all the time. The only difference is that I'll be on the other side of the desk." Being on the other side of the desk can make all the difference in the world:

My interviewing feedback was disconcerting, to say the least, since I have been dealing with people individually and in groups for many years. It was like watching a video of my golf swing: I didn't like what was being pointed out, but I couldn't deny it. I was presenting myself much less effectively than I had ever imagined.

INDEPENDENT CONSULTANT, HBS '60

Salespeople and others whose jobs involve frequent contact with strangers are particularly prone to the "what's-different-I-interview-all-the-time" attitude. In fact, salespeople are so accustomed to subordinating themselves to the product that often they are very inept at selling *themselves.* Job interviewing involves shifting gears.

Whatever your background, avoid being cocky about interviewing. If you're thinking, "I don't have to read this chapter, since [you fill in the blank]," we mean you! If you think that you are a natural-born, spontaneous interviewer and especially if you pride yourself on your ability to wing it, that bravado could lose you the job of your dreams. Give yourself the self-confidence that comes from solid preparation.

SETTING UP THE INTERVIEW

Each interview stems from a prior event: a networking contact, a letter sent as part of your marketing campaign, a phone call from a recruiter. The other chapters in this part of *In Transition* discuss in detail how to go about these activities, all of which have as their objective *the interview.* So congratulations if you've succeeded in getting the interview! Don't slack off now!

The impression you make on a prospective employer begins with your first contact with the organization. If you are dealing with support staff in setting up your interview, be efficient, courteous, and professional. Act as you would want someone to act who was making an appointment for an interview in *your* office: courteous to your secretary, considerate and understanding of your tight schedule, and willing to be flexible. That should be your model—not playing the busy executive. (But don't go overboard; your time is valuable.) Set up the interview recognizing that both sides are dealing with a valuable commodity—time.

TELEPHONE INTERVIEWS

An interview situation that trips up many managers without their even being aware is the telephone interview.

NUGGET: If you have not prepared a script and practiced for the telephone interview, you simply will not make as good an impression. Don't blow an opportunity by skipping these steps.

The phone interview sets the stage for the face-to-face interview. You may recall instances where your secretary, after setting up an interview with someone, made a favorable or unfavorable comment that proved to be very prescient, ranging from, "She sounds very good" to, "I don't think he's going to fit in here." Such comments influence how a candidate is viewed because telephone impressions can be accurate. Recall a situation where you made the initial screening call to a prospective candidate with a promising resumé; if afterwards you thought, "Did I catch him at a bad time or is he always like that?" that candidate was already off to a bad start.

As a candidate, your first telephone impression is very important. Do everything possible to ensure that it is positive.

- Have a script prepared, possibly several three-by-five cards with key points and phrases. Your script will help allay your initial jitters, give you some wording that is comfortable to you and impressive to the listener, and ensure that you don't forget any important points.
- Be natural; be yourself. The "natural you" is not infallible or omniscient, but the self-assessment section should make you comfortable with your particular area of expertise. You are valuable; let that come across.
- If a call catches you at a bad time, mention it at the outset and arrange for a follow-up call. Rather than coming across as stressed or impatient, plan to speak when you'll be focused and free from deadlines or other pressures.
- Don't ramble. A telephone interview is not a chat with a friend but a business call. Some telephone interviewers, either as a testing technique or out of inexperience, may get chatty. Don't fall into the trap; be natural, courteous, and cooperative, but give the clear impression that you have much to do. You know the process: this call is that first cut to establish whether there seems to be a fit worth pursuing.

THE FACE-TO-FACE JOB INTERVIEW

You have an interview with the line manager responsible for your target area. You're ready to talk knowledgeably about the company based on research, network contacts, and recent media articles. Your best interviewing suit or dress is ready, and you've scheduled a booster breakfast with a friend who always makes you feel particularly good about yourself. This one should lead to a job!

Your task in each job interview is similar to that of a person selling a product: ascertain the buyer's needs, and then communicate convincingly and succinctly what you-the-product can do to fulfill the needs articulated. The distinction in the job interview is that you-the-product must not only do a good needs-benefits sell, but be mindful that your very presence is a *product demonstration.*

How do you "demonstrate" yourself as a manager? You demonstrate organizational and communication skills by the manner in which you communicate and react to questions. Your effective use of resources is reflected in how well you budget your time in the interview. You demonstrate interpersonal skills at every step of the interview. How balanced and well-grounded you are in the face of conflict or threatening situations shows through during discussion of past difficulties. The extent to which you would fit into the organization is revealed before, throughout, and after the interview in your contacts with the receptionists, secretaries, and everyone who formally interviews you.

NUGGET: Everything you do during a job interview is a demonstration of you-the-product, for good or for ill. Develop an effective way of handling difficult questions. Don't spend too much time chatting during an interview. Act like an executive without coming across as arrogant. Don't alienate the interviewer by trying to control the interview. Take your candidacy seriously: prepare and present as the competent manager you are.

INTERVIEW POINTERS

Hard and fast rules for interviewing are suspect; circumstances differ and the effective interviewee adapts to the situation at hand. Over the years at the HBSCNY Career Seminar we have developed these interview pointers:

Determine What Is Appropriate Here and Now

Behavior appropriate in the initial stage of the first interview differs from behavior appropriate in the latter stages, after things have warmed up and are going well. How you conduct yourself in a follow-up interview differs once again. And after you have met everyone, discussed everything, and are being measured for compatibility, you will act in yet a different fashion. Keep checking: at what stage am I? What is appropriate?

Keep Your Antennae Working

Use your gut instincts to get a reading of the other person, and plan your responses accordingly.

Gut Instinct	Action
Where does he or she seem to be headed with this line of questioning?	Come up with crisp, pointed responses; help the interviewer to get there sooner, and give yourself more time to make other points.
I get the feeling that he or she is getting impatient.	Cut it short; you just saved yourself from being labeled verbose.
I'm getting the sense that he doesn't think a woman/someone my age/a finance type/an engineer could handle this position.	Without stretching, give some examples of how you've handled similar situations. If that doesn't do it, be up front about your gut instinct. Better to get that unspoken reservation on the table and addressed.

Trust your instinct and your empathetic abilities.

Remember the Initial Minutes Are Particularly Important

Within the first five minutes of an interview the person with whom you are speaking will form a subconscious impression and possibly make a "decision" about you. Skilled interviewers try to defer this judgment until they have acquired more data, but even they rely on their initial gut feel and intuition. The interview will usually go on for much longer, but in the remaining time the interviewer is looking for reinforcement for that initial impression. Keep in mind these ramifications for *you* in an interview:

- Be aware that those first minutes are *key*. Use them effectively. That does not mean that you shortcut all small talk to get to your sales points. It does mean that the image you project in the initial minutes must be consistent with you-the-product.
- Your "aura" is highly influential in the initial impression you make. Self-confidence and self-acceptance are key factors, as discussed in

Part 2. If you don't feel good about yourself, other people can sense it. Conversely, if you do feel positive about your campaign and confident about you-the-product, that comes across in a powerful, impressive way. Check yourself for mannerisms and habits that create negative impressions. (See the trial interview technique further on in this chapter.)

"Control" the Interview by Making Your Points

Much common wisdom exists about controlling the interview. This is *not* done by your contesting the interviewer's legitimate role in choosing conversation topics; this only frustrates and alienates the interviewer. The way to exert an appropriate degree of control is to have your sales points ready and to insert them naturally but effectively into the conversation.

- Prepare a script consisting of a concise description of each of your sales points plus several well-crafted but brief examples from your career. Write out a page minimum for each point, and then boil that down to several paragraphs. Commit these *short* paragraphs to memory so that you can make each selling point naturally and effectively.
- Think of these well-crafted sales points as arrows in a quiver at your side. During the interview, look for "openings" into which you can shoot one of the arrows, using a transitional phrase such as, "That sounds very similar to my experience in our South American subsidiary."
- As the interview progresses, keep track of your *remaining* sales points. Your task is to introduce each one into the discussion, preferably in the first half of the interview.
- Just before the conclusion of the interview look for an opportunity to *summarize* your abilities relevant to the position discussed. Add one or two brief examples you did not use earlier.

Consider the Interviewer's Checklist

At each stage of the conversation an experienced interviewer is seeking particular information. The following checklist is one framework used by interviewers:

- ☐ The *skills* required to do the job
- ☐ The relevant *experience* to do the job
- ☐ *Compatibility* with the workplace

☐ Appropriate *potential* (high or low) given the growth possible in the position

☐ *No surprises* after the hire

Keep in mind that at any point in time the interviewer is focusing on one of these areas. The process will go more smoothly and the interviewer will give you high marks if you take your cues from his or her questions and stay on point. In most cases the areas are addressed in the order they appear above:

- *Skills* and *experience* are usually dealt with at an early stage in the interview process.
- *Compatibility* and *potential* are measured with increasing levels of intensity as the interview process proceeds. The final meetings will focus exclusively on how well you will fit in—on whether the "chemistry" is right.
- All through the process the interviewers will be on alert to anything that suggests you may be concealing something that would compromise your ability to do the job. Every interviewer has gone through the unpleasant surprise of having the boss say, "How on earth did you ever decide to hire *him?*"

During call-back interviews be alert to where each person you speak to is on the above list. You may be well into the compatibility stage with several people you have spoken to repeatedly, and then be introduced to a person for the first time who needs to discuss your skills and experience.

Recall the distinction between *skills and experience* discussed in Chapter 7: skills are transferable, experience is not. *Compatibility* is largely related to the values, styles, and organizational fit issues discussed in Chapters 6 and 8. Don't fool yourself on the *potential* issue; in a position with limited growth possibilities, an aggressive, fast-track manager simply is not a good candidate. Finally, alert the interviewer to any *surprises* that could be misconstrued; be natural and candid about your limitations and, where appropriate, describe the compensating techniques you use.

Manage the "Small Talk"

"How much small talk is the right amount?" is a tough but important question. Small talk is important in establishing your compatibility; too much small talk wastes time. At the start of the interview respond warmly but briefly to small talk by the other person, but don't initiate any on your own. Later on, *after* you've had the opportunity to cover your skills and experience and *if* things seem to be going well, it might be appropriate to engage in small talk. You might refer to one of the interviewer's personal mementos in the office or a common interest. Again keep in mind where you are in the interviewing process; how much small talk would you like if your roles were reversed?

Guide the Poor Interviewer; Treat Every Minute as Precious to You

Your interviewing skills are tested when you find yourself with someone who lacks the skill, training, or experience to conduct an interview efficiently. The first and most important thing is to not take the situation personally. Think like a salesperson: "How can I turn this situation to my advantage?"

You might ask, "Would it be useful if I were to go over the experience I've had that relates to the position as I understand it?" Or if no position has been described, you might say, "In preparing for this job search I developed a summary of my skills; would it be useful for me to review that with you now?"

Another effective technique is to mention time and work pressures. If you run into someone who is so interested in small talk that you can't get a word in edgewise, try, "I realize that your work schedule will limit our time together. May I run through a summary of my skills and achievements?"

Display Enthusiasm and Good Humor

Don't get so absorbed in the planning and execution of the interview process that you stifle your spontaneity, enthusiasm, and humor. These characteristics carry considerable weight in the interviewing process. Don't tell jokes or engage in otherwise inappropriate behavior that suggests your discomfort; this is no time to pull a comedy club routine! But don't take yourself so seriously that you forget to communicate the range of your personality.

Send a Follow-Up Letter

A follow-up letter is not only a common courtesy, it is an essential aspect of the interview (see Chapter 15). Most important, it gives you an opportunity to reinforce the key points made in your interview and to add additional information or emphasis.

HOW TO HANDLE THE QUESTIONS YOU DON'T WANT ASKED

As you prepare for interviewing, you will quite likely find yourself thinking, "I hope they don't ask me about *that.*" The questions you *don't* want to be asked represent a threat to your interviewing expertise: even if an interviewer never asks these questions, the very prospect has a negative influence on your presentation and your self-confidence. The natural tendency is to try to avoid dealing with these questions, hoping against hope that you can maneuver the interview around certain topics.

But then the day comes when an interviewer asks, "How did you happen to leave that company?" This may very well be an innocuous question, possibly even a transition question to get from one subject to another. But as discussed in Chapter 9, if you have not worked on the emotions such questions trigger, your response will undoubtedly be inappropriate.

Defuse those difficult questions. Begin by making a list of *all* the questions and issues you would prefer not be discussed. Taking one at a time, review the facts of the situation. Then write out a well-worded response that doesn't compromise your integrity. Balance your response in terms of assuming and assigning blame, and make sure you are comfortable with the wording. Remember that your response must square with reference checks. This scripted response should have two parts—a *one-sentence* comment giving the basic facts, possibly in a semihumorous manner, and a three- or four-sentence *amplification* with more information phrased very objectively. Memorize your chosen responses! In most cases the one-sentence comment will suffice; use the expanded backup if necessary. This preparation will ensure that you are no longer inhibited by questions you hope they won't ask.

SOME ELEMENTS OF POOR INTERVIEWING

- *An inflated sense of entitlement* will lead you to act as if you don't have to play by the generally accepted rules and conventions.

- *A propensity to play the chameleon* will prompt you to contort yourself to fit the job, telling interviewers what they want to hear rather than being yourself and focusing on your priorities for this transition.
- *An inability to gather data during the interview* due to insensitivity to nuances will hamper your ability to stay on track with the interviewer.
- *Poor preparation* leads to asking questions that indicate minimal interest in the job, a lack of commitment to the search, and a general arrogance.
- *Self-sabotaging and overcompensating behavior,* such as treating the interviewer inappropriately, milking descriptions of past experiences, undermining your image with self-deprecating turns of phrase, or being a "know it all" needlessly compromise your candidacy.
- *Not responding to questions* gives the impression that you are not listening, or actively avoiding the interviewer's probe. Both leave a bad impression.

These patterns are best caught through the trial interview technique described below. Most likely they stem from some unresolved issues (see Part 2). Get those issues resolved! They create inappropriate behavior that you are unaware of and that is therefore out of your control (see Chapter 9).

THE MOCK INTERVIEW

A sensible and reliable method for getting an objective assessment of your interviewing skills is the mock interview. Just as you tested your resumé with a neutral third party, the mock interview enables you to identify any parts of your presentation that need additional work. Here are the basics:

1. Schedule a mock interview before you do any actual interviewing, but only after you have determined your product attributes—what you are selling—and have read this chapter.
2. Have a friend set up a short interview for you with an associate who is an experienced interviewer and does *not* know you. This might be someone in the human resources department who is regularly involved in the hiring process, a line manager adept at interviewing, an executive recruiter, or any person whose work involves interviewing at the executive level.
3. At the time of the interview, conduct yourself as you would in a regular job interview. Describe your goals and the benefits you would

bring to the job, and respond to the interviewer's questions. Leave after the agreed-upon time period.

4. Have your friend debrief the interviewer as soon as possible after the interview, writing down all comments, favorable and unfavorable. Ask your friend to get as much detail as possible on the *unfavorable* reactions; they point to areas needing work. Your friend will in many cases give you this feedback over the telephone. Ask for his or her written comments; you have a more reliable record and you undercut the natural tendency of a friend to sugarcoat feedback.

5. Do a number of mock interviews. Avoid rationalizing negative feedback, especially when you hear similar comments from several sources. Work to *perfect* your interviewing skills without resorting to pat answers or losing your spontaneity; that is the entire purpose of this technique!

Once you are satisfied with your mock interview feedback, you are ready to start interviewing. When you do, it will be with a sense of confidence and self-assurance that will enhance your credibility and build toward a successful marketing campaign.

THE "SUCCESSFUL" VERSUS THE "UNSUCCESSFUL" JOB INTERVIEW

The success of a job interview should not be judged on whether you get a job offer but whether it advances your marketing campaign. Focusing excessively on a job offer can lead to myopia, causing you to overlook potential leads and tangential opportunities. Think in business terms, just to ensure that you do not consider the interview some kind of popularity test. The job interview is the *sales call*, during which you-the-salesperson articulate the attributes and applications of you-the-product convincingly and in a manner that befits the product. In the selling business every sales call does not result in an order; similarly, in your marketing campaign every interview will not result in a job offer.

A *successful* job interview yields a number of positive results:

- If the prospective buyer has an unfilled need and your price and performance requirements are reasonably in line, you will be invited to take further steps in the interview process. These follow-on interviews may result in a job offer, which you may or may not accept after suitable negotiations. Or you may decide, alone or in consultation with the buyer, not to take the process to the offer stage. If you do this in a constructive and congenial manner, the door is open for future possibilities.

- If, on the other hand, the position of interest within a company is presently filled, consider the possibilities open to you if your presentation has been extremely impressive. Another closely related need may exist within the company for which you-the-product are the ideal fit. If there are no prospects within this company, your interviewer may be sufficiently impressed to refer you to someone else with an unfilled need. If in the future a vacancy occurs, you could be at the top of the buyer's list. Finally, if the company has consulting needs in line with your abilities, you may be offered contract work.

In other words, a successful job interview is not only characterized by an immediate job offer. At managerial levels, that seldom happens, since most hiring decisions are influenced by many people who must be consulted before an official decision is made. One manager we know was so impressive in an interview with a CEO that he was asked to do a consulting project to investigate a new market; he now heads the marketing efforts of a subsidiary of that company.

The ramifications of an *unsuccessful* job interview are seldom obvious to the interviewee. The interviewer is unconvinced that you-the-product perform at the level you're advertising. You have little or no chance of being considered for other positions in the company because you've shot your credibility. The interviewer is uncomfortable referring you elsewhere, since your poor presentation could compromise his or her relationships.

All of your preparation to this point—your self-assessment, your market assessment, your careful courtship of companies of interest, and your well-rehearsed interviewing style—come together in the interview. You have as much control over an interview as the preparation you're willing to do. Stay at the helm: this is when it will all pay off.

17

RECRUITERS: THE BROKERS OF THE JOB MARKET

THE MYSTIQUE OF EXECUTIVE SEARCH

You are marketing you-the-product to one or more segments of the job market. In that market are brokers who match buyer and seller. These brokers have a variety of names: recruiter, headhunter, executive search consultant. In this chapter we refer to all people and firms providing this brokerage function as *recruiters.*

The recruiting industry has a certain mystique to many outsiders. Managers know that every day someone gets that unexpected call from a recruiter that can propel him or her into an exciting and rewarding new position. Many managers maintain contact with a handful of recruiters in hopes of one day receiving that magic call. Ironically, most managers are also aware of the questionable practices of some recruiters. Most people have at least one negative recruiter story—sometimes heard second- or thirdhand, sometimes a painful chapter in their own past.

Begin by learning the basics: how recruiters are compensated, who makes up the industry, their function as job-brokers, and how they do—and do not—fit into your job search.

My first move, after I was fired, was to contact several recruiters who had worked for our firm. They were friendly, but the weeks went by and nothing happened. Finally, I came to the realization that the recruiter works for the recruiter, not for you! That wasted a lot of time in my search.

VP, CONSUMER PRODUCTS, HBS '78

NUGGET: When you clearly understand the function and limitations of these brokers, you can use recruiters effectively in your marketing campaign. Failure to do so could result in missing out on some great jobs or in your being used by recruiters. Avoid the frustration caused by having unrealistic expectations of recruiters.

RECRUITERS ARE PAID BY THE EMPLOYER

Recruiter or broker fees are paid by the *employer* (the *client*) for *presenting* properly qualified candidates to fill an employment need. Employers work through a third party for any of a number of reasons: confidentiality (both inside and outside the firm), better access to the employees of competitors, enhanced discipline to the process, greater objectivity in defining the position and assessing candidates, prescreening of prospective candidates, and less burden on staff. Since the fee is customarily *one-third* of the new hire's annual cash compensation, the client has determined that the cost of using a recruiter is justified by access to a better pool of candidates, faster and more objective results, and less wear-and-tear on management than if recruiting were handled in-house.

During your job search you may encounter firms who at first glance appear to be recruiters but offer a different kind of broker function: connecting you with the job market in exchange for a fee paid by *you*. These are *not* recruiters but comprise a shadow part of the industry dealing with (some might say preying upon) people looking for jobs. We recommend against using such services; for more details see Chapter 19.

NUGGET: Recruiters work for the corporate and institutional *client* who pays the fee, not for you. Never deal with a recruiter who charges *you* a fee. Job seekers who speak of "my recruiter" or who expect recruiters to carry out their job campaigns for them don't understand how the game is played.

TWO CATEGORIES OF RECRUITERS

Recruiters can be grouped into two broad categories, according to the nature of the client relationship and compensation and expense reimbursement arrangements.

- *Retainer firms* have an exclusive on their assignments; no other firm is engaged to fill the position. Customarily they are paid one-third of their fee when the contract is signed to initiate the search, with the remaining two-thirds paid over the course of the assignment, whether or not the position is filled. Expenses incurred are reimbursed by the client company. Retainer firms may or may not specialize in certain fields or industries but generally will accept a search assignment in any field.
- *Contingency firms* may or may not have an exclusive assignment from a company. They are paid a fee *only* if they fill a position. Their expenses are often *not* reimbursed by the client. They may have good contacts in particular industries or segments of the job market and under extraordinary circumstances will "shop" a particularly attractive candidate.

The pros and cons of working with each type of recruiter depend on the goals of your campaign, your professional history, and your seniority in your field. Retainer recruiters normally handle assignments for higher levels of management, and they generally have a more professional reputation. Contingency recruiters handle a wider range of situations and include in their ranks a broader cross-section of players, from the very successful and principled recruiter who has developed expertise and a niche to the individual in a tight financial situation willing to bend the rules for a fee.

Elegantly appointed offices may be enjoyable to visit, but you should focus on what role a recruiter can play in your marketing campaign. Contingency recruiters are capable of marketing someone who might earn them a fee even if they are not aware of any actual openings; this is seldom if ever done by a retainer firm, which works only on specific client assignments. The universe of recruiters is large and varied; the most recent *Directory of Executive Recruiters*[1] lists 900 retainer firms and 1,196 contingency firms in the United States. Within that group may be several who could assist your marketing campaign—and some who could complicate it. It's your job to know how to use the recruiter or broker effectively.

Whenever you are dealing with a recruiter, determine in which cate-

[1]Kennedy Publications, Templeton Road, Fitzwilliam, NH 03447.

gory he or she belongs. Ask early in the conversation, "Does your firm do contingency or retainer search?" Recruiters with *retainer* firms will indicate clearly that they do *only* retainer work; *contingency* recruiters will often respond, "We do *both.*" Just knowing enough to ask that question is a signal to the recruiter that you would like to use—but not *be* used by—a job broker.

RESPONDING TO A RECRUITER'S INITIAL CONTACT

It's happened! You answer your phone to hear a professional-sounding voice say, "I'm Reg Percival with Truss Steward. We're working on a very interesting assignment for a client, and I'd appreciate your input and reaction. Is this a convenient time for you to talk?" You excuse yourself to close the door and return to the phone with anticipation. What to do next?

- It is best to talk with the recruiter now; he or she is making lots of calls, and you may not connect again. By this point you should have your priorities clear, your skill set firmly in mind, and the parameters most important to recruiters (such as your geographical flexibility) well considered. If you cannot speak at length say, "I'm in a meeting," take the recruiter's number, and establish a callback time.
- *Listen* to what he or she has to say; don't be impatient to start your sales pitch.
- *Respond* to what has been said. Most likely the recruiter will describe the assignment and leave it to you to indicate interest yourself or mention the names of people you know who fit the specifications. In some cases the recruiter is not interested in you as a potential candidate but is "sourcing"—seeking only what names or information you might offer; this should be clear from his or her initial comments.
- *Indicate interest* if the position appeals to you. Ask some reasonable, intelligent questions that demonstrate your knowledge about the field generally or the function specifically. Do *not* probe for information that the recruiter says is confidential. Mention your most relevant qualifications; don't exaggerate. Respond to a reasonable number of relevant queries. Don't be preoccupied with selling yourself at this point. The recruiter is interested in you; *don't risk disqualifying yourself* by pushing yourself too aggressively.
- *Let the recruiter propose the next move.* Be prepared to set up an appointment or to hear, "We'll be back in touch with you." Quite possibly, the person with whom you are speaking is not the recruiter

but works in the firm's research department. In that case, he or she will be reporting on you and other potential candidates to the recruiter, who will set up a face-to-face meeting. Your appointment may be with a senior recruiter who is the primary liaison with the client or with a more junior person doing preliminary screening.

- Be sure to *get the full name and contact information* of the person who called you: name, firm, mailing address, telephone, fax number. If within several weeks they have not followed up as indicated, you may wish to call them, although a lack of follow-through generally indicates a lack of interest.

INITIATING A CONTACT WITH A RECRUITER

As you are working on your marketing campaign, in all likelihood somewhere a recruiter is working on an assignment to fill your ideal job. How do you get in touch with that recruiter? Unfortunately, there is no sure way of gaining the attention of a recruiter working on a search assignment in your target area. However, do the following to increase the probability of coming to the attention of recruiters:

1. *Network, network, network!* The more people you have made aware of your availability and qualifications, the greater the chance that one of them will mention your name to a recruiter working on an assignment along the lines of your interests.
2. In most job searches *sending your resumé to recruiter firms* is an appropriate part of your marketing campaign; it involves a certain expenditure of time and money but may bring results. However, be realistic about the chance of results. Most recruiter firms are inundated by unsolicited resumés; the larger firms get *thousands* each week, overwhelming the process of categorizing and logging in resumés, let alone matching them with current searches. A resumé sent to a smaller, less well-known recruiter firm is more likely to be read, although the number of searches per firm is smaller.

NUGGET: When sending your resumé to a search firm, be practical, not fancy. Address a brief, businesslike letter to a specific individual. Summarize your interests, your compensation range, and your views about relocating.

---

3. Establish contact with *recruiters who have placed colleagues* in your target field or function. Understand that their *current* list of assignments may be in completely different fields; however, they may be aware of related assignments being worked on by other recruiters in their firm. Don't hesitate to call more than one good contact at a firm: communications within a firm, or even in the same office, are not always flawless.

4. *Research the contingency recruiters* who specialize in the sectors of the job market you have targeted. Contact them early in your selling phase; they can be a source of market intelligence, and they may choose to market you. Be sure you understand the ground rules and maintain control.

5. *Contact recruiters with whom you have a special relationship,* such as personal friends or recruiters who have worked for your current or former employer. They will no doubt be very supportive and may have some good advice. However, don't develop unrealistic expectations.

POINTERS FOR WORKING EFFECTIVELY WITH RECRUITERS

1. For recruiters, time is money. Don't waste their time.

2. You create a good impression with recruiters by being organized, by describing yourself in a clear, concise, and objective fashion, and by dealing with them in a straightforward manner.

3. Many people disqualify themselves during the initial telephone screening because they are not prepared and rely on their ability to extemporize. Prepare a script in anticipation of a recruiter calling, with a concise overview of your background, a skills summary, and a synopsis of your goals for this transition. You'll sound managerial and impressive in your comments.

4. If you are dealing with a contingency recruiter who is interested in marketing you, *proceed with caution and stay in control.* Some contingency recruiters have very good contacts and are respected in the industries they service. A well-placed telephone call to a prospective employer could net you a job. However, if your resumé is mass-mailed around the industry by a recruiter with a bad reputation, it can cause considerable damage to your marketing campaign. Insist on ground rules in advance. For example, you might insist that any firm the contingency recruiter wishes to contact on your behalf be run by you first. If you have already made contact with the firm, you'll avoid any

conflicts over fees, and preserve your straight-line communications with a potential employer.

5. Most recruiters are hardworking and honest. However, as in any field, some recruiters behave irresponsibly and unethically. Learn the ropes and look out for yourself. Never let a recruiter submit a falsified resumé on your behalf. Never let a recruiter pressure you into making a decision before you are ready. Think twice when a recruiter calls your spouse or significant other to plug a job he or she wants you to take. Most difficulties people have with recruiters are caused by poor communications, a lack of clear ground rules, and erroneous expectations.

6. Some recruiters are not above taking advantage of prospective candidates who permit themselves to be exploited:

   • If you are working with a recruiter who repeatedly arranges interviews that you find ego-gratifying but seldom in line with your objectives, watch out! The recruiter may be using you to make a favorable impression on a client, even to string a client along until he or she finds a suitable candidate. You may elect to gain interviewing experience and exposure by taking such interviews, but examine your motives to be sure this is a good use of your time and energy.

   • Recruiters may contact you as a source of information on other people in your firm. Thinking that you are the object of the recruiter's interest and trying to make a favorable impression, you cooperate fully, only to be dropped after the recruiter has obtained the necessary sourcing information. *If the recruiter's focus is more on the company you work for than on you, gracefully exit the conversation!* For example, "I've got another call coming in. Please call me again if you have an assignment related to my interests. Good luck on this search."

   • Once the client likes a candidate, recruiters can be very persuasive in convincing him or her to take a position that is a force fit. Stay clear about your priorities and your goals for this transition. Don't compromise your objectives.

7. If you are looking for an entirely new line of work, recruiters are unlikely to help your marketing campaign. Recruiters are hired to locate and present candidates with qualifications and career paths directly related to the client's needs. Their role is not to make the case for the off-specs candidate.

8. If you are unwilling to relocate or are highly selective about geographic areas, recruiters will find you less attractive as a potential candidate. However, if you do have geographical criteria, *make them known to the recruiter early in the discussion.* All too often search firms have presented a candidate and the client made an offer, only to learn that the candidate of choice has decided against a move to a new location. There is no *surer* way of alienating recruiter and client.

9. Recruiters do not pursue candidates who are employed by companies on their current list of clients. This seldom effects the job searcher but is another reason to contact many recruiters rather than just a few.

UNDERSTAND THE "COURTESY INTERVIEW"

Shortly after you lose a job, a good friend may say, "I talked about you with Mary Stuart of Softwick and Strangles; they've done a number of searches for our firm. She said she'd be happy to meet with you." Wow! A personal introduction to a top-flight headhunter! You thank your friend.

On entering the impressive offices of Softwick and Strangles, you receive a warm welcome from the receptionist and are ushered into Mary Stuart's office. She is very friendly and interested in your situation, asks a lot of questions, and makes some good suggestions. After a while her secretary reminds her it's time for another appointment, and you leave, expressing sincere thanks for her help and feeling very good about yourself.

Reflecting back on the meeting the next day, you realize that nothing specific was said about what the next step would be or what Mary Stuart would be doing for you. Still you're thinking, "Certainly it can't hurt to have someone like that on my side. As a matter of fact, this job search may not be as complicated a process as I had feared."

Quite likely, you won't be hearing from Mary Stuart soon, if at all. Your meeting is a service commonly offered by recruiters: the courtesy interview. A good client asks for help for a friend; to maintain the relationship the recruiter agrees to meet you. In some cases such meetings are a useful orientation to the job search process, with the recruiter giving practical advice and direction. The danger is that you may come away with completely unrealistic expectations, thinking the recruiter will take an active role in finding you a job.

High-level managers, with many friends in close contact with recruiters, may even go through a *series* of courtesy interviews and come away convinced that the phone will ring any day with a new job. Don't underestimate the negative impact of this thinking. In all likelihood none of the recruiters who were so pleasant and attentive had an assignment that matched your background and attributes. The more probable scenario is your waiting in vain, becoming frustrated and less and less sure of your marketability. Too often the real bottom line of courtesy interviews is the loss of valuable time and a devastating blow to your self-confidence when the balloon of unrealistic expectations bursts.

DIRECTORY OF EXECUTIVE RECRUITERS

The most current and complete listing of recruiters is published by Consultants News, Fitzwilliam, NH 03447. Call them at 603-385-2200 to order by telephone. They also supply pressure-sensitive mailing labels that can be purchased in subgroups of recruiter specialization.

EXECUTIVE TEMPORARY PLACEMENT FIRMS

The temporary employee concept has expanded to include upper-level managerial and professional positions with the recent growth in the number of executive temporary or interim management firms. Interim executives are a logical option in turnarounds, in crisis management situations, or under circumstances where the longer-term prospects of the position are unclear. Another advantage to the prospective employer is the speed with which the need is filled. When a prospective corporate client contacts such a firm with a specific need, the executive temp firm undertakes to provide a suitably qualified person within several weeks.

Interim placement jobs typically last for three to twelve months. Fees are comparable to recruiter fees, in the range of 30 percent of actual compensation, and paid by the hiring corporation—with additional fees if the interim placement results in a permanent hire, a fairly common occurrence.

Executive temp firms maintain lists of prescreened individuals, including job seekers, retirees, and others in transition. Of particular interest are people with clearly defined skills and a willingness to relocate on short notice. If you fit these criteria, you can find out more information on executive temp firms, including a current directory, from Kennedy Publications, Templeton Road, Fitzwilliam, NH 03447 (603-385-2200).

You now have a clearer understanding of these "facilitating agents" in the job market—the brokers who earn a living locating candidates for corporations. Use their services intelligently where appropriate; they can be valuable in your campaign. Keep your priorities uppermost and your self-esteem intact, and you'll avoid being used by them.

18

CAREER HELP FOR HIRE

At various points in your self-awareness and marketing campaign, you may augment your efforts with professional career assistance. Familiarize yourself with the various resources available: outplacement firms, career counselors, "matching services," special task firms, and college and graduate school career development offices.

In assessing any such service—whether offered by your employer or paid by you—your question should be, "What benefits does it offer me?" With the exception of outplacement, the services discussed in this chapter will be hired by you, and in most cases you will pay a fee.

OUTPLACEMENT

You may well be "on outplacement" as you read this, or anticipating that possibility. Outplacement services are contracted for by an employer to help in the transition of one or more employees out of the company and into a new situation. The extent and type of outplacement assistance purchased vary widely. At minimum, it may consist of one or more workshops on resumé writing, interviewing, and other job hunting skills, with several one-on-one consultations with an outplacement counselor. At the other extreme, outplacement assistance may include briefing and preparation of the manager doing the firing, including advice on the time, place, and details of the dismissal meeting; intervention by outplacement personnel immediately after the employee is dismissed (termed a "take-out" session); intensive counseling of the dismissed employee and spouse in the ensuing weeks; detailed assistance in job search techniques; and office space and secretarial assistance at the outplacement firm's facilities.

Because the nature and duration of outplacement packages vary widely, some dismissed employees spend as little as several hours with an outplacement counselor. Others have access to outplacement services until they find a new position. It all depends on the product your former employer has chosen and the amount the company is willing to pay. At the low end, fees currently run in the range of $500 to $1,000 per employee. At the high end, outplacement firms charge a percentage of annual salary (ranging from 10 to 20 percent) with discounts depending on the number of individuals being outplaced and the competitive situation.

Outplacement is a relatively recent concept. The industry grew rapidly during the career dislocations of the late 1970s and 1980s. Currently, over 200 firms offer outplacement service as their primary business; in addition, some career counselors provide outplacement assistance. Some outplacement firms also offer "preventative" services to clients—to identify poor fit situations at an early stage and design corrective action that avoids the trauma of an abrupt and unexpected dismissal. Others offer retirement counseling for clients whose candidates for outplacement are more interested in planning for that phase of life than in securing a new position.

Since most employers decide on the outplacement services offered departing employees, you may have little say in the outplacement arrangements made for you. *However,* most managers have *more* leverage in these situations than they exercise. Here are our guidelines to maximizing the benefits of outplacement:

1. *Ask for outplacement assistance.* Do your homework (see below) so that you are clear on what will further your campaign. Have a good idea of the outplacement services of greatest importance to you, and those you would trade off. *Don't forego a benefit that may well be yours for the asking. You are entitled!*

2. *Outplacement or money?* Some firms may offer you the equivalent of all or a portion of the outplacement fee in cash. Only you know your financial circumstances, your access to comparable services, and what is critical to your campaign. Again, do your homework: ascertain exactly what you are being offered, and meet with the person who will be counseling you (as opposed to the engagement manager). Company-paid outplacement has a practical advantage: you will not be tempted to spend the money on something else. And depending on the outplacement firm and your employer's management of that relationship, you may receive more assistance than if you arranged for your own counseling.

3. *If possible, select your outplacement firm.* If your outplacement program is part of a package deal, you may not have this option. However,

if your employer has decided to pay a certain fee for your outplacement and is open to your input, shop around among several outplacement firms. Your ex-employer may use multiple vendors, for example, each with a different package and approach. Some may be real estate intensive, providing offices and support functions. Others may be counseling-intensive, giving you more one-on-one counseling time. Even if people from the outplacement firm are already in the next room to speak with you, you have the right to ask about the possibility of considering alternatives. Ask friends who have been through the process to give you their recommendations. At a minimum, be sure you have confidence in the individual who will be your counselor. This is no time to work with someone with whom you feel uncomfortable. Trust your instincts here. Further information on outplacement firms, including a current directory, is available from Kennedy Publications, Templeton Road, Fitzwilliam, NH 03447 (603-385-2200).

4. *Criteria for selecting outplacement firms.* When assessing various firms, ask to speak with people who are going through the firm's outplacement process or who have completed it. An outplacement firm that does a good job should not have reservations about letting you talk with managers they have counseled. Have your priorities for outplacement in mind, and ask clear, direct questions to understand a particular firm's approach. If you will be using their facilities, check out where you'll be working. Will you be working in a different space every day, or do you have a designated area? Where is the support staff located? How are phone calls handled? Meet the counselor who would be working with you. Get in writing the specifics of the services you will receive for the fee your employer is paying; don't assume you are getting the same package as a colleague who had outplacement from the same firm. Determine the period of time they will assist you; is there a cap on the hours of counseling time or the number of months you can use the office?

5. *Work with the outplacement firm.* After you have chosen a firm, give it your enthusiastic cooperation and full attention. Buy into the process. The outplacement process may take some adjustment, and it may not always be enjoyable, but it can give you useful guidance and an all-important discipline.

CAREER COUNSELORS

This category refers to firms or individuals who charge for their services *on an hourly or task basis.* Many firms and individuals offer career assistance for a fee, some highly qualified and working to high standards, others not. The fees range widely and do not always indicate quality. Group career assistance is usually less expensive than one-on-one; you may choose to split your budget for career assistance between group participation and individual counseling.

To find an effective career counselor for your particular situation, explore a variety of avenues. Ask your friends, especially those who have gone through a career transition. Consult the people you know in counseling roles: ministers and rabbis, guidance counselors, therapists and human resource professionals. If you are in the market for a career counselor, we recommend the following:

1. *Meet with the person who will be your counselor* for one session. This worthwhile investment will give you a good sense of the fit between you, the services offered, and the fee arrangements. Ask all of your questions about the process: how frequently you would meet, the likely duration of the process, what you will be expected to do, and what your counselor will do. Register how comfortable you are with the person. Let your instincts guide you.

2. *Ask to speak with current or previous clients.* Every reputable counselor has satisfied clients who are willing to speak with prospective clients. If a counselor balks at this request, citing confidentiality or any other rationale, move on to your next name.

3. *Make a change* if you don't feel you're getting your money's worth after the first several sessions. A good counselor should make you work hard, with lots of homework between sessions. If you are failing to do the homework, a responsible counselor will address the issue by altering his or her approach to suit your situation or, in some cases, questioning the value of your continuing with appointments at this juncture.

4. *Expect solid coaching, professionalism, and support.* A competent counselor will take you through a combination of self-awareness exercises and practical job search techniques. He or she will give you impartial insights and strong support. A counselor will not find you a job, any more than your tennis coach will play in the tournament for you. That's up to you, and never forget that.

5. *Recognize if and when you need a career counselor.* If you have the discipline to plan and implement a self-assessment and marketing campaign and the willingness to seek out the help and support of friends, you are capable of working on your own. Even in this case it may be useful to have a good counselor to check in with periodically,

just to ensure you're not overlooking anything. If you know yourself well enough to know that you need a superimposed structure or that you won't get around to forming a board of advisers, find a good career counselor. Doing so is the most responsible step you can take.

"MATCHING SERVICES" OR "EXECUTIVE GUIDANCE" FIRMS: WATCH OUT!

Preying on the vast number of people who are out of work or in other career difficulties are a number of organizations often more skilled at eliciting fees than providing services. They take a variety of forms and guises, but the common denominator to their spiel is, *"Leave the work to us; we'll find you a job."* This type of firm has a seductive appeal to the average manager, especially the executive accustomed to hiring specialists. Take a look at the classified ads in the *Wall Street Journal* or other business publications and note the skillful wording: "Your time is too valuable to waste in looking for a job." "Maximize your career opportunities." "State-of-the-art information." "We know how to find the top positions." "Get maximum market exposure in the shortest amount of time." "Employ the services of a firm that will match you up with a better job—at more money." Lump-sum fees of $5,000 or more, paid up front, are not uncommon with these firms.

If they delivered on their promises, matching services would be a prominent factor in the career market rather than a fringe group. The attractive concept of all current job openings computerized for matching with the right candidate remains an elusive dream. Some firms have lists of positions, and some may offer introductions to people you'd like to reach. If you could work with a number of these firms and pay only the firm that "matched" you with the right job, this might be a logical part of your job search. But if you are asked for a fee up front, decide whether you are spending money on a valid service or on a wishful expectation.

SPECIAL TASK FIRMS

Among the resources available to the job-changer are firms or individuals who perform specific tasks for a fee: resumé writing, interview training, letter typing and mailing, telephone answering, and video-taped rehearsals for upcoming presentations. These firms offer attractive services to the executive accustomed to delegating menial tasks. And in particular cases, an interviewing workshop or letter service can make all the difference to your campaign.

Your use of these firms will be dictated in part by your financial situation. However, even if money is no object, certain tasks should *not* be delegated. The primary example, in our opinion, is the preparation of your resumé. This is a very personal item; to be an effective marketing piece it must reflect *you* in every way. Each resumé preparation service develops a certain way of doing things, a "look" that can be spotted by knowledgeable people in the business. As discussed in Chapter 15, we feel strongly that the design and contents of your resumé need to be *your* decision. Hand over the mechanics of layout and typesetting to a specialist firm, if you like, but the choice of typeface, the color and weight of the paper, and the "look" of your resumé are your responsibility.

NO- OR LOW-FEE SUPPORT SERVICES

Look for other kinds of career services, particularly those sponsored by an organization that defrays some or all of the cost to you. This is no time to isolate yourself, and any one of these services might provide invaluable support during this transition. Some examples:

- An increasing number of churches and synagogues have set up career support groups. For example, fifteen are meeting in Fairfield County, Connecticut, alone as of this writing. Check your area.
- Some mutual interest groups facilitate networking and job search contacts. For example, at the New York Venture Group's monthly breakfast meeting, which brings together management candidates, investors, consultants, and professionals in various aspects of business, time is allotted for anyone to stand up and make a one-minute announcement. Check your area to find similar opportunities.
- Your college or graduate school career development office, your alumni/ae association, or your local college club may provide a wide range of services, including sponsoring formal or informal programs dealing with career issues. Harvard Business School has an Alumni Career Services Office. Yale University provides a list of alumni/ae resource people arranged by industry to the local Yale club in every city. In New York, the Yale Alumni Association of Metropolitan New York has a sophisticated network of over a dozen coordinators and

several thousand resource people. If you aren't a member of your own alumni/ae association and local club, join and keep your eyes open!

Not all of these resources may serve your needs and interests, but you won't know until you check them out. Of the many career assistance resources available, you must determine which represent attractive cost/benefit potential for your specific situation, and verify—as you would with any consultant or vendor of services to your company—that the promised services will be delivered.

19

CLOSING THE SALE: THE FINAL STAGES OF THE JOB SEARCH

Your marketing campaign has resulted in successful contacts with all your target firms. In each situation, based on your prior research of the company's situation and your well-practiced presentation, you have articulated and demonstrated your relevant attributes in a manner that has impressed the people you have met. As the tone of the interviews shifts, the emphasis is no longer on whether you can do the job. Companies are now in a selling mode, doing their best to convince you to come with them.

In an unforgettable week, you receive offers from three firms (or make it four or five—this is your fantasy). Negotiations ensue, each firm bidding against the other. Finally, the last offers are in, and you select the best package—which is much richer than you had ever anticipated. The successful firm is ecstatic, the losers are gracious and promise to keep in touch with you. Your new boss enthusiastically agrees that you deserve a one-month vacation before you come to work and generously puts you on the payroll *now* so your benefits and salary will be accruing while you're basking on the beach!

A delightful fantasy, without question, but seldom do searches wrap up so neatly or so effortlessly. Job offers tend to come in one at a time—frustrating your efforts to compare *A* versus *B*. The job offer you most want gets snarled up with politics or key-people-on-vacation factors, and you are forced to make a go/no-go decision on a less attractive offer you had been planning to save as a fallback.

"How can I keep offer *A* on hold until I can get company *B* to make an offer?" That's a frequently asked question at the HBSCNY Career Seminar, and there's no easy answer. You may be able to buy some time by requesting additional information, a visit to a job-related location, or further discussions with people in the firm. Slowing down the process requires careful strategizing, influenced by factors such as the strength of your negotiating position, the availability of backup candidates, and the firm's sense of urgency. As you can recall from your hiring experience, once a company makes an offer, management will be impatient to get your response, fill the job, and move on to the many matters set aside during the recruitment process.

Some how-to-get-a-job manuals recommend orchestrating your initial contacts with prospective employers to increase the probability that offers will come in simultaneously. In real life, the job search process does not progress at a predictable rate. Rather than be dismayed by your inability to orchestrate the conclusion of your search, regard it with the perspective of the CEO of your job search (see Chapter 3). Accept that you have only limited control of the situation, and identify the factors over which you *can* exert some influence. Understand your role in this critical phase of the job search, particularly the do's and don'ts that many job seekers overlook. This chapter does not cover all the facets of this complex topic, especially since the factors involved in salary negotiations vary widely according to the size and nature of the company and the level and bargaining position of the candidate. Rather, we offer an overview of topics for your awareness and mastery.

ELEMENTS IN THE FINAL PHASE OF THE JOB SEARCH

If you are at the *beginning* of your job search and marketing campaign, become familiar with the final-stage elements discussed in this chapter now. Certain elements are best considered as you move through your campaign: when you reach the final stages of your search, you may not have sufficient time or patience to assemble all of the necessary information.

Here is an overview of the final-phase elements:

I. Line up your references.
   A. References to validate facts (education, employment, job titles, dates)
   B. References with comments on your work effectiveness
   C. High-priority endorsers

II. Prepare for the negotiations.
   A. Research relocation factors.
      1. Cost of living in the new area (taxes, housing costs, need for private schools, etc.)
      2. Moving expenses that are customarily reimbursed by the employer

      3. Other relocation costs and probability of reimbursement (loss on house sale, increased mortgage rates, spouse visits to new location, temporary housing, etc.)

      4. Your spouse's employment prospects

  B. Line up the employment/compensation package.

      1. Exact job description (reporting relationships, responsibilities, scope of authority, accountability, goals, critical success factors, etc.)

      2. Base salary; time of next salary review

      3. Incentive compensation (commission, incentive formula and payout, deferred compensation, profit-sharing, performance shares, stock options, restricted stock, etc.)

      4. Bonus (range, likelihood, how determined, recent track record)

      5. Perquisites (car, club memberships, enhanced insurance, low-cost loans, free legal assistance, etc.)

      6. Employment contract/termination agreement (customary? possible?)

      7. Sign-on bonus

  C. Evaluate the fringe benefits.

      1. Pension plan (relative contribution by company and employee)

      2. 401K plan

      3. Insurance (life, disability, travel, and accident); who pays?

      4. Medical plan (limits, deductible, waiting period, restrictions for pre-existing conditions, employee's share of premiums)

      5. Vacation policy

      6. Education assistance

      7. Savings and thrift plans

III. Negotiate your employment/compensation package.

IV. Formalize your acceptance.

  A. Written summary of terms.

  B. Wrap up your search.

  C. Spread the good news.

REFERENCES AND REFERENCE CHECKING

As you formulate your marketing campaign, identify individuals to serve as references. Organize your references into three categories:

1. People who can verify employment term, compensation, and responsibilities at the preliminary stages of reference checking;
2. Individuals who have observed you in action and can describe your performance;
3. Senior executives who, while they may not have had a day-to-day working relationship with you, are prepared to give you a very favorable and substantive endorsement.

Do not give out your references until the appropriate stage of the interviewing process: unnecessary calls will wear out their patience and goodwill. A good interviewer will contact other references outside of your list, but have a ready list of people to support your candidacy.

Take time to brief your references on the role you would like each to play. Make sure references in the first category are clear about the years, salary, title, and scope of your employment. Check back with them periodically to give an update on your search and to determine which of your prospective employers have been in contact.

Speak to references in the second and third category *each time* you give their names to a prospective employer. Describe the position, your most relevant skills and experience, and the hot buttons you have determined to be most important to the potential employer. Remind each reference of one or two specific accomplishments that reinforce your fit with the job. Convey your enthusiasm; it will spur their efforts on your behalf and it won't hurt you if they communicate your eagerness to your prospective boss. That said, beware of excessive coaching that could compromise the effectiveness of your references.

Use your third category of references to promote your candidacy in the final stages. After briefing them on the position and your key selling points, ask them to call a pivotal person in the hiring decision. "You have a terrific candidate in Karen. As [one CEO to another] I'd like you to know what a contribution her work made to our firm." Calls like this can be key to closing the search—in your favor.

If you are currently employed, organize the reference process to guard against word of your candidacy getting out prematurely. Except where you would be fired on the spot or severely compromised in your ability to do your job, your boss should be aware of your job search or at least aware that you are not completely satisfied with your present situation. You may be able to line up one or two trustworthy confidants in your present firm who can be contacted in lieu of your boss to satisfy reference checking requirements. If not, ask prospective employers to contact your other references and to make the job offer *contingent* on verification of your present employment after you have accepted the offer and are ready to give notice.

One final word. Offers contingent upon references are a fairly common practice. This is where lack of integrity can have unfortunate ramifications. A candidate accepts an offer, severs ties with his or her current job—only to have the offer retracted because of a discrepancy between final reference checks and resumé or interviewing statements. We know of candidates who have been persuaded to falsify their resumés—claiming to still work at a job they've left months earlier or inflating a job title—only to have the offer retracted when reference checks proved the data false. Be honest in your claims. Brief your references to eliminate any chance of miscommunication.

NEGOTIATIONS

Negotiating the employment package—including salary, other forms of compensation, perquisites, other-than-standard fringe and employee benefits, and relocation expenses—is yet another part of the job search process where you can bring your business experience to bear. Perhaps negotiating has been a significant part of your business life; if so, make sure you bring to *this* negotiation the experience and skill you use on the job. If your business experience has not included much negotiating, look back over past negotiation experiences—for a used car, for example—and learn from them. Where you have succeeded, remember the critical success factors. Where you might have done better, call on the expertise of your board, and use your network to find an experienced negotiator who can coach you. Be sure you feel confident in your negotiating abilities before the negotiations begin.

Assets and Liabilities

If you've followed the *In Transition* process, you are undoubtedly better equipped for the upcoming negotiations than you realize:

- You are very clear about what you have to offer the company; you are professing to be no less or no more than you are.
- Your market research has generated information about the company's salary structure and other compensation practices, which puts you in possession of key negotiating data.

- You have set the stage for a negotiation based on cost/benefit considerations by presenting your skills and experience for the job in a convincing manner.
- You have made a positive impression as someone who will fit in well with the company culture, so the people with whom you will be negotiating are predisposed to close the deal.

Assess your negotiating position, particularly the points in your favor. Be aware that subtle points can be very important. As one recruiter with many years of experience put it, "If there's a love affair, money becomes a secondary matter."

A word of caution: just as some competent salespeople have difficulty selling themselves, managers not uncommonly encounter internal obstacles to negotiating on their own behalf. Assess your feelings about negotiating to detect any self-sabotaging tendencies, such as these:

- You may back off when the negotiation phase arrives, using rationalizations such as, "I don't want to alienate my future boss" or "I'm sure the company will pay fairly." If throughout your life, both in your upbringing and in your work experience, the message has been, "Take what you're offered, do as you're told, don't question directions or authority," it will be particularly difficult to recognize this tendency to retreat from negotiating
- You may see negotiating situations as a commentary on your *self-worth* rather than your talents related to this position. You may lose your objectivity and become involved in negotiations on a personal and even emotional level. In such circumstances you are at a negotiating disadvantage and will raise doubts about your competence in the minds of people who would be working with you.
- You may resent that negotiating is even *necessary*. "Why is the prospective employer holding back on what I am entitled to? Perhaps this is not the kind of firm to work for if I have to *fight* for what I'm worth."

These are just a few of the ways people handicap their ability to negotiate effectively. Be honest with yourself about anything that could sabotage your negotiating the best possible package. Discuss strategies to compensate with your board and your personal advisers. Have a clear understanding of the employment negotiation process for what it is: a means of obtaining appropriate compensation for skills and experience of significant value to your prospective employer. The more diligently you have done your self-assessment and market research, the easier negotiating will be.

Prior to and throughout the negotiating process, put on your *marketing hat* for a fresh perspective. As a marketer your responsibility is to get the best possible price for you-the-product; the buyer's responsibility is to pay the lowest price. Negotiating is completely appropriate in these circumstances. And remember, the higher the agreed-upon price, the higher your perceived value, so you are working in your best interest to negotiate well.

Negotiating Pointers

Now that you are persuaded of the importance of negotiating, it's time to develop specific strategies and techniques. Tailor these to the situation: the company culture, your bargaining position, the nature and level of the position, the degree of risk involved, the complexity of the compensation package, and whether or not attorneys are involved in the negotiating process. Seek, assess, and heed the counsel of advisers with negotiating expertise.

Keep in mind these pointers:

The More Information You Have, the Stronger Your Position

As you approach the negotiation stage, use your network and market research contacts assertively to gather information on the company's policies, estimates of specific salary ranges, and other pertinent data.

Reveal Little Salary Information during the Early Stages of Interviewing

Some discussion of salary is difficult to avoid, since a prospective employer needs to know whether your requirements approximate the compensation specified for the position. Develop interviewing techniques that respect the employer's need without disadvantaging yourself. Remember that it is appropriate to defer discussion of your salary requirements until the job has been fully defined and you have described your relevant skills and experience.

Below are several techniques to consider, depending on your circumstances:

1. Focus on the *position* each time the subject of salary arises. For example, "My impression from both our discussions and my knowledge of the industry is that this position is in line with my compensa-

tion requirements, but perhaps this is a good time to confirm that; has a salary range been set?" or "You know this job well; what is it worth in this company?"

2. Prepare several techniques for handling questions about your current or previous salary. You might stress that your present or previous job circumstances were determinant—a booming market on Wall Street, an underfunded nonprofit—so your past salary may not be relevant to the position under discussion. Your response should emphasize that you want to fit into *this* organization's culture and compensation structure.

3. While well-prepared responses may enable you to parry salary questions in a constructive manner, you must have an answer ready if push comes to shove. You might talk about salary in terms of the *future:* "I would judge that this job, if done in an exemplary manner, would pay in the range of $____ two or three years from now. That would be acceptable from my standpoint." Or if you have solid data, "My research indicates that this job probably pays about $____ [name the *high* end of the salary range you've determined by your market research]. Given the nature of the job and its prospects, that seems reasonable to me."

4. If you have demonstrated capabilities relevant to the job, you might respond to a question about salary by joking, "Is this a job offer?" The question of price arises only when the buyer is interested. By confirming that you are considered right for the job, you further strengthen your negotiating position.

Be Clear about Your Value

If you are currently employed, a switching premium of at least 10 to 20 percent is customary. If you are not employed, the prospective employer may begin with a lower figure. Your state of mind and clarity about your value vis-à-vis the position can have its strongest influence in these circumstances. Establish an air of self-assurance in the early stages of interviewing, based on a strong sense of self-esteem—the fruit of your self-assessment. Make sure you don't undervalue yourself as you move into the negotiations.

Manage the Salary Discussion Phase

When the interviewing process has reached the point where both parties feel positive about the fit, salary will come up again. Unlike earlier rounds of screening questions, this time the interviewer has a salary range in mind, as well as a starting point within that range. If your research has given you a good idea of that range, name a figure on the high end. Otherwise, get the interviewer to name a figure, saying something like, "Our discussions have indicated I could bring a great deal to this company, but I'd like my salary to be consistent with your company's culture as well as my value. I'm sure your compensation structure is fair; what salary do you have in mind?"

Keep Your Mouth Shut

Whatever salary figure is named, keep quiet and give it respectful consideration. Quite possibly, the interviewer will raise the figure during your silence. When you do speak, first reaffirm your interest and enthusiasm about the position and the company. Then—unless the figure exceeds your wildest expectation—indicate that you feel the figure is on the modest side. Use wording that avoids criticism, such as, "Is this a figure we can increase?" Leave the door open for further negotiations by regarding the figure as indicative but not definitive, to be considered in the context of the total employment package. *Never accept or reject a salary offer on the spot.*

See the Entire Package before You Accept

It is very difficult to negotiate for anything once you have accepted an offer. An employer may try to get your acceptance of each piece of the package as it is offered. Remember that it is in *your* best interest to hold off until all parts of the package are on the table. Only then should true negotiations begin.

Don't Resist Third-Party Involvement

Another variable in the negotiations is the person or persons with whom you negotiate. You may not have much say in this, but consider how you might influence this aspect of the process. At some point, you want to negotiate directly with the person who has the greatest need of your services and the greatest sense of urgency about bringing you on board. However, if the company puts a human resources person or recruiter into the negotiating role, it *can* work to your advantage. An intermediary can put forth negotiating positions on behalf of you or the company. Both sides can maintain a certain flexibility, thereby avoiding a premature "take it or leave it" stance.

Keep in mind the role and relative authority of each person in the process. A third party is not a *neutral* party. Any one person may have limited authority to modify or enhance the terms of your offer. To allow for internal consultations, be agreeable to carrying over your discussion until the following day. Consider taking the initiative by asking for a day to think things over.

Weigh the Elements of the Package

Know the importance to you of the *compensation package* in relation to the *entire* employment package. Try to address what is important to you first and reach a tentative agreement on that priority, contingent upon the results of further negotiations. For example, if you are facing a loss on the sale of your home, relocation reimbursement will be a high priority. Conversely, your compensation package may be all you really care about. As with other negotiating factors, you may not have much control over the sequence of negotiations, but you *can* influence at what point you agree on each part of the package.

Maintain a Good Sense of Timing

If negotiations finalize too quickly, you most likely have left something on the table. If negotiations drag on too long, you risk jeopardizing your image as an incisive manager or even having the offer withdrawn. To guard against bringing up a new issue late in the negotiations or appearing to nit-pick, be sure to touch on *all* relevant issues early on, based on the list you have prepared in advance and checked with your advisers. Resolve the easy issues quickly so you can spend more time dealing with the major issues. If you handle employment negotiations well, you will enhance your stature with your new employer.

Use One Offer to Improve Another

If you are fortunate enough to have *more than one* offer, you are in a strong negotiating position provided you take advantage of the opportunity. With your board or negotiating coach, formulate your strategy for using one offer to leverage another. Avoid anything that hints of blackmail or bluff; be sincere and tactful. To compare offers objectively, prepare a worksheet, and write down the financial packages side by side. Use your product specifications and the conclusions from your self-assessment exercises as a yardstick to assess the fit of each position. Use your board to ensure objectivity in case one of the companies has done a particularly good sales job.

Get It in Writing

When all points have been negotiated and a verbal agreement reached, get it in writing—a simple letter listing all the elements of the package. Take a day to think over the list, but don't drag your feet. Once you make a decision, give your acceptance directly to your new boss if at all possible. Leave yourself some time before your start date to organize things, as we discuss below.

NEGOTIATING THROUGH A RECRUITER

If you were introduced to the firm by a recruiter, he or she will have a major role in orchestrating the closing phase of the search. This is particularly true for *retainer* recruiters, who have a close working relationship with the client; in the case of *contingency* recruiters, the employer may choose to take a more active role. An experienced, responsible recruiter can be a great asset in negotiations. The recruiter is representing the client's interests; however, he or she knows the market and in most cases will earn a fee based on a percentage of your compensation. Whatever the arrangements, cooperate with the recruiter but do not rely on him or her to look after *your* interests.

A recruiter's role in discussing compensation changes over the course of the search. In the initial stages the recruiter determines whether your salary requirements are in line with the client firm's compensation specification for the position, and gives you a ballpark indication of that compensation range. As the interviewing process unfolds, the recruiter explores more fully your thoughts about the employment package and compensation in particular. Maintain some flexibility in these early discussions.

Prior to substantive discussions about compensation, use your network to get an estimate of the salary for the position and for equivalent positions both within the organization and at other comparable firms. Discuss your findings with the recruiter in a low-key but assertive fashion. If your market information is accurate and your reasoning sound, you may influence the salary offered you. If the figure you name is out of line with the salary for the position, you can clarify the reasons (possibly factors you have not considered) and decide whether to remain in the running.

When you become a finalist, the recruiter takes an active role in the offer and negotiation process. If the compensation package is large or complex, lawyers representing the company's and your interests will also be involved. Some recruiters are quite expert in the role of honest broker, shepherding the negotiations along, avoiding counterproductive or confrontational situations, ensuring clear communications, and dissuading either side from taking unreasonable positions. Especially in situations of differing cultures or customs, such as recruiting situations that cross national borders, the recruiter can perform a useful interpreter role to avoid disruptive errors in perception.

That said, don't rely solely on the recruiter in your negotiations. Have face-to-face discussions with your prospective boss to demonstrate first-hand how competently you handle negotiations. Establish that your request for a better package is based on competence and confidence about your fit for the position. A recruiter is an intermediary in the negotiations who wants to conclude the search—but is likely to have one or more reserve candidates to fall back on if you and the client cannot reach an agreement.

After all the elements of the package have been agreed on, be sure the recruiter gets it all down in writing. The deal should not be wrapped up until both parties have read the description of the package and agreed it is correct.

EMPLOYMENT CONTRACTS AND OTHER CONTRACTUAL AGREEMENTS

The term *employment contract* is a misnomer; a contract does not—and cannot—bind the employee to the employer. Such agreements are essentially anticipatory separation/termination agreements, covering what will happen if employment ceases. For that reason it may be difficult to propose such a contract as a significant part of your employment package without appearing to contradict expressions of enthusiasm and optimism about the job.

If the position involves a significant degree of risk, your request for such an agreement is more likely to be perceived as appropriate. Joining a severely undercapitalized new venture, stepping in as part of a turn-around management team, taking a position in a war-torn country, or working for a foreign employer might each qualify as a risky situation. If there is no such obvious justification and you are not in a strong negotiating position, insisting on an employment contract could prejudice your candidacy. If you feel strongly about getting a contract, determine the firm's policy well in advance of negotiations. If you do decide to go forward, discuss your strategy with your advisers, and have a third party (the recruiter, human resources contact, or—if he or she is already involved in the process—your attorney) present your proposal. Be ready to respond to questions such as, "Do you have doubts about taking the position?"

As an alternative to a separate contract, consider including in your letter of agreement several key provisions. For example, you might specify a minimum term of employment or a certain level of outplacement, terms agreed to in the negotiations but less controversial in this form.

THE CONCLUSION—AND THE BEGINNING

Congratulations on successfully completing the negotiations! You rightfully feel a sense of accomplishment—and relief. Your new boss can't wait for you to begin; there is much to be done, and you are eager to get back in the saddle.

Hold it! Take a little time to wrap up your job search campaign properly; it will be in your long-term interest.

1. Ensure that your entire employment package—the results of your thorough negotiations—is in a written form satisfactory to your advisers, including your attorney if size or complexity require.
2. Contact *all* the people who assisted you in your job search campaign to share your good news. They represent an ongoing resource for information, contacts, and advice related to your new position. They deserve a personal "Thank-you!" Call some; write others; for many, a letter with your new business card will suffice.
3. Arrange some kind of special recognition for the members of your board.
4. In the enthusiasm about your new opportunity, don't forget family and close friends who hung in there with you during the peaks and valleys.

Organize your *In Transition* materials, and put them in an accessible file. Refer back to your self-assessment notes periodically to ensure that you're still headed in the correct direction. Keep your product specifications clearly in mind, particularly your top six priorities and bottom six trade-offs, to avert any tendency to revisit your decision under a cloud of "shoulda done's." If you encounter a particularly sticky situation at work, check back to find out if you're reverting to an old pattern; review your options, and use the helpful questions, "What game are we playing?" and "Do I want to play that game?" You may find it helpful to use some of the *In Transition* materials on the job: the Myers-Briggs, for example, is extremely useful for facilitating day-to-day organizational interactions.

Finally, you will quite likely find yourself referring back to your job search file when you encounter friends and acquaintances in career difficulties. Having successfully gone through the *In Transition* process, you have something valuable to offer: how-to-do-it advice, words of assurance, and the wisdom to step aside when your involvement would put you in that invested advice category discussed in Chapter 2. Many past participants of the HBSCNY Career Seminar have recounted their satisfaction at being able to pass on to others the good news about the potential inherent in a transition as well as specific empowering techniques. As one person put it, "The process made such a positive change in my life, I regard it as a gift to be shared with others."

20

A RECAP OF THE *IN TRANSITION* PROCESS: A CHECKLIST

USE YOUR CHECKLIST

Even the most experienced pilot wouldn't think of taking off until he or she had gone through the preflight checklist. There are too many items to remember, some of which must be done in a certain sequence. And memory is unreliable at times, especially when dealing with routine or unexciting tasks. This chapter contains an exhaustive checklist covering all aspects of a career transition. Not all of the items listed will apply to your situation, but you may find them useful in a future transition. The checklist serves several purposes:

1. To provide an overview of the *In Transition* process;
2. To ensure that you don't overlook any aspect of the process;
3. To give you a document that can be reviewed with those close to you so that they can understand what you're doing and, where appropriate, provide useful input;
4. To help you keep a perspective as you proceed on your job search;
5. To facilitate, along with your written marketing campaign, discussions with your board about actual versus projected progress;
6. To help you decide on modifications or enhancements to your campaign.

The sequence of the items on the checklist is important; the actual time spent on each will vary with the individual. In practice, many of the items overlap and occur simultaneously. Use the list to manage your job search effectively.

> When you're in a career transition, it's a lot like starting up and running your own business. After I realized that, it got easier. I just told myself

each morning that I was in the business of getting a job. First thing each day I would have a management meeting (myself and the dog) where we'd go over the business plan, review the goals for the week and set up the tasks for the day. Then I'd put on my salesman hat—or production hat or whatever the task was for the day—and get cracking. Putting the job search in a business context made it a lot easier to organize and get things done—especially the tasks that I hate doing.

FOUNDER, NONPROFIT CONSULTING FIRM, HBS '68

A REMINDER: DON'T OVERLOOK THE SELF-ASSESSMENT PROCESS

The temptation with a list like this is to skip the preparatory part and plunge into the *action* portion. Although understandable, that approach is risky. Keep in mind these analogies:

- A pilot must systematically go over the preflight checklist to avoid potential mishaps.
- An explorer starting out for a trek across the desert must recheck provisions to ensure all is in order to prevent a shortage of critical provisions midway through the journey.
- A sailor, impatient to take advantage of the tide and wind, must keep mindful that an oversight in preparation can have dire results at sea.

Management theory experts stress that managers should spend more time thinking, planning, and strategizing. Most likely, your life—business and otherwise—is typified by *action.* What does the "ideal manager" (your perception or model) do when faced with a problem, obstacle, or low morale? Act! Get results! Leave contemplation and introspection to philosophers and theorists. But planning *does* save time. Do your homework and *then* get going.

As we discussed in Part 2, in more than ten years of using the *In Transition* process in the HBSCNY Career Seminar, the most successful case histories involve people who did a *thorough job of self-assessment.* Some changed careers; some remained where they were. They consider themselves more successful because each understands what success means for him or her. Personal priorities inform their allocation of time and energy. For each, life has become more fulfilling.

A MINICHECKLIST FOR RECENTLY DISPLACED MANAGERS

If you've suddenly lost your job:

Don't Immediately

- Update your resumé.
- Start interviewing.
- Radically change your life-style.
- Go on an extended vacation.
- Sign a contract with someone who will help you for a lump-sum fee.
- Put your house on the market, sell stocks, auction antiques, cash in your insurance policy, or otherwise act precipitously.

Do

- Make a complete list of all your network resources (see Chapter 14).
- Do the list of life accomplishments for the Intrinsic Skills Exercise in Chapter 7. This should take at least *five* hours, spread over the course of a week; don't rush it!
- List the support systems available to you (see Chapters 3, 13, and 14 and item IV of the following checklist).
- Read "Congratulations on Your Good News" (Chapter 1).
- Review the remainder of this outline.
- Start at Chapter 1 and skim through the book.
- If your ex-employer has offered you *outplacement,* read Chapter 18 thoroughly.

The checklist below consists of three broad categories: getting perspective (items I, II, and III), practical realities (items IV and V), and the *In Transition* process (items VI and VII). *Work on practical realities and the In Transition process concurrently.*

THE CHECKLIST

    I. Give yourself a break.
        A. Dealing with your own career issues is *not* easy.
            1. The "my job/my identity" syndrome
            2. The "stigma" of joblessness
            3. Internal issues

B. Your managerial experience *is* applicable, once you realize it.

C. The fact that you're considering the *In Transition* process means you've taken a positive first step.

D. Resolve to use the current situation to your advantage and to give *yourself* top priority.

E. Stretch your perspective.

    1. Acknowledge that, just as in business, you may not yet see the whole picture: what looks like a setback or a failure may, in reality, be an *opportunity*.

    2. Read *The Road Less Traveled* by M. Scott Peck (New York: Simon & Schuster, 1978) or another similar book[1] to broaden your perspective.

II. Get an overview of the process you are about to undertake.

  A. Skim through this book.

    1. Introduction and Part 1: a warm-up and perspective on the self-assessment and self-marketing process

    2. Part 2: the self-assessment process: essential to knowing you-the-product

    3. Part 3: the self-marketing process: market assessment and self-marketing, techniques you are already familiar with in other contexts

  B. Familiarize yourself with other resources.

    1. Buy *What Color Is Your Parachute* by Richard N. Bolles and *skim* through it, including the numerous resources listed in the final sections.

    2. Speak with friends who have successfully gone through a similar experience; find out what resources were useful to them.

    3. Consider working with a career counselor to facilitate the process, but only one who works on an hourly fee basis (Chapter 18).

III. Adapt your management habits to the new situation.

  A. Balance your two roles of executive and implementer.

  B. Spend *one hour each day* reviewing and planning.

---

[1]Other recommended titles: Mary Catherine Bateman, *Composing a Life* (New York: Atlantic Monthly Press, 1989). Alice Koehler, *An Unknown Woman: A Journey to Self-Discovery* (New York: Bantam Books, 1983). Gerald O'Collins, *The Second Journey* (Mahwah, N.J.: Paulist Press, 1987). Carol Hyatt and Linda Gottlieb, *When Smart People Fail* (New York: Simon & Schuster, 1987). Daniel J. Levinson, *Seasons of a Man's Life* (New York: Ballantine Books, 1986). George Vaillant, *Adaptation to Life* (New York: Little, Brown & Co., 1977).

C. Practice being a *fair boss* to yourself.
  1. Set reasonable work loads.
  2. Reward yourself when the work is up to date.
D. Establish objective standards to measure progress.
  1. Beware of the clerical accomplishment syndrome; number of letters mailed or telephone calls placed may not be the best yardstick of productivity.
  2. Maintain objectivity by setting up and using your board (Chapter 3).
E. Remember that you have managed projects before, in a somewhat different situation. Transition territory is not as unfamiliar as it may seem at first.

IV. Assess and organize your support resources.
  A. Financial resources
    1. Set up a realistic budget; involve your family.
    2. Do a fallback budget and contingency plan which assumes your transition will last twice as long as you envision.
    3. Assess on a case-by-case basis the merits of involving members of your family as well as close friends. They are going through this with you; to what *extent* you involve each is your judgment call. Address their worst-case scenarios, which may be more terrifying than any conceivable reality.
    4. Reduce expenses.
      a. Be realistic: you must be able to live within your budget.
      b. Don't punish yourself: this is no time to cut the gym, stop seeing friends, or eliminate dry cleaning expenses.
      c. Keep some recreational activities: they are particularly essential during this time.
      d. Examine how cutting expenses will affect your life-style. A decision to cut down on home entertaining has both financial and social ramifications.
    5. Set up your borrowing resources.
      a. Bank lines of credit
      b. Home equity loan
      c. Borrowing against insurance policies
      d. Relatives, friends (hard to do, but better to discuss it early instead of when things get tight)

      6. Other fallback sources of financing
        a. Sale of assets (examples: heirlooms you are not attached to; get a current appraisal)
        b. Rental of idle second house
  B. Your personal support systems
      1. These support systems are as important as your financial support system.
      2. Your state of mind is the key factor: it depends on an effective support system.
      3. Appoint yourself CEO of your job search and form a board (Chapter 3).
      4. Your spouse or significant other may need to augment his or her support systems; you will be focused and sometimes distracted; discuss that reality.
      5. Test your support system: it should come through even when you don't ask for help or just want to hide out.
      6. Reconnect with the medical community. Get a physical, and ask your doctor for any symptoms you should bring to his or her attention.
  C. Internal support techniques
      1. Acceptance: of yourself, the people in your past, those you encounter in your search, your friends and family, your situation
      2. Humor: still the best tonic

V. Set up your office and business systems.
  A. Office facilities
      1. Assess the pros and cons of working at home; it requires *dedicated* work space.
      2. Consider office space with a friend or associate.
      3. Investigate rental suites with secretarial and communication services already set up; assess cost versus benefits.
  B. Communication systems
      1. Your telephone interface with the outside world must be reliable and businesslike.
        a. Home: evaluate answering machine versus answering service.
        b. Home: instruct everyone (including children, cleaning staff, and visitors) on answering the phone and message-taking procedure.

         c. Borrowed office: make arrangements for your calls to be effectively handled; be considerate of the extra work for the staff; pick up messages frequently.

         d. Call your number several times a week to make sure the appropriate image is coming through to callers.

    2. Fax machine options

         a. Arrange access to a friend's machine or a service.

         b. Purchase your own machine with a dedicated phone line.

C. Your "office services"

    1. Printed supplies

         a. Order stationery: business and personal size.

         b. Order calling cards.

         c. Aim for a high-quality, refined look; no gimmicks.

    2. Filing system

         a. Keep it well organized, in a place of its own.

         b. Set up effective follow-up system.

         c. Develop a cross-reference system to keep track of networking contacts.

    3. Typing/word processing

         a. Outside service

            (1) Get one, if only as a backup for overload times.

            (2) Selection factors: turnaround time, size of staff (if it's a one-person shop, check the backup), cost, location, and hours (you'll have to go there frequently), alternative means of relaying instructions to them (hard copy drop-off or fax is most reliable), word processing facilities for storing and retrieving your standard paragraphs, mail merge for standard mailings to multiple recipients

            (3) Check their references: obtain a list of clients, and call several.

         b. Doing your own typing

            (1) Be realistic: typing everything yourself risks overload, distraction from more important activities, and correspondence delays.

            (2) Beware the unproductive diversion of the job hunter, such as spending hours generating a typo-free letter.

            (3) A word processor is fast, has text storage capabilities, and does mail merge, but don't use a cheap-looking printer.

       (4) If you are not proficient on a word processor, take instruction: you'll save time and reduce frustration.

       (5) Word processors fail at the worst times. Have a typewriter or other backup means of self-generating "managerial" looking letters for the quick turn-around or other special situation.

    4. Other machines: purchase only the *essentials* at the outset; you'll find out what else is important as you go along. Don't waste money on the tempting toys in office supply stores and catalogs.

VI. Do your self-assessment (Part 2).
  A. Prepare your product specification file (Chapter 4)
  B. How Would You Like to Be Remembered? (Chapter 5)
  C. The Feature Magazine Article (Chapter 5)
  D. Your Life Mission Statement (Chapter 5)
  E. Your Priorities (Chapter 5)
  F. Your AVL Values Profile (Chapter 6)
  G. Your Myers-Briggs Type (Chapter 6) (do with someone trained in this instrument; see Chapter 6 for details on finding a qualified practitioner)
  H. Your McClelland Motivational Profile (Chapter 6)
  I. Your Intrinsic Skills (Chapter 7) (phone your order for the workbook per the instructions on the first page of Chapter 7)
  J. Your Environmental Fit Inventory (Chapter 8)
  K. Your Ideal Job (Chapter 10)
  L. Your Constraints (Chapter 10)
  M. Pulling it all together: Your Product Specification Sheet (Chapter 10)

VII. Develop a plan for marketing yourself in the job search (Part 3)
  A. You've completed your *product assessment.*
    1. Life goals
    2. Near-term priorities
    3. Skills
    4. Other attributes
    5. You-the-product defined in a product specification summary
  B. Next, do the *market assessment.*
    1. Develop your screen/sieve to evaluate the market in view of your product specifications (Chapter 12).

    2. Identify market segments of visceral interest; ask only, "Would I look forward to working in that field/function/position?"

    3. Develop a contact in each field or function of interest (see Chapter 14 on Networking).

    4. Conduct investigative interviews to determine your *fit* with markets of interest and the *probability* of employment (Chapter 12).

    5. Define your target market segments, based on a review of information gathered during investigative interviews; verify your conclusions with your board.

C. Develop your *marketing campaign.*

    1. Have an action-oriented plan with a timetable.

       a. Each phase with its goals

       b. Methodology for achieving each goal

    2. Recognize and provide for the realities of the job search (Chapter 13).

    3. Develop your list of *networking resources,* and strengthen your networking ability (Chapter 14).

    4. Prepare your *sales tools* (Chapter 15).

       a. Your *resumé:* draw from your list of accomplishments (Chapter 7); draft it, test it, redraft it, retest it—until it *works!*

       b. *Letters:* draft standard forms and paragraphs: give different categories of letters differing amounts of time.

       c. Your *basic networking pitch:* write, rehearse, revamp. Use!

    5. *Ads:* establish a procedure for screening publications and responding to ads for positions in your target market (Chapter 15).

    6. Develop your *interview techniques* (Chapter 16).

       a. Telephone interviews

       b. Face-to-face job interview

    7. Define how you will use *recruiters* in your campaign (Chapter 17).

VIII. Implement your campaign!

    A. Keep on keeping on: maintain the daily discipline and commitment to yourself to forge ahead.

    B. Course correction: be alert to indications that a change in direction or methodology may be needed; consult your board and act decisively.

C. Look after your well-being: if you sense you are flagging, reinforce your support systems (join a local group that meets weekly, hire a career counselor, get together with your board members more often).

D. If you start spinning your wheels, call a board meeting and reevaluate your strategy.

E. Stay the course. Keep your expectations *realistic.* Your efforts will pay off.

APPENDICES

APPENDIX A
PRIORITIES-GRID INSTRUCTIONS

STEP 1: Put your eighteen cards in alphabetical order, and beginning with co-workers, number each card in the right-hand corner (co-workers: 1, workplace: 18). Stack your cards in numerical order, 1 on top.

STEP 2: Take 1 (co-workers) and placing it directly to the left of your stack of cards, read your definitions of 1 and 2, or co-workers and contribution to society. Decide which is more important to you at this time. Looking at the grid, you will see that the first pair of numbers in the first column on the left are 1 and 2; circle your "forced choice" priority.

STEP 3: Turn over 2 and begin a "discard stack." You are now looking at 1 versus 3; again ask yourself to make a forced choice and circle your selection on the grid. Repeat this process with 1 versus 4, 1 versus 5 right on through to 1 versus 18. You are now finished with your 1 card.

STEP 4: Turn over your discard stack, now consisting of priority cards 2 through 18. Just as before, move 2 directly to the left of your large stack, to facilitate your doing the forced choice exercise with 2 as the constant. Again create a discard stack as you work your way through the second column on your priorities grid (2 versus 3, 2 versus 4, etc.).

STEP 5: Move across the priorities grid, repeating the process above until you have circled one of each pair of numbers. *Alert:* Avoid reading *any* one of your constant priorities (left side of column) and thinking, "I *know* this is more important than anything else so I won't bother to compare here." *Force yourself to examine each pair before selecting one priority.*

STEP 6: Tally the number of times you selected each priority.

Alert: Only 1's are in a vertical column exclusively; be sure to include horizontal selections in your count.

EXAMPLE: Take in every circled 7, not just those in the column beginning "7 8":

1 7   2 7   3 7   4 7   6 7   7 8
                                7 9
                                7 10
                                (et cetera)

Alert: In case of a two-way tie (for example, 4 and 16 each having been selected a total of seven times) find that pair on the grid. If you circled 4, consider that the more important priority of the two; similarly, if you circled 16, that is the more important.

Alert: In the case of a three-way tie, again look at the priority pairs involved. If 3, 12, and 13 were selected an equal number of times, consider these pairs: 3 12   3 13   12 13. If one priority was selected twice, one once, and one not at all, you have your tie broken. If each priority was selected once, you have a genuine tie.

PRIORITIES GRID

```
1 2
1 3   2 3
1 4   2 4   3 4
1 5   2 5   3 5   4 5
1 6   2 6   3 6   4 6   5 6
1 7   2 7   3 7   4 7   5 7   6 7
1 8   2 8   3 8   4 8   5 8   6 8   7 8
1 9   2 9   3 9   4 9   5 9   6 9   7 9   8 9
1 10  2 10  3 10  4 10  5 10  6 10  7 10  8 10  9 10
1 11  2 11  3 11  4 11  5 11  6 11  7 11  8 11  9 11  10 11
1 12  2 12  3 12  4 12  5 12  6 12  7 12  8 12  9 12  10 12  11 12
1 13  2 13  3 13  4 13  5 13  6 13  7 13  8 13  9 13  10 13  11 13  12 13
1 14  2 14  3 14  4 14  5 14  6 14  7 14  8 14  9 14  10 14  11 14  12 14  13 14
1 15  2 15  3 15  4 15  5 15  6 15  7 15  8 15  9 15  10 15  11 15  12 15  13 15  14 15
1 16  2 16  3 16  4 16  5 16  6 16  7 16  8 16  9 16  10 16  11 16  12 16  13 16  14 16  15 16
1 17  2 17  3 17  4 17  5 17  6 17  7 17  8 17  9 17  10 17  11 17  12 17  13 17  14 17  15 17  16 17
1 18  2 18  3 18  4 18  5 18  6 18  7 18  8 18  9 18  10 18  11 18  12 18  13 18  14 18  15 18  16 18  17 18
```

CIRCLE. Count total times each number is circled:

```
1 —  2 —  3 —  4 —  5 —  6 —  7 —  8 —  9 —  10 —  11 —  12 —  13 —  14 —  15 —  16 —  17 —  18 —
```

Adapted from Richard N. Bolles, *The New Quick Job-Hunting Map* and *What Color Is Your Parachute?* © 1985 by Richard Nelson Bolles.

APPENDIX B
YOUR INTRINSIC SKILLS GROUPING ACHIEVEMENTS: A SAMPLE

Athletic

- High jump at age 13—3 inches from world record
- Fifth in state high school pentathlon
- Held city high school triple jump record
- Lettered in track and cross-country in high school and college

Business

- Changed governance structure at law firm to permit mergers
- Shaped new cardiac care program
- Reorganized and redirected strategy for $1 billion bank

Culinary

- Self-taught cook

Literary

- Writing poetry
- Edited college literary magazine
- Edited national college poetry journal
- Wrote article on favorite writer
- Finished dissertation in under two years

Military

- Best bayonet fighter in basic training mock competition
- Platoon machine-gunner

Natural Science

- Developed extensive collection of butterflies as a boy and into twenties

Miscellaneous

- Top-flight *Scrabble* and *Trivial Pursuit* player
- Section representative at HBS
- Gave speech at college that left audience in shock
- Planned trips around Low Countries and France
- Developed and taught poetry course
- Introduced couple who subsequently married

APPENDIX C
YOUR INTRINSIC SKILLS
NARRATIVES: A SAMPLE

PENTATHLON

In 1968, as a senior in high school, I finished fourth in the state pentathlon championships. The pentathlon consisted of a 100 yard dash, the high jump, the 120 yard hurdles, the discus throw, and a 1 mile run. In other words, it was a scaled down decathlon and in that sense a real measure of the all round athlete—a test of speed, spring, coordination, strength and stamina. You cannot do this and not be balanced and complete and self-reliant and tough.

Though not exceptionally fast, I was gifted with unusual spring in those days, and I worked hard enough to master the technique (hurdle and field) events and to build my endurance. I ran 100 yards in 11 seconds—adequate at best—but scored the maximum allowed in the high jump by clearing 6 feet. (The high jump was and is my favorite event. It entails protracted drama and high aesthetics; it pits man against himself, but ends always in failure: it is the most Aeschylean of field events.) I was an accomplished hurdler, and managed to keep a three step rhythm through all ten to finish in 16 seconds. Though I weighed but 155 lbs. a quarter century ago I managed to throw the discus 115 feet, and concluded with a 5:10 mile, 20 seconds above my best, but not bad.

The boy who finished first later went on to play tight end for the Pittsburgh Steelers; the boy who finished behind me in fifth went on to quarterback at the University of Colorado and halfback for the Baltimore Colts. I ran track in college and continue to waddle and flail in a losing struggle with time and gravity.

COOKING

I taught myself to cook. In point of fact I had always made a decent spaghetti carbonara and a tasty kheer, but these were mere stunts, bearing the same relation to genuine cooking that a parrot's mimicry bears to genuine speech.

I taught myself to cook because one does not want always to eat out; because sandwiches and canned soup can be depressing; because, if one wishes to entertain, someone has to make the food; and not least because cooking is effort followed by immediate reward, and at a time in my life when cause and effect seemed otherwise decoupled this provided a welcome hedge against frustration.

My simple trick is to find a good recipe and follow it slavishly with good ingredients. I like some reasonably elaborate orchestrations—an exceptional arroz negre (Catalan paella of rice, tomatoes, squid, mussels, shrimp, and monkfish), a terrific kulebyaka (a turnover of salmon, rice, peas, cream), and a positively lubricious cassoulet. But I also like simpler dishes—vichyssoise or gazpacho or asparagus. The meal itself ought to be a succession of movements, like music, of different texture and force and cadence. The machinery by which it is made—the whirr of the Cuisinart, the peeling of potatoes, the way an onion resolves itself into rings under a knife, the odor of basil releasing its esters—these are tactile and more private pleasures reserved for the cook.

APPENDIX D
ORGANIZATIONAL FIT

Below are a representative sample of qualities HBSCNY Career Seminar participants listed in their best-case/worst-case boss, peers, and environment exercises. Use these only as a guide!

Boss, Best Case	Boss, Worst Case
Open-minded	Arrogant
Secure	Arbitrary
Forthcoming	Evasive
Well-connected	Humorless
Respects me	Short-term oriented
Has the guts to take risks	Manipulative
Shares my values	Takes credit for my work
Goal-oriented	No guts
Competent	Blames me for his or her mistakes
Confident	Nonconfronting
Loyal	Fails to support
Coach	Plays favorites
Can make things happen	Abusive
Experienced	Cheap
No boss!	Ruthless
Team builder	Incompetent
Communicator	Dictatorial
Delegator	Dishonest
Rolls up his or her sleeves	Belittling
Gives feedback quickly	Wants a "yes" every time
Explains the full picture	Lazy
Ethical	Suspicious
Good sense of humor	Intense
Sets clear goals	Not respected

Boss, Best Case (cont.)

Emotionally stable
Shares my work ethic
Intelligent
Enthusiastic
Available
Leader

Peers, Best Case

Conscientious
Well-rounded
Highly motivated
Principled
Not competitors
Self-motivated
Professional
Secure
People I can have fun with
Agree on common goals/work on
  group problems/present a
  united front
Cooperative
Stimulating
Trusting
Creative
Nonpolitical
Varied ages and styles
Team players
No attitude problems
Contribute ideas
Bright
Knowledgeable
Complementary skills
Don't smoke
Good on follow-through
Diverse life-styles—single/married
Similar values
Positive thinkers
Reliable

Boss, Worst Case (cont.)

Permits factional warfare
Controlling
Paranoid

Peers, Worst Case

Cutthroat
Don't carry their load
Cliquish
No outside lives
Prima donnas
Unmotivated
Unreliable
Bitter
Back-stabbers
Related to the boss
Gossips
Nongossips
Devious
No big picture interest
Sneaky
Grand-standers
Prejudiced
Not helpful
Absorb all the credit
Incompetent
Judge on superficials
Bureaucrats
Dishonest
Exploiters
Nasty
Don't share information
No peers!
Traitors
Lazy
Defensive

Environment, Best Case	Environment, Worst Case
Growing	Darwinian
Profitable	Bureaucratic
Well-staffed support system	Pretentious/stuffy
Big city	High turnover
Task orientation	No individual rewards
Privacy	No leadership
Resources available	No trust
Unstructured	No training
Structured	All smokers
Quality conscious	No smokers
Team performance counts	Radically changing
Attractive	Fluorescent lights
Industry leader	Boring
Ethical	Cramped
Fast paced but not all out	Technologically backward
Informal	Noisy
Professional	Poor morale
Intellectually challenging	Poor compensation
Smaller group	Not progressive
Creates some stress	Weak leadership
Has windows	Frantic pace
High tolerance for experimentation	Rampant nepotism
Organized chaos	Anything goes as long as it is profitable
Sense of urgency	
Lack of pretense	Turf warfare
Easy commute	Screaming and yelling
Quiet	Longevity counts more than raw brainpower
Sane	
Multinational	Four people in the space of a small bathroom
Highly computerized	

APPENDIX E
CLARIFYING CONSTRAINTS

On the following pages is a list of typical constraints—the roadblocks, real or apparent, within which a job hunt is conducted. Take a few moments to fill in *your* constraints (use only the relevant squares). First define the constraint; then verify, not justify, each; and finally note the impact of that constraint upon your career direction or job hunt.

Internal Constraints (Related to me, people close to me)	Explain What is the constraint?	Verification How real is this constraint? What would happen if I dropped it?	Impact How is this constraint modifying my goals/search?
Financial (e.g., "I am unwilling or unable to work for less than x thousand dollars per year.")			
Family-related (e.g., "My spouse wants to stay close to my in-laws" or "My children are at a critical point in their schooling.")			
Geographical (e.g., "I'm single and I won't consider anyplace other than a large urban center" or "I grew up in this area and want to stay here.")			
Psychological (e.g., "I could not stand to be without a job for more than x weeks" or "I seem to have a subconscious resistance to going after this job assertively.")			
Physical health (e.g., "I don't have the stamina to travel 50 percent of the time.")			

Internal Constraints (Related to me, people close to me)	Explain What is the constraint?	Verification How real is this constraint? What would happen if I dropped it?	Impact How is this constraint modifying my goals/search?
Time (e.g., "I don't have the time to research the small company option.")			
Readiness to accept support (e.g., "I'd never ask for advice/a loan/a place to stay" or "I'm not willing to tell people I'm looking.")			
Other Internal Constraints			

External Constraints (Related to the market)	Explain What is the constraint?	Verification How accurate is my perception? Should I validate it further?	Impact How is this constraint modifying my goals/search?
Experiencial (e.g., "My work experience gives me no creditability in applying for investment banking jobs" or "My experience suggests I'm too senior for what I'd really like to do.")			
Appearance (e.g., "People put me in a box as soon as we meet, and I just don't look like the type for the position I'm seeking.")			
Discrimination (e.g., "I could get hired, but for me the 'glass ceiling' would be there.")			
Skills (e.g., "I'm not good at financial analysis" or "I just don't have the talent.")			

External Constraints (Related to the market)	Explain What is the constraint?	Verification How accurate is my perception? Should I validate it further?	Impact How is this constraint modifying my goals/search?
Marketplace Realities (e.g., "There are only a handful of such positions" or "That industry is contracting: too many people are chasing too few jobs.")			
Other External Constraints			

APPENDIX F
INVESTIGATIVE INTERVIEWING: FIELDS, FUNCTIONS, AND POSITIONS

Below is a list to get your thinking started on possible new arenas for the next phase of professional life. See Chapter 12 for a more comprehensive resource.

FIELDS

Academia	Interior design
Accounting	Investment banking
Advertising	Investment management
Architecture	Law
Arts	Market research
Banking	Media
Computers	Medicine
Consulting	Ministry
Cosmetics	Packaged goods
Education	Public relations
Energy	Publishing
Executive search	Real estate
Export/import	Restaurants
Fashion	Retailing
Financial services	Robotics
Foreign affairs	Social services
Foundations	Television/entertainment
Government	Training
Health care	Transportation
Hotel/club management	Travel

FUNCTIONS

Account management	Long-range planning/forecasting
Accounting	Market research
Affiliate relations	Mergers and acquisitions
Association management	Mortgage finance
Budgeting	New business concepts
Commercial lending	New business development
Consulting	Office management
Convention planning	Operations management
Corporate affairs	Product management
Corporate events	Programming
Corporate finance	Project finance
Corporate licensing	Project management
Credit administration	Public finance
Curriculum design	Research/development
Customer service	Sales
Financial modeling	Securities analysis
Fund-raising	Strategic planning
Human resource management	Trading
Leasing	Treasury
Leveraged buy-outs	Trust and estate management

POSITIONS

Academic dean	Banker, commercial
Accountant	Banker, investment
Actor/actress	Banker, mortgage
Administrator	Banker, private
Analyst	Broker, business
Analyst, bond	Broker, real estate
Analyst, budget	Buyer
Analyst, financial	Caterer
Analyst, policy	Community organizer
Analyst, sales	Compensation specialist
Analyst, securities	Consultant
Appraiser	Consultant, management
Architect	Consultant, political
Artist	Controller
Artist, graphic	Counselor, career
Auctioneer	Counselor, guidance
Auditor	Curator

Positions (cont.)

Designer	Nurse
Designer, interior	Photographer
Designer, landscape	Photographer's representative
Doctor	Planner
Editor	Planner, personal financial
Engineer	Planner, strategic
Executive director	Planner, urban
Executive recruiter	Producer, broadway
Fund-raiser	Producer, corporate video
Human resources director	Producer, film
Investment adviser	Producer, television
Journalist	Professor
Lawyer	Program officer
Lawyer, general counsel	Psychologist
Lawyer, patent	Publisher
Lawyer, public interest	Real estate developer
Legislator	Researcher
Literary agent	Salesperson
Lobbyist	Seminar coordinator
Manager	Software designer
Manager, banquet	Special events coordinator
Manager, investment	Stockbroker, institutional
Manager, marketing	Stockbroker, retail
Manager, portfolio	Teacher
Manager, product	Therapist
Manager, real estate	Tour director
Manager, sales	Travel agent
Manager, station	Venture capitalist
Minister	Writer

BIBLIOGRAPHY

We strongly recommend these two extensive annotated bibliographies:

Bolles, Richard N. *What Color Is Your Parachute?* (Berkeley: Ten Speed Press, 1991), pp. 287–327.

Jaffe, Betsy. *Altered Ambitions* (New York: Donald I. Fine, Inc., 1991), pp. 215–217. (Especially for women; over 50 titles dealing with all aspects of professional life.)

In the HBSCNY Career Seminar our preference has been to recommend our favorite "companions for the journey." We hope these books add perspective and even inspiration during your journey:

Daniel J. Levinson. *The Seasons of a Man's Life* (New York: Alfred K. Knopf, 1978; softcover: Ballantine Books, 1986). The research on all stages of life popularized in *Passages* will steady anyone who imagines career transitions to be the exception rather than the rule.

M. Scott Peck. *The Road Less Traveled* (New York: Simon & Schuster, 1978). We know firsthand that this is a life-changing book. It suggests ways in which confronting and resolving problems—and suffering through the changes—can lead to a higher level of self-understanding and fullness of life.

Gerald O'Collins. *The Second Journey: Spiritual Awareness and the Mid-Life Crisis* (Mahwah, N.J.: Paulist Press, 1987). This is slim volume that makes a powerful argument about the organizing elements before mid-life, and the possible breakthrough to a new agenda after mid-life. One of Mary's favorites; worth ordering from your local bookstore.

George E. Vaillant. *Adaptation to Life* (New York: Little, Brown & Co., 1977). The longitudinal study of Harvard College graduates, interviewed every five years over multiple decades. Another view of the changing outlooks and altering perspectives of men as they move through life.

These books are referred to in the text:

Allport, G. *Pattern and Growth in Personality* (New York: Holt, Rinehart and Winston, 1961).

Bateman, Mary Catherine *Composing a Life* (New York: Atlantic Monthly Press, 1989).

Bolles, Richard N. *The New Quick Job-Hunting Map* (Berkeley: Ten Speed Press, 1985).

Bridges, William. *Surviving Corporate Transition* (New York: Doubleday, 1988).

Directory of Executive Recruiters (Fitzwilliam, N.H.: Kennedy Publications, 1991).

Directory of Outplacement Firms (Fitzwilliam, N.H.: Kennedy Publications, 1991).

Hirsh, Sandra Krebs and Kummerow, Jean M. *Introduction to Type in Organizations* (Palo Alto, Calif.: Consulting Psychologists Press, 1990).

Hyatt, Carol and Gottlieb, Linda. *When Smart People Fail* (New York: Simon & Schuster, 1987).

Koehler, Alice. *An Unknown Woman, A Journey to Self-Discovery* (New York: Bantam Books, 1983).

McClelland, David C. *The Achieving Society* (New York: D. Van Nostrand, 1961).

McClelland, David C. *Human Motivation* (New York: Irvington Press, 1982).

McClelland, David C., Atkinson, J. W., Clark, R. A., Lowell, E. L. *The Achievement Motive* (New York: Appleton Century Croft, 1953).

Myers, Isabel Briggs and Myers, Peter. *Gifts Differing* (Palo Alto, Calif. Consulting Psychologists Press, 1986).

INDEX

INDEX

ABOUT THE AUTHORS

MARY LINDLEY BURTON began her professional life as an aspiring securities analyst at F.S. Moseley in Boston after graduating from Smith College in 1972. Following a subsequent stint at Bankers Trust in New York, she received an MBA from the Harvard Business School. She spent two years working in marketing for IBM, and then started her own consulting practice. Now in its fourteenth year, Burton Strategies provides career strategy consulting services to individuals in professional transition. In addition to one-on-one consulting, Mary runs small groups of career changers and lectures widely on career enhancement. She lives in New York City.

RICHARD A. WEDEMEYER has over twenty-five years of varied management experience with large and small organizations in the United States and abroad. After receiving a BS in chemical engineering from the University of Rochester and an MBA from Harvard Business School, he spent fifteen years in technical and financial management. Then, in a 1979 mid-career course correction, Dick joined Jim Henson's small, privately held company that produces the Muppets. As Vice President Administration of Jim Henson Productions, Inc., his responsibilities have included day-to-day operations, facilities and systems, human resources, and organizational development. He lives in Riverside, Connecticut.

In 1980 the Harvard Business School Club of Greater New York asked Mary and Dick to take over the career program that had originated in the 1950s with Carl Boll. They have since developed and taught a new curriculum which balances self-awareness with adroit self-marketing. The career seminar has received recognition for its effectiveness from sophisticated attendees representing a wide range of ages and career situations.